Fables & Distances

Also by John Haines

FABLES
and
DISTANCES

New and Selected Essays
JOHN HAINES

 Graywolf Press
Saint Paul

Publication of this volume is made possible in part by a grant provided by the Minnesota State Arts Board through an appropriation by the Minnesota State Legislature, and by a grant from the National Endowment for the Arts. Significant additional support has been provided by the Andrew W. Mellon Foundation, the Lila Wallace-Reader's Digest Fund, the McKnight Foundation, and other generous contributions from foundations, corporations, and individuals. Graywolf Press is a member agency of United Arts, Saint Paul. To these organizations and individuals who make our work possible, we offer heartfelt thanks.

Published by Graywolf Press
2402 University Avenue, Suite 203
Saint Paul, Minnesota 55114
All rights reserved.

Printed in the United States of America.

ISBN 1-55597-227-6

2 4 6 8 9 7 5 3 1
First Graywolf Printing, 1996

Library of Congress Catalog Card Number: 95-80236

Acknowledgments

The author gratefully acknowledges the editors of the following publications in which the essays in this book were first published.

"Within the Words: An Apprenticeship" first appeared in *My Poor Elephant*, Ed. Eve Shelnutt, Longstreet Press, 1991; and in *George Washington Review*, 1991.

"What Are Poets For?" first appeared in *AWP Chronicle*, March/April 1995.

"In and Out of the Loop," Review of *Hotel Lautréamont* by John Ashbery, first appeared in *The Hudson Review*, Summer 1993.

"Less than Holy," Review of *The Bread of Time: Toward an Autobiography* by Philip Levine, first appeared in *The Hudson Review*, Autumn 1994.

"Introduction" was first published in *The Estate of Poetry* by Edwin Muir, Graywolf Press, 1993.

"On Robinson Jeffers" was published in *The Gettysburg Review*, Vol. 2, No. 2, 1989.

"Formal Objections," Review of *Expansive Poetry*, Ed. Frederick Feirstein, first appeared in *The Hudson Review*, Summer 1990.

"Something for Our Poetry" first appeared in *Northwest Review*, 1983.

"*You and I and the World*: Some Notes on Poetic Form" first appeared in *Poetry East*, Nos. 20 & 21, Fall 1986.

"Reflections on the *Nature* of Writing" was written for a symposium sponsored by and published in *Mānoa*, Vol. 4, No. 2, Fall 1992.

"On a Certain Attention to the World" first appeared in *The Ohio Review*, Winter 1993.

"Notes, Letters, and Reflections" first appeared in *The Ohio Review*, No. 43, 1989 and was revised in 1994.

"Foreword" was first published in *The Story and the Fable* by Edwin Muir, Rowan Tree Press, 1987.

"On the Writer in a Nuclear Age" first appeared in *New England Review/Breadloaf Quarterly,* Summer 1983.

"In the Woodland Still," Review of *Forests: The Shadow of Civilization* by Robert Pogue Harrison, was first published in *The New York Times Book Review,* June 7, 1992.

"The Creative Spirit in Art and Literature" was published in *The Nature of Nature,* Ed. William H. Shore, Harcourt Brace Inc., 1994. The essay was first presented as a paper on creativity at Ohio University, April 1990, and subsequently revised.

"Notes from an Interrupted Journal" is revised and excerpted from "The View from Buckeye Dome," which first appeared in *Alaska Journal,* 1982; and later in *The Ohio Review,* No. 41, 1988; and in *Place of the Wild,* Ed. David Burks, Island Press, 1994.

"Fables and Distances," Review of *Thomas Merton in Alaska: The Alaska Conferences, Journals, and Letters* and *Alaska: Recollections on Land and Spirit,* Eds. Robert Hedin and Gary Holthaus, first appeared in *The American Book Review,* 1989.

"John Muir's Alaska" was first published in *Travels in Alaska* by John Muir, Sierra Club Books, 1987.

"Days in the Field" first appeared in *Alaska Quarterly Review,* September 1994.

"Shadows and Vistas" was first presented as an address to the Alaska Environmental Assembly in Anchorage, May 22, 1982.

"Another Country" first appeared under the title "Death" in *Witness,* Vol. V, No. 2, 1991.

"Leaving Alaska" first appeared in *Alaska Magazine,* December 1992.

"Interview" first appeared in a different form in *Northwest Review,* Summer 1989.

"*The Eye in the Rock*: Toward the Understanding of a Poem" first appeared in *45 Contemporary Poems: The Creative Process,* Ed. Alberta Turner, Longman, 1985, and was written in response to questions put to the author by the editor regarding the genesis of the poem, its structure, and its meaning.

"On Hunting," Review of *Deer Camp: Last Light in the Northeast Kingdom* by John M. Miller and *A Hunter's Road: A Journey with Gun and Dog Across the American Uplands* by Jim Fergus, first appeared in *The New York Times Book Review,* August 15, 1995.

"*To the Wall*" first appeared in *Writer's Digest,* July 1993.

"The Far Country of Sleep" first appeared in *Cream City Review,* Vol. 7, No. 2, 1993.

"Early Sorrow" first appeared in *The Ohio Review,* Fall 1990.

Grateful acknowledgment is due to the following for financial assistance while this collection was in preparation: The Academy of American Poets, The American Academy of Arts and Letters, The Author's League Fund, and PEN.

Contents

For my wife Joy
With love and gratitude

Preface

I have never felt it necessary or appropriate that a poet be limited to writing about poetry. In support, I look back to a figure like Matthew Arnold, whose range of interest included classical literature, public education, and the whole of European culture in his time. Among the great moderns there have been many who, like Hermann Broch and Robert Musil, used their skills and voices in the widest social and political context. A writer I admire among my contemporaries, Wendell Berry, whose range of interest and competence includes literature, agriculture, and the necessary health of rural communities, seems to me exemplary in this respect. His notes on the unspecializing of poetry should be required reading in any graduate or undergraduate writing program.

There is room, in the general or critical essay, for speculation on both the work under review and the world from which it emerges and, rightly taken, must return to. If I have learned little else in my life as a writer, I feel strongly that the specialized mind, or attention, is a form of attenuation and leads to death—death of the spirit, death of art and language.

Many years ago I set out to know a country, to settle in it as deeply as I could and, as it turned out, make of that living knowledge a book. As a writer, I could do nothing else. In the end I could not separate art and nature, the country and the writing. They depended on each other, and with good fortune would make a single work.

In comparing the work collected here with what I wrote in the 1970s, published in *Living Off the Country* (1981), I realize that, though the major themes remain constant, I have in certain ways outgrown the place of most concern in my adult life. If there is less of Alaska here, compared with that previous work, this is in part because over the past decade and a half—a transitional period during which I have often lived and worked elsewhere—I have gone beyond a particular locality, while at the same time I have repeatedly returned to it as a means of checking on myself, and because it has been, both actually and symbolically, home as no other place could be.

I had at one time considered giving this new collection the title, *Another Country.* To the extent that it reflected back on that earlier work, this would have been a congenial choice. I had in mind also that other community, scattered and not always apparent, of individuals who have sought in one way or another to further the effort in thought and art by which we may know ourselves in this world. For it is, often enough, another country we seek and hope to find, intellectually and esthetically, if not actually. In a more immediate sense, it has been obvious to me for some time that our present country—as nation, as society, as spiritual home—has shown increasing signs of instability and political unrest. Presidential homilies notwithstanding, I see at present little evidence of insight or understanding among our administrators and elected people, little immediate promise of rescue or renewal. Wherever one looks, beyond our perennial public distractions, the growth of bureaucratic, corporate control is much in evidence, and all values, including those traditionally associated with higher education, are subverted by that influence.

Given this, what is the serious writer to do? Join the corporate lists in their academic guise and thereby impose on oneself a discrete professional silence? Leave the country and become an exile? Seek out some remnant of a lost bohemia; settle down in a remote region, tend one's garden, and try to get along? Or is there some means of understanding and expression by which one might, however tentatively, affect events and persuade at least a few of one's contemporaries toward something more positive and hopeful?

In this connection, it was significant to me, while briefly associated with one of our regional universities, that when the Gulf War broke out early in 1991, amid all the media uproar and patriotic promotion of what was at best a violent and dubious business, not one member among the general faculty spoke out against it. A handful of concerned students organized a protest; one or two individuals in the department of political science spoke up in opposition; but no professors of literature and language, and no creative writers among them. I do not call attention to this merely to be contentious, for it has seemed to me all too typical, an academic prudence carried to extremes.

Partly with the foregoing in mind I conceived my essay, "What Are Poets For?" At the time, I was unaware of an essay with the same title by the philosopher, Martin Heidegger. That essay, concentrated on the spiritual destitution of the modern world, derives much of its impulse and substance from the eighteenth-century German poet, Friedrich Hölderlin, whose original question was, "What are poets for in a destitute time?" Heidegger's response to the question is profoundly searching, and deserves to be read by anyone concerned with the fate of poetry.

My own essay has a more immediately practical motivation in calling attention to the characteristic self-absorption of contemporary American poets, and to the absence in their work of social and political comment—indeed, of any intellectual content—especially when compared with outstanding examples from the work of traditional masters and from many of our prominent moderns. In attempting an answer to the question, I do not, by any means, feel that I have exhausted the possibility of reply.

When I gathered the essays for *Living Off the Country,* I was faced with an arrangement of miscellaneous pieces written for one occasion or another—book reviews, reflections on nature, autobiographical sketches, and so forth. The present collection is not an exception. Though it is more ample and varied, and features a selection of letters, it too includes reviews of individual books of poetry, a group of writings on Alaska, speculations on art and nature, and one extended interview. The whole of it is framed by two autobiographical essays.

As always, when collecting work done over a period of time, we are reminded of the help given by friends and fellow writers—of the sources and texts, the many clues and hints—without which the work might never have been done at all, or done inadequately. Here, especially, I wish to acknowledge my debt to Dana Gioia, to Scott Walker, and to Donald Hall, all of whom at one time or another read through a draft of these essays and offered both criticism and encouragement. My lasting thanks goes to these friends and editors.

At some future time it would seem appropriate to have all of my literary criticism collected in one volume, my writing on Alaska and related themes in another. For the moment, I hope the present arrangment will seem justifed.

JOHN HAINES
April 1995

I

Within the Words

For the first time it struck me that to be a poet must be something exceptional . . . that poetry, the real thing, had within it a power that might change, if not the world, at least the life of an individual. And I was not alone. . . .
JOHN HAINES

Within the Words: An Apprenticeship

Let me begin at the beginning and attempt to say why I believe, against most current thought and practice, that poetry is neither a profession or a career, nor can it in any genuine sense be understood as a choice, but comes, as it were, to the chosen, as a gift or, it may sometimes be, an affliction. In the true instance it becomes an obsession, something that cannot be refused. If this is not the case, then in all honesty I believe that it would be far better to have done some more practical and humanly useful thing in life.

I would trace my own interest in, my respect and love for, the spoken and written word, back to my father, to his reading to me from the old tales: from *Treasure Island* and *The Jungle Books*, and on occasion from such weightier works as *Moby-Dick*, though it was unlikely that at an early age I understood much of what Melville was saying. I listened to "Gunga Din" and "The Road to Mandalay," to stories of Brer Rabbit and Tar Baby, and to much else that was then considered reading matter for young people. This reading aloud was perhaps the finest thing my father did for me, though he did much else besides. I suspect that in that echo of a voice, of the words within the voice and the voice within the words, comes our earliest and most lasting sense of the language, its traditions and its possibilities. Certainly it was so in my own history. And from that followed an early interest in reading on my own, while I did not suspect for many years that I too might write and be listened to.

My second clue comes from a class in my junior or senior year in high school. I had a teacher, a man named Roy Burge, who loved English poetry and managed to convey that love to many young people in Coronado High School over the years. During one fall term we were reading Chaucer and Shakespeare, as well as other English poets. We were asked to read aloud and pronounce as well as we could those portions of *The Canterbury Tales* that were assigned to us. And one thing above all that Roy Burge did for us in that class sticks firmly in mind. One day he brought into class a record player and a disk on which a well-known English scholar read, with care and precision, selections from the *Tales* in Middle English. Thus, struggling along with the text as well as we could, we were treated to someone reading from the poem as an expert. Listening to that cultivated voice speaking the lines with their memorable cadences and inflections, I was entranced. For the first time it struck me that to be a poet must be something exceptional and marvelous; that poetry, the real thing, had within it a power that might change, if not the world, at least the life of an individual. And I was not alone in that impression; I recall more than one of my classmates taking a renewed interest in the poem, and reciting along with me some of the lines we had learned. Some years later, while at sea during World War II, I could recite, for my own consolation and for the entertainment of my shipmates, portions of the text—long passages from the *Prologue*. And without subsequent reference to the text, I could still do this many years later. Something in that music had caught me, and it never let go.

After the war, as much as I may have been attracted to the spoken and written word, I was still far from being decided on a life in poetry. Instead, with a related inclination, I was attracted to art, to painting and drawing, and to sculpture. And it was to this discipline that I began to devote myself soon after getting out of the service in 1946. If I read much poetry then, it was more apt to be Whitman or Tennyson, Omar Khayyám, Kahlil Gibran, or someone else in a popular vein. I remember a long-ago girlfriend and I reading together one evening from *The Prophet*; or perhaps it was she who read and I who listened, not overly impressed, but for her sake attentive and respectful.

Then, before my first year in art school was over, came my decision to leave school, to seek adventure and a home in Alaska. From that decision and its consequences I date my beginning as a poet. For it was during my first solitary winter at the Richardson homestead that I began to write seriously for the first time.

When I had built my small house, had put up a woodpile, and settled in for the winter, I had time on my hands; time to read and, as I had thought, time to paint. At some point during that fall I had ambitiously built an easel. Now I looked over my meager art supplies, the canvas, paper, and paints I had brought with me. It seems to me now that I tried a few sketches, perhaps a watercolor or two. But with the advent of early winter the sunlight departed and the nights grew longer. Moreover, the outdoor scene with its snowmass and its slanting and fugitive winter light, its mountains, and its icebound river, struck me as so overwhelming and dominant in itself that my halting efforts to reproduce some of it on paper or canvas seemed to me more and more futile. After a few weeks I grew despondent and cast about for something else to do.

That first winter, with all of its newness and mystery, its strange power, had a profound effect on me, and I had to find some way, aside from the more obvious and practical measures, of responding to it. I had built a house, the first true project of my young life. I had begun to explore some of the country around me, and I was coming to know a few of the older inhabitants of the area, individuals who were, to all appearances, still steeped in nineteenth-century life and, in some important way, representative of it. In all of this there was an intensity of impression and feeling, and without in the least understanding what I was letting myself in for, I looked about for some means of making my impressions clearer to myself if not to others.

I no longer remember what books I had brought with me. I could not have had many, but I did own a three-volume set of art history by the Frenchman, Elie Faure, and I probably had an anthology of poetry, of romantic or conventional verses. Somewhere at midpoint during that long winter, and provoked by whatever internal sign, I began to write, and once begun I wrote steadily for some weeks. I have kept with me all of these years a few of those early efforts; they were long-lined and prosy, made up from God knows what model, but it certainly wasn't Chaucer. I was attempting to set down, in what seemed to me then the only appropriate form, something of what I was seeing and coming to know, far-off there and alone in a strange country. I was at the same time attempting to clarify, for myself and for some future reader, something of that lone-liness and its effect on me, a thing at once painful and strengthening.

I wrote many poems; or I should say that I wrote a great many of what I thought were poems at the time. I had no one to show them to, no one to tell me that they were good or bad, promising or a waste of time. Looking at them now, some forty years later, I see a rudimentary form of the kind of poem I would later write with better success, and an unmistakable sign of the subject matter it would take me many years of work to clarify and embody in a true poem. What does impress me now in those early efforts is the abundance of energy and imagination, of the basic inspiration that seemed to drive me. Once I began, I found it easy to write, all too easy per-haps. There was nothing evident to tell me that I should write, no one to tell me what I should write about; but I sensed that this was what I had to do, at least at that moment, and the lines and homemade stanzas poured out. Only later did a self-critical faculty take firmer hold in me, and with that came an inevitable dwindling of motivation; or I should say that I learned to write less and became harder to satisfy. Nonetheless, that early motivation carried me a long way, and provided the necessary energy for many years.

In my second summer at the homestead, with a house built and noth-ing more of pressing importance to do there, and before me the knowl-edge that in the fall I would have to leave and return to school, I spent much time reading. While in Fairbanks one day I went to the one book-store then in town and bought a hefty anthology of American poetry, edited by Louis Untermeyer or by another editor or critic prominent at the time. And for the first time I began to read and to pay close attention to poems I had not known before. Just who the poets were that most im-pressed me I am unable to say now, but certainly E. A. Robinson was one of them. I recall being excited by his long poem, "The Man Against the Sky," and before long I made my own attempt to write something like it, long-winded and philosophical. Of that brief summer period a handful of poems survive, written in one style or another, with little direct or dis-cernible influence. Reading them now, I find them not embarrassing, only inadequate. I did not know how to say, nor did I yet know what it was I most needed or wanted to say.

That summer, prompted by some obscure impulse, I joined the Book-of-the-Month Club, and I acquired through the mail, among other things, a set of *The Great Thinkers,* and Sigrid Undset's long trilogy, *Kristin*

Lavransdatter. I read these books during the long summer evenings, sitting on the screened porch of my house, with the sound of the river in flood downslope below me, and outside the screening an incredible whining from the worst mosquito infestation I have known in the North.

In the late summer of 1948 I left Fairbanks and returned to school in Washington, D.C. I enrolled in the art program at American University as a returning veteran and quickly became absorbed in painting and drawing again after a long absence. My girlfriend had taken up with a fraternity man in the meantime, and I was on my own again in a totally new situation.

Just when it was that I resumed writing poems I am not certain, but it must have been early in that fall. Many things — hopes, fears, loves, obsessions, discoveries, and deprivations — were stirring in me, and I had to find the means of getting them out. I assumed that I would be able to continue my art life and be a poet too. It required some painful and drawn-out time for me to give up that illusion; a long year in which I half-starved on my inadequate GI allowance, and turned out poems as well as paintings, and two serious pieces of sculpture.

My return to the city opened up the book world to me, and I began reading furiously. What I read then owed much to one particular event. While still in Alaska I had sent to my former girlfriend a few of the poems I was writing. She in turn showed them to her mother, a woman who had become a good friend to me quite apart from my having been at one time a prospective son-in-law. This woman, intelligent and generous, far ahead of her time in being what has become known as "liberated," saw the germ of something in those rough and early poems of mine. When I returned to Washington, she suggested that I show my poems to the poetry consultant at the Library of Congress. Robert Lowell had just departed from the post, and his place had been taken by Leonie Adams, a poet of whom I knew nothing at the time. I was myself far too diffident to approach such a person, but my old friend, not at all hesitant, called and arranged a meeting. This meeting took place late one September morning in the office occupied by the consultant.

Leonie Adams was a shy, quiet woman. After some brief conversation I gave her my sheaf of verses, and we all sat there in silence while she looked through them. She had little to say about the poems in detail, but was quick to appreciate what there was of merit in them. Inevitably, she asked who I was reading. I don't remember what I replied to her, but it was bound to be obvious that I knew next to nothing of modern poetry. She asked me if I had read this or that poet, and named a few of them, famous at the time: Eliot, Ransom, Cummings, Frost, and others. She then did something for which I will always be grateful. She put a recording on a machine that stood against the wall in her office, and played for us brief moments of these poets reading from their own work. We listened to Frost, to Ransom, and to several others whose names have slipped away. These voices, unknown to me, and unlike anything I had read before, stirred a new interest in me. Before we left her office she wrote down for me a list of the poets I might find worth looking into.

Such is that obscure, almost accidental service we render to others at the right time in life. I took her list and her comments with me, and in no time at all I launched myself into modern poetry with an appetite born of long deprivation. It was to be quite a while before I met and talked with another poet.

I lived then, an impoverished art student, on the top floor of a rooming house on N Street, near Dupont Circle. I occupied one room with a skylight and a closet, with a bath across the hall, for twenty-five dollars a month. I had a single bed, a small table, and a hot plate to cook on, donated by my father and his second wife who lived then a few blocks up Connecticut Avenue. N Street was then a fairly cheap and bohemian neighborhood. On the other side of the street and half a block down, under the green copper dome of St. Matthew's Cathedral, was St. Matthew's Court where Peter Blanc, an older artist I came to know, had his studio. A few blocks away, across Connecticut Avenue, the Phillips Gallery was within easy walking distance. And not far up the avenue was Whyte's Bookstore where, as I soon learned, almost everyone in literary and artistic life in Washington came to browse and might be met there. I recall now one early fall evening at the bookstore a reception for someone in the area. Wandering around the store, listening to people I did not know, I heard from a corner of the room where a handful of people were gathered, the recorded voice of T. S. Eliot reading from "The Waste Land." My ear was caught by that music and the tone of that voice, as obscure as I found the verses then, and I was soon deep into the work of that poet, echoing his imagery and his cadences, composing from moment to moment and from day to day my own version of an urban wasteland, one I was to know all too well before I was finished with my art studies in Washington and New York.

It was an intense year and a half. With the energy left over from reading and studio work, I wrote poems almost automatically, with the cadences of one poet or another running in my head. I would stop, as it were, in midstride while walking the streets, to jot down a line or an idea, while at the same time thinking of the artwork I had begun or was to do. I had no car, and I rode the bus and the trolley between N Street and American University. My friends and fellow students were all in one way or another seriously occupied with art, intent on becoming painters and illustrators, or perhaps headed toward a teaching career or, in one or two instances, a museum directorship. I knew no other writers. All the same, it seemed to me that I found ample fellowship among the people I studied with, many of whom, like myself, were veterans recently returned from the war.

Once again I was fortunate in having an outstanding teacher, one who gave me, in example and encouragement, precisely what I needed at that time. Leo Steppat, who taught both drawing and sculpture, was a refugee from Hitlerite Austria. He was highly intelligent, a good artist in his own right, and dedicated to the teaching of art. He was also literate, knew German poetry well, and was one of the few people to whom I could show my poems and receive an intelligent comment on them. He gave me exactly the hearing I needed, and something more: an adult companionship at a critical time. It was not that I needed encouragement; I would have prevailed, I think, had the whole world been stone deaf. It was something more than that, and of profound significance in human life: that individual who appears to us as a guide and a guardian, at a time when we are, if not lost precisely, perplexed and needing confirmation and assurance. Leo Steppat, with his own perplexities, his nail-biting, and his perpetual migraine headaches, was that to me.

There was also a young woman, a fellow art student, with whom I became involved, and whose interest in me, I now understand, was that of a fairly conventional person attracted to someone who appeared to be anything but conventional. She brought me an intermittent joy, much pain, and finally an intensity of emotional abandonment when she lost interest in me. But she also gave me the first good poem I was to write. It was influenced by the voice and the imagery of Dylan Thomas, but was still a poem I could call my own, stricken as it was, filled with images of late autumn and of doomed love—all the classical symptoms, in fact, and in the background a student garret where we met and loved and finally took leave of each other.

I was somewhat older than many of my fellow students, and may have appeared to my instructors as more serious than the average. But for whatever reasons, I often fell into company with a few of the older artists and teachers during that period, and I was sometimes invited to events and gatherings not often attended by the other students. And this fact led to a brief meeting with the poet Charles Olson.

Caresse Croseby, of Black Sun Press, at that time kept a gallery off Connecticut Avenue and within a block or two of the Phillips. I recall stopping by the gallery one day to talk to her about something or other, and to look at a show of paintings by the French surrealist, Robert Delaunay. She also kept the press going, and had recently issued a small book of poems by Olson, called *Y & X*, and illustrated by an Italian artist. As I understood it, Olson was then working as a postman to support himself, his wife, and small child. One evening in late fall I was invited to a gathering to be held at Olson's home somewhere in the northwest section of the city. The purpose of the gathering was, in part, to raise money for some medical expense concerning Olson's wife. Along with the fund-raising, there would be a film showing and a reading by Olson from his new book.

Many people from literary and artistic Washington showed up that evening; there was a good deal of talk and drinking. We were shown the Cocteau film, *Blood of a Poet,* and I seem to recall one other and briefer film. After the film showing, Olson rose to the center of the room to read. He read two of the poems in a ponderous and pontifical manner, staring out over the small audience from behind his eyeglasses, looking rather like a stranded walrus. It was my first poetry reading, and I found the poems for the most part impenetrable.

After a brief reading, copies of the book were auctioned off. As it turned out, there were only one or two bidders among the audience, and I found myself wondering at the lack of interest and concern in these people, at their unwillingness to contribute. I felt ashamed for them, and after some hesitation I raised my hand and voice and bid, as I recall, ten dollars for a copy of the book. That was a lot of money to me then, money I could ill afford, but on looking back on that evening I am glad I made the gesture. Olson signed my copy for me, looking up at me from where he sat, as if he did not know quite what to make of me. Somewhere in my dislocations of the past twenty and thirty years I seem to have lost that copy, and where it ended I cannot say. I did not see Olson again, and it was only many years later that I read of his visits with Ezra Pound who at the time was still confined to St. Elizabeths Hospital, not far from the city.

I did not seek the company of other poets and knew none while I lived in Washington. So far as I could determine then, painting and sculpture were to be my field of work, and poetry would be something I would also do on the side. I spent the winter of 1948–49 in a fever and grind of work, of study in art and poetry, my energies divided between them.

To live then on a GI allowance without other means was extremely difficult. I worked intermittently as a draftsman for an architect I knew, but most of my time was spent at school, working in one of the studios, and otherwise at home in my small, skylighted garret on N Street. It was a year of privation, materially as well as emotionally, but it seems clear to me now that the poet in me was nourished and strengthened by that condition.

Later, when the school year was over, and I had taken a temporary job with the Navy Department, my feelings were in serious conflict. For some time an old friend and fellow art student had been urging me to move to New York where all that mattered in art was then taking place. My mood shifted about from day to day and from week to week. New York City, what I had seen of it in one brief visit, terrified me. But there in Washington my energies were increasingly consumed by my job as a statistical draftsman, and even the better part of my weekends went to the Navy Department in a hectic postwar period when the armed services were being unified and each of them was competing with the others for their funding. Whether I wrote more than one or two poems during that summer and fall I cannot now be certain. I recall one isolated episode: while waiting for my girlfriend in a doctor's office one morning, I had a sudden flash of inspiration and wrote down some verses I still have a copy of; they were dark and passionate, filled with foreboding.

For a time I entertained the notion that I might remain at my job, keep a studio, and do my artwork in my spare time as some with whom I worked in the office managed to do. I went so far as to rent a separate living space while keeping the upstairs room as a studio. But in the end I was able to do very little creative work during that summer and fall, working a long night shift and saving my money.

Like many plans in life, mine, as tentative as they were, eventually ran up against abrupt reality. I was called into my supervisor's office one day and informed that after December my contract would not be renewed. I no longer remember the reasons given for this decision, but it was the signal I had been waiting for. I decided to leave Washington and move to New York. In early January of 1950 I took the train from Union Station, and a whole new phase of life began.

I went at first to live with my old friend and his wife in a run-down three-room apartment on Stanton Street, near the Williamsburg Bridge. Soon afterward I enrolled as a student in Hans Hofmann's School of Fine Art on Eighth Street, in the Village. It may have been a month, or a little more than that, after a few sessions at Hofmann's school, that I decided to abandon art and devote my life to poetry. At what moment, motivated by what particular event, I made this decision, would be impossible for me to say now. But there was one striking fact connected with it: for some time I had suffered from severe headaches of a migraine sort; it seemed significant that once I made my decision, the headaches vanished.

Many pages might be written on my two years in New York, on the summers spent in Provincetown on the Cape where Hofmann's school moved for the season; on the people I met with, and about the changes that were taking place within me. With the abandoning of art came a renewed passion for poetry and for literature generally. I continued to attend classes once or twice a week at Hofmann's, to draw from the model and participate in his occasional and half-puzzled criticism of my drawings. I say puzzled, because Hofmann was never able to understand why I did not bring in more work to be viewed and discussed. I could hardly tell him why, and simply avoided classes as much as I decently could. My thoughts were no longer in art except as a witness.

I spent my days walking the streets, visiting libraries and bookstores, reading voraciously, muttering to myself verses from other poets or some lines of my own in formation. I steeped myself in the atmosphere of the city, or as much of it as I could know. I lived nearly within sight of the East River and its famous bridges, and I read Hart Crane with a kind of religious passion: "The Harbor Dawn," "The Bridge," and many other of his poems. I read Whitman also, and rode the ferry to Staten Island and back. I walked from the Battery and the Fulton Fish Market uptown to the Museum of Natural History, and back; and I came to know firsthand the silence of Wall Street on a windy and freezing Sunday. I knew that my time in the city would be limited, that once my government subsidy was exhausted I would have to leave; and I knew also that one day I would return to my house and land in Alaska, to a project looming though still far-off.

Sometime during that year of 1950 Dylan Thomas gave his first American reading, at the 92nd Street Y. I went with an artist friend to hear him, and we listened enthralled to that sonorous voice reading from Hardy and Yeats, from Auden and Edward Thomas, and finally from his own startling poems. Inspired, I was soon writing in a new style—needless to say, one not yet my own.

Other poets came to read from time to time, at the 92nd Street Y or the New School, and I was privileged to hear, long before I knew their work well, Edith Sitwell, Cummings, William Carlos Williams, Mary and Padraic Colum, and once Carl Sandburg, who sat on a stool with a guitar and, along with a reading of his own poems, sang for us a few of the old ballads. Besides these, there were the gallery openings and receptions, the student gatherings, and other events of the art world in which I mainly moved.

When school moved out to the Cape for the summer I went along, like many others, to escape the city heat. That first summer I lived in a tent on the dunes, and walked the three miles into town over sandhills and through a scrub oak forest. With the sound of the ocean in my head day and night, I began reading *Four Quartets* for the first time. The poems I wrote were long and sequential, filled with the seawind, with the cries of gulls, and with occasional news from the town itself. I wrote continuously, and destroyed the better part of what I wrote.

After Labor Day nearly everyone returned to the city and to school. I stayed on alone for a few weeks, haunting the empty streets and the beaches, composing my verses, aware of my slow progress, but aware also that I was learning to write and that the time would somehow be sufficient for me to find myself.

I had no declared or public ambition to be a "writer," only that more secret ambition to learn as much as I could from the example of poets from the recent past as well as from the contemporary writers I had become familiar with; and, finally, to render justice to all that I was seeing and coming to know, the evidence for which I somehow understood was far more universal than my own limited experience of it. There was a voice, or so it seemed, not wholly mine, and through which I might learn to speak if I lived long enough and continued to write and to learn.

I made little effort to publish. I read my poems to friends, but seldom sent them out to magazines. I was more or less ignorant of the entire literary culture of magazines, editors, and schools of writing. I published one poem, my first, in the summer of 1950, in a small magazine called *Gale* that originated from New Mexico. The one poet of importance whom I met in my two years in New York was Weldon Kees, who showed up at a reception one evening in Hofmann's Eighth Street studio. I knew Kees not as a poet, but as a figure in the art world, a painter and a critic. My friends and acquaintances otherwise were painters and sculptors; some, like David Smith, Franz Kline, Willem de Kooning, and Jack Tworkov, already well known, others about to become so, and many who would never be.

Poetry for me was something that might grow of its own accord and in its own time, fed by whatever experience life sent my way, and nourished by the poets I was reading and whose work I was slowly absorbing and making in some way a part of my own potential esthetic. And not only the poets, but writers of fiction also, the writers everyone was reading in those days: Mann, Joyce, Proust, Kafka, Gide, Hamsun, and the prominent English and American modernists. It was an intense and fruitful time, the best of times, possibly, to have lived in New York.

What I have described here, as incomplete as it is, is the sum of one individual's early experience. To what extent it will prove valid for poets generally, I will leave to others to ponder and decide. I know that it does not describe the normal course for a poet nowadays, located as most of us are within the university.

As for *vision*, that abused and elusive word, I am convinced that it cannot be an acquisition. It is given, along with the elementary talent, in a confused and rudimentary form, to be nourished and struggled with, clarified through experience, and verified by the example of others. It is part of the world in which the poet lives and of which he too is a part, some portion of which may be realized and given form in a poem or a book.

What one's vision amounts to in its completed form, as incomplete as it must remain, will be mostly up to others to determine. Inevitably, one will feel at times that he has fallen short of his best inspiration, that the utmost in him has not been realized. Yet, in all fairness and generosity, the effort has not been wasted. Finally we have done the best with what we were given, have not held back from the required commitment in a conventional safety. In art, as in love, only the whole thing, the complete and consuming passion, really works.

It goes without saying that one must do something in order to live. How one chooses to live may to some extent be a matter of deliberate choice, as was Williams's decision to become a doctor, or Stevens's choice of insurance law as a profession. But the choice in such cases is surely related to the original impulse and cannot be arbitrary. When one is lucky and driven toward a goal he cannot see, the choices are apt to be the right ones, even when we cannot be certain that they are. It is a matter of faith, of steadfastness, along with a certain indifference to fashion. One's models are the great poets, the great examples, and no others.

It follows from what I have said, and drawing again on the example given us by the great work of the past, that we are the better for knowing many things, and for having immersed ourselves in life, in the world of people and events. One's sensibilities require, not specialization, but amplitude and depth in order to be nourished properly.

The sum of available knowledge for a poet has diminished considerably in recent times, and with this has come, inevitably, a reduction in resources. We have lost much of the ancient material of poetry, nearly the whole of its mythological background with all of its natural and supernatural transformations and embodiments — dragons and demons, metamorphic types, and so forth. That we can no longer look into the night sky and see there gods and heroes, whole constellations of beasts and actors, means that the world as imagination has been reduced in scope and value. It is in part the mission of poetry to keep these and all related things alive, to renew their character and their meaning, and in so doing keep alive the language we speak to ourselves and to others; and keep fresh also the heart and the spirit from which the words must come.

1991

II

On Poetry and Poets

The fate of modern poetry as a whole is the consciousness, born of the history of literature, of its relationship to the poetry of all times and peoples. On that background it appears as an imitation or an echo.
JACOB BURCKHARDT

What Are Poets For?

If I were to attempt to describe briefly what I see as the situation of the arts today in America, and confine myself primarily to literature, I might begin with the following quotation from Thomas Hardy:

> Literature is the written expression of revolt against accepted things.

I have found this quotation useful for any number of reasons. If it does not speak for all literature at all times, it seems to me to speak clearly enough for our own time, and particularly for this present moment.

In any period, literature, and I mean imaginative literature mainly, will carry a certain minimum content. In our time, whether we like it or not, that content has its political implications, even if one sign of that is silence—silence in the face of, not simply injustice, but in the face of all forms of social subversion, ethical misconduct, and so forth. This ethical content is already implied in the quote I have given from Hardy. By "revolt" one understands at the very least some form of protest; by "accepted things" we understand certain policies and practices—the public lies and deceptions, the "insolence of office," or simply a prevailing attitude that has become fixed and false to contemporary reality.

With these ideas in mind, I would link the quotation from Hardy with another, from Robert Furneaux Jordan, a man of whom I know next to nothing except that he is quoted in a collection of writings devoted to the Scottish poet, Hugh MacDiarmid:

     ... the step great artists have to take, from intrinsic beauty to
     social passion, ethics and political economy.

A statement like that deserves careful study. On reflection it seems clear enough that the step proposed by Jordan is that taken by nearly all major poets sooner or later, and by writers of fiction also. It is the step taken by Neruda in our time, by Brecht, by Jeffers, and in one way or another by Eliot, by Williams, by Auden, and by Pound, etc. It was the step taken in the novel, preeminently, by Hermann Broch, by Robert Musil, and other writers in Central Europe. It was the step taken by Milton, and on occasion by Wordsworth before he became an official poet:

           ... Statesmen! ye
   Who are so restless in your wisdom, ye
   Who have a broom still ready in your hands
   To rid the world of nuisances;

These lines from an early poem, "The Old Cumberland Beggar," seem to me to strike the authentic note. In modern poetry in English it is Yeats, I suppose, who stands as the supreme example. And there is always Dante.

A brief reading through any representative anthology of poetry in English reveals how often poets in the past have turned to this public rebuke of persons and policies; it is difficult to recall a major poet in whom this capacity and its expression are entirely absent.

By way of historical illustration, listen to Dryden's brilliant and caustic depiction of some of the principal actors in British public life in his time; for example, his ranking of political villains in "Absalom and Achitophel," of which these lines are typical and famous:

   Of these the false Achitophel was first;
   A name to all succeeding ages curst:
   For close designs and crooked counsels fit;
   Sagacious, bold, and turbulent of wit;
   Restless, unfixed in principles and place;
   In power unpleased, impatient of disgrace:

And farther on in that long poem we find these still contemporary lines:

So easy still it proves in factious times,
With public zeal to cancel private crimes.

How easily, with a few changes and additions, in names and nouns, these lines will fit any number of public individuals today. The nature of intrigue, of corruption and falsehood, does not change.

Or we might quote from Jonathan Swift's satiric verses on the death of a famous general, the Duke of Marlborough:

'Twas time in conscience he should die.
This world he cumbered long enough;
He burnt his candle to the snuff;
And that's the reason, some folks think,
He left behind so great a stink.

As well as being serious criticism, such things can be high fun, both apt and memorable. Once again, the verse lines and the thought they carry can easily apply to certain persons in public life today and in the recent past.

The range of poets and examples is nearly unlimited. We can turn to Blake, who put into his compact lines and stanzas the most telling of images, as in these from "Songs of Experience":

How the Chimney-sweepers cry
Every blackning Church appalls;
And the hapless Soldier's sigh
Runs in blood down Palace walls.

Elsewhere in the poem, two lines speak for every political state in existence:

The strongest poison every known
Came from Caesar's Laurel Crown.

The world has universally become a far more dangerous place than it was when Blake wrote, but the truth in these lines still holds.

From Oliver Goldsmith's "The Deserted Village" we recall the following:

And, trembling, shrinking from the spoiler's hand,
Far, far away thy children leave the land.
   Ill fares the land, to hastening ills a prey,
Where wealth accumulates and men decay;

These lines are famous, and rightly so, for they are as true today as when they were written. There is nothing, absolutely nothing, in the thought that is strange to our own time and place, especially now in this era of closing factories, vanishing towns, and dispossessed people.

In modern poetry this ardor, this ethical passion, freed in part from the old metrical rigor but with a renewed intensity, comes into its own again. D. H. Lawrence was a moralist of the first order, and with all of his characteristic venom, more often right than wrong:

> How beastly the bourgeois is
> especially the male of the species—
>
> Presentable, eminently presentable—
> shall I make you a present of him?
> .   .   .
> And even so, he's stale, he's been there too long.
> Touch him, and you'll find he's all gone inside
> just like an old mushroom, . . .
> under a smooth skin and upright appearance.
> .   .   .
> How beastly the bourgeois is!
> Standing there in their thousands, these appearances,
>   in damp England
> what a pity they can't all be kicked over
> like sickening toadstools, and left to melt back, swiftly
> into the soil of England.

This passion for denunciation, too, is part of the inheritance of poetry, and if we take poetry seriously we cannot do entirely without it.

Not long after the First World War, in his "Mauberley" sequence, Ezra Pound wrote the following lines summing up his reaction to that war in England. The lines refer to returning British veterans:

> walked eye-deep in hell,
> believing in old men's lies, then unbelieving
> came home, home to a lie,
> home to many deceits,
> home to old lies and new infamy;

usury age-old and age-thick
and liars in public places.

And this too seems both old and new, as fresh in its way as anything written since. The lines quoted are as good an illustration as might be found of Pound's well-known statement that great literature is "news that stays news." And Pound was not reluctant to use his immense talent in writing verses of another sort, slighter perhaps, yet in their own way just as effective, as in these lines on members of the postwar British Parliament:

We are six hundred beefy men,
    But mostly gas and suet;
And every year we meet to let
    The other feller do it.

Change the numbers, and this verse applies equally well to our own often irresolute and ineffective Congress.

Many years later, in wartime, William Carlos Williams expressed a mood of disgust and despair, in the poem that begins:

These
are the desolate, dark weeks
when nature in its barrenness
equals the stupidity of man.

Reading these lines, with their plainspoken energy and decision, one wonders what became of that larger spirit, the impulse that encouraged Williams in a number of poems to address himself openly and directly to "my countrymen," and that drove him to write the devastating critique that begins:

The pure products of America
go crazy—

And which ends with what must be considered a kind of prophecy:

as if the earth under our feet
were
an excrement of some sky

and we degraded prisoners
destined
to hunger until we eat filth

while the imagination strains
after deer
going by fields of goldenrod in

the stifling heat of September
Somehow
it seems to destroy us

It is only in isolate flecks
something
is given off

No one
to witness
and adjust, no one to drive the car

It is a poem that Randall Jarrell once called "terrible," and he did not mean that it is incompetent.

We would not ordinarily think of Dylan Thomas as a "political" poet, and as the description generally applies, he was not. Yet in response to one of the infamous partitioning treaties of the 1940s he wrote a poem beginning:

The hand that signed the paper felled a city;

And which continues in the following stanza:

The hand that signed the treaty bred a fever,
And famine grew, and locusts came;
Great is the hand that holds dominion over
Man by scribbled name.

Or we can cite E. E. Cummings, who along with sentiment and conventional seasonal complements, never relinquished his social criticism, writing, for example, of "the Cambridge ladies who live in furnished souls"; and addressing another poem to "Lord John Unalive." On another occasion he begins a poem with this rather fabulous statement:

there are possibly 2½ or impossibly 3
individuals every several fat
thousand years.   Expecting more would be
neither fantastic nor pathological but

dumb. . . .

And he opens another of his surprising sonnets in this way:

pity this busy monster, manunkind,

not. Progress is a comfortable disease:
your victim (death and life safely beyond)
plays with the bigness of his littleness

He ends the poem in that unfailing, seriously playful manner of his:

. . . pity poor flesh

and trees, poor stars and stones, but never this
fine specimen of hypermagical

ultraomnipotence. We doctors know

a hopeless case if—listen, there's a hell
of a good universe next door; let's go

Perhaps what I have been talking about can be more pointedly illustrated
by a useful comparison. The English poet, A. E. Housman, wrote some
lovely verses, and a good many insipid ones as well. Among the latter is
the following, a poem called "Epitaph on an Army of Mercenaries":

These, in the day when heaven was falling,
    The hour when earth's foundations fled,
Followed their mercenary calling
    And took their wages and are dead.

Their shoulders held the sky suspended;
    They stood, and earth's foundations stay;
What God abandoned, these defended,
    And saved the sum of things for pay.

Which is rather like referring to certain Central American mercenaries as "Freedom Fighters."

But the Scottish poet, Hugh MacDiarmid, many years later, made of the idea something extraordinary, in a brief poem written in reply to Housman's, and which he called "Another Epitaph on an Army of Mercenaries":

> It is a God-damned lie to say that these
> Saved, or knew, anything worth any man's pride.
> They were professional murderers and they took
> Their blood money and impious risks and died.
> In spite of all their kind some elements of worth
> With difficulty persist here and there on earth.

It is in this passionate rebuttal by MacDiarmid that poetry, rescued from Housman's conventionality, is most alive.

The poet and critic Edwin Muir was of too gentle a nature to write with the kind of denunciatory fervor available to Lawrence or MacDiarmid. Nonetheless, he wrote a number of poems that make quite clear that he understood very well the sort of age we are living in. Among these is a poem called "The Refugees," from which I quote:

> A crack ran through our hearthstone long ago,
> And from the fissure we watched gently grow
> The tame domesticated danger,
> Yet lived in comfort in our haunted rooms.
> .   .   .
> We saw the homeless waiting in the street
> Year after year,
> The always homeless,
> Nationless and nameless
> .   .   .
> . . . we watched the wrong
> Last too long
> With noncommittal faces . . .

Muir was writing of events that took place in Europe during the late 1930s and the early 1940s, but the astonishing thing is just how contemporary his poem is in its imagery and in its meaning.

So much, for the time being, for what I will call my *classical* examples. By way of instructive comparison, let's turn to a few examples from more recent poetry; to this from an issue of the *New Yorker*:

> I don't know anyone at the table except
> the friend who's brought me, who knows only
> the host and hostess. I perch on my chair
> like an egret, snowy and attentive. The man
> on my left is the youngest son of an onion farmer.
> The crop was ruined this year by rain . . .

And so on, in a tone of voice that could as well have been kept to a personal letter, and to no one in particular.

Or listen to this, from *The Best American Poems of 1989:*

> I could digest the white slick watery mash,
> The two green peppers stuffed with rice and grease
> In Harry's Cafeteria, could digest
> Angelfood cake too like sweetened sawdust.
> I sought to extend the body's education . . .

Or this, from an issue of *Mānoa*:

> I could write about fog, pre-Christmas
> gloom, our new little cat named "Doc"
> (after "Doctor Jesus" by the Viloinaires),
> the Mexican meat ball soup for lunch,
> coffee full of black lightning, a cold sore . . .

And this, from an issue of the *American Poetry Review*:

> And while my brain was being fried
> I was led gently by the hand,
> leaving my son to urinate alone by the trees

picking me dandelions and taking
care of Linda's drum . . .

And, finally, from another past issue of the *New Yorker*:

My father in a broth-stained undershirt
as he laughs in our weak-light kitchen
sounds like a mouse running—raspy chuckle,
fear-scurry, a grain of rice seized and bitten.
How small one life is . . .

To which one can only respond: Exactly.

I don't think it unfair to quote from these poems as I have been doing. In their cozy domesticity, in their dominant subjectivity, they are fairly typical of the better part of current verse. No more unfair than to quote from Dryden, from Lawrence, or from Muir, as I have also done. Whether arranged in a more or less formal stanzaic pattern, whether metered, or measured by syllabic count, whether capitalized or in lower case—in whatever poetic mode, they are alike in their trivializing habits of speech, in their absence of any moral urgency, of any lesson to teach us, except perhaps that it is possible to write badly and be acclaimed for doing so. And we are concerned here with the additional problem that many people reading these lines cannot, or will not, notice the difference.

What are poets for? In a poem called "Dedication" the Polish poet Czeslaw Milosz phrased the question in this way:

What is poetry which does not save
Nations or people?
A connivance with official lies,

And he continues with the following:

That I wanted good poetry without knowing it,
That I discovered, late, its salutary aim,
In this and only this I find salvation.

Following on the catastrophe of the Second World War, another Polish poet, Leopold Staff, published a poem I have never forgotten:

> Three small towns,
> So small that all of them
> Could be contained in one.
>
> They are not on the map.
> They were destroyed in the war,
> For in them lived people
> Who were hard-working, quiet,
> Peace-loving.
>
> O tepid, indifferent brothers!
> Why does none of you look for those towns?
> How poor is the man who
> Asks no questions.

Rereading this poem after many years, I remembered an article in the *New York Times* some months ago, discussing in detail the problems of that city's water supply. And the one detail that struck me most forcibly was the fact, casually admitted, that at the bottom of one of that region's major reservoirs, under many fathoms of water, were *thirteen* villages. I had to read that figure twice in order to understand it, as impressive in its implied violence as any act of declared warfare. What became of those small towns, of the people and the creatures who lived in them? Did no one write their memorial poem?

In partial answer to the foregoing question, and to offer an example of verse that would express an appropriate anger in response to so drastic an event, let me turn the reader to a poem by H. Phelps Putnam, a poet little remarked on now, but whose "Ballad of a Strange Thing" deserves consideration as one of the more remarkable poems of our time. I quote from the poem's final lines:

> Thereafter the rains beat down
> The autumn, the drenched leaves came down
> From the black trees, choking the ditches,
> And over the sea came sons-of-bitches
> With a hollow quarrel, the talking rats

Of England and of Europe slithered
Down the hawsers, doffed their hats
And squealed; and the plague spread and came,
Taking the cleanly name
Of honor for its strange device,
Even to our town . . .

It would be difficult to find in recent American verse anything to equal the metrical precision, the clarity of image, the energy and force of these lines.

It is worth a moment's time to return to Wordsworth, to a particular passage from the *Preface* to *Lyrical Ballads* of 1800:

> . . . The subject is indeed important! For the human mind is capable of being excited without the application of gross and violent stimulants; and he must have a very faint perception of its beauty and dignity who does not know this, and who does not further know that one being is elevated above another in proportion as he possesses this capability. It has therefore appeared to me that to endeavor to produce or enlarge this capability is one of the best services in which, at any period, a writer can be engaged; but this service, excellent at all times, is especially so at the present day. For a multitude of causes, unknown to former times, are now acting with a combined force to blunt the discriminating powers of the mind, and, unfitting it for all voluntary exertion, to reduce it to a state of almost savage torpor.

These thoughts, and those that follow them, written down nearly two hundred years ago, are as fresh and applicable as when they were first conceived. Certainly, the situation as Wordsworth describes it has not improved, and has indeed become worsened and more universal. And he says further:

> . . . poetry is the most philosophic of all writing . . . its object is truth, not individual and local, but general and operative . . . carried alive into the heart by passion; truth which is its own testimony,

And perhaps as important as anything else, he adds, "But poets do not write for poets alone, . . ."

Thinking about the poems I have quoted—from Dryden, from Blake, Goldsmith, Lawrence, etc.—and there are many more I might have referred to (I have no more than mentioned Yeats, for example), it seems to me that it is just this moral, this ethical passion that informs the great poetry of any period. Which is to say that there is a tradition in poetry for the kind of poem I have been quoting, and for one reason or another that tradition has pretty well disappeared. But when did poets stop writing that poetry? When did we stop taking our words seriously, and cease to believe that what we had to say really mattered?

In order to write such poems you must have a certain conviction, and be willing to submit that conviction to scrutiny, to questioning and, if justified, to doubt. One assumes, in other words, a public voice and an audience, even if that audience must, to some extent, be imagined, as Yeats suggested; or projected into another time, as Robinson Jeffers felt was essential.

That earlier poetry, together with its more modern counterpart, assumed a society and a place for literature within it, however estranged and at odds with society a poet might be. The poets assumed the possibility of a dialogue, however interrupted that might be. And where there is no true dialogue the art itself is in question, and the result will be a poetry of increasing isolation and narcissism, more or less what we have today in abundant measure.

If the purpose of poetry is to instruct, and I mean *instruct* in the profoundest and truest sense—and I think this is reasonably true of what we have called literature—how can one learn from a poetry conceived and written in a vacuum? In a state of mind, or a condition, in which no meaningful dialogue is possible?

Most of us understand, even when we do not admit it aloud, that poetry and serious imaginative literature have for some time been overtaken by other forms of semiofficial truth. We no longer look to poetry for that acute and comprehensive sense of reality in life that we need. We poets have handed over a critique of society to journalists and writers of nonfiction. Yet it has always been true of great poetry that it contains, or embodies, a critique of life, of society and its values. And I think it fair to say that, no matter what additional forms of criticism may contribute, social discourse will be much the poorer lacking the participation of poetry.

(At the center of my argument, though I have not until now emphasized it, is that ancient, myth-dominated relation to the world that has been called magical. Words, thoughts, forms, and acts, once constructed and set in motion, might have an effect on the world — on nature, on the enemy, on the object of one's desire, and so forth — and often enough were intended to do just that. If poetry loses that conviction entirely, it loses the better part of its energy, and will lose as well its justification for existence.)

"How beastly the bourgeois is . . ." This moral outrage, and the tension it carries into the writing, is something that poetry cannot do without. And already, by Tennyson's time, it was apparent that poetry had lost much of its moral force and had declined into sentimentality and to saying things "beautifully." It was this situation, in part, that Yeats had to struggle against; and I think it correct to say that it was this decline that the modernist movement sought to reverse, even when the poets and artists would not have identified the problem in quite this way.

"My countrymen . . ." "My townspeople . . ." That this address, characteristic of many of Williams's poems, was ever possible, and is assumed throughout *Paterson,* for example, seems now to be a notion terribly out of date. What poet in this country today would attempt it?

Nonetheless, the question persists: How is a poet to undertake an effective criticism of the system that employs him, that makes possible his position, his tenure, and his safety? Other than, say, as a tentative and timid questioning of techniques in teaching? Yet it seems to me that this criticism must be attempted if poetry is to regain vitality and relevance. The notion that creative writers have no responsibility is a definition of adolescence.

It has been said, and it was Auden who said it, in his elegy on W. B. Yeats, that "poetry makes nothing happen." And a reasonable person would agree, though if we were to be honest about it we might find it worthwhile to define that "nothing" and make clearer that other key word "happen." It is true, for example, that Goya's series of etchings, *The Disasters of War,* did not change the nature of warfare, nor did its terrible images diminish the cruelty in human nature. On the other hand, the moral passion in that work, combined with its unclouded vision and skill of hand, did result in a memorable art. And was that *nothing?* And did nothing *happen?*

If a single poem, or a single line of poetry, has become lodged in one individual's memory, to be recalled and repeated at an appropriate moment, and has as a consequence changed or enlarged that individual's understanding of existence, and has in some further way educated or intensified his appreciation of values — would that be *nothing?*

It's worthwhile to consider all of this from yet another point of view, and to be reminded of what this art of ours is all about. The following is quoted from the critical writings of Ford Madox Ford:

> The only human activity that has always been of extreme importance to the world is imaginative literature. It is of extreme importance because it is the only means by which humanity can express at once emotions and ideas. To avoid controversy I am perfectly willing to admit that the other arts are of equal importance. But nothing that is not an art is of any lasting importance at all, the meanest novel being humanly more valuable than the most pompous of factual works, the most formidable of material achievements, or the most carefully thought out of legal codes.

It has been customary in recent times to refer to poets in other languages, from Eastern Europe and Latin America, whenever we discuss poetry in conjunction with politics. We do so, often enough, with a certain envy that so immediate and necessary a relation should be available to these poets. But it has been my intention, in part, to recall that a tradition for that poetry exists in our own language, and it is that tradition we most need to revive and nourish. The poems I have been quoting from do not simply belong to the past; they are alive and relevant today, will stand for us as models, if not precisely in their verse structures, at least as examples of what a certain kind of poem can be and do. In other words, they are useful to us.

Aside from its intrinsic value, perhaps the most important thing about the quotation from Thomas Hardy that I gave at the beginning, is that it served another poet, Hugh MacDiarmid, as a kind of signpost during his creative life. In search of something I did not know that I needed, I came upon it, and it spoke to me immediately and personally. If what we vaguely, or carelessly, call and sometimes dismiss as, *tradition*, means anything, surely it means this much.

It seems only reasonable at this point to ask if there are not poets now in whose work this moral and ethical passion can at times be found. Certainly, and I would mention, among others, Hayden Carruth, Philip Levine, Denise Levertov, Louis Simpson. In recent decades this voice has surfaced on occasion in the poems of Robert Bly, James Wright, John Logan, and Robert Duncan. It was certainly present in the poems of Elizabeth Bishop. Perhaps the most consistent voice of conscience and conviction in American letters in recent years has been that of Wendell Berry, among whose recently published poems the following lines from "The Reassurer" are characteristic in their clarity and decision:

> The President smiles with the disarming smile of a man
>   who has seen God, and found him a true American,
>   not overbearingly smart.

But rather than indulge myself in that sometimes dubious, and often unfair, ranking of talents and dispositions, I would prefer that the reader consider carefully what I have said here; then turn back to the poetry itself and judge independently the justice of my argument. For, far from being merely another pronouncement on contemporary poetry, this essay of mine is at once an inquiry and an invitation.

Needless to say, you cannot simply make up such poetry, cannot invent it from having read the books, nor by stealing from other peoples' histories. You must have known that place and that time, and that particular state of mind and of being. You must know what you are writing and why you are writing it. An adequate emotional or, it might be better to say, an authentic, response to the world is possible only in the presence of an intellectual understanding of that world and its condition. In the end it is not a matter of meters, nor of free verse, nor anything of the sort, though many things are important. It is a matter of courage, of intelligence, and of character. The poets I have quoted were not merely playing with words, with rhymes and meters; they meant what they said, and that makes all the difference.

It is true also that all that I have attempted to say here, have quoted from, can be placed in context with that profound insight of Hermann

Broch: "Political indifference is ethical indifference." It might be said also that in the end ethical indifference becomes esthetic indifference.

What is the most conspicuous feature in American life today? One answer to the question would be the complete lack of content in conventional politics. This emptiness, this vacuity, penetrates everything else, and affects ordinary life with a peculiar and anxious falsity. The situation reminds one of those institutional monarchies whose style and public gestures have been overtaken by history, and whose sole objective must be to maintain an appearance of reality when reality itself has assumed another form. In all such cases, the new reality may announce itself as a universal apathy, or as a vigorous protest; failing any other appeal, it may impose itself in the form of a necessary violence.

The question returns: What has all of this to do with poetry? For the sake of emphasis let me repeat the words I quoted earlier from Robert Furneaux Jordan:

> . . . the step great artists have to take, from intrinsic beauty to
> social passion, ethics and political economy.

One need not be a madman in a city park, shouting slogans of salvation, nor be a messenger of doom; yet it does not seem to me to be inevitable that a responsible criticism of society should be beyond the grasp of a poet in our time. This does not, need I say, necessarily imply the writing of "political" poems. It does mean finding the will, or the ambition, to think through the predicament of society at this time; it means having the will, and the imagination, to seek the appropriate form for that thought. And more than that, it means having the will and the courage to speak out, clearly and forcefully, even at the risk of exposing oneself to official and professional retaliation.

And if this criticism should prove to be beyond the capabilities of a poet now, and if the criticism must be left to an establishment press, or to a few independent scholars and critics, then perhaps the question I have asked, "What are poets for?" is even more to the point.

I will end with one final quote, from Hugh MacDiarmid. As cryptic as it may at first appear, I hope its relation to what I have said so far will, on reflection, become clear. The quotation is as follows:

> . . . watertight compartments are useful only to a sinking ship.

1990–94

JOHN HAINES   35

In and Out of the Loop

Review of John Ashbery's Hotel Lautréamont

The first thing that struck me on opening John Ashbery's new book was the endorsement by Harold Bloom on the inside jacket, and from which I quote in part: "And more than ever Ashbery seems to be to the second half of our century what Stevens and Yeats were to the first." Having considered the apparent preposterousness of a claim like that, I thought that I might have missed something in my years of reading poetry, had misread the moderns as well as the classics, and had mislaid entirely my understanding of poetry's place and purpose in our lives.

In what sense, then, might Bloom's claim be understood? In order to answer that question I considered several possibilities, which I would frame as follows.

Imagine a Stevens who had lived into senility; had completely lost sight of what he had meant to say, his vision of poetry and imagination, and had yet retained his facility with words, a certain playful elegance of expression, a style inherited from his former, more active self:

> The midgets who stand on giants who stand on midgets
> in Palookaville . . .
>
> ("From Palookaville")

Or, imagine an Eliot who had mistaken his direction on his way to the *Quartets*, and had ended in repeating, with variations, the more gossipy and trivial parts of "Prufrock," "Portrait of a Lady," and certain other poems of his early period. Had said, in effect, "Let us go, then . . ." and proceeded to an unending description of cakes and ices, of balding bachelors and teatime ladies, with hurried glances into a countryside completely altered from the one he began with, and with no apparent direction, no resolution, and no hope. As if he had said, "Ah, my friend, you do not know what life is . . ." and had proceeded to demonstrate that he also did not know where he was nor the significance of anything he had described to us, but had simply walked off and left us with a heap of incomprehensible fragments.

Or, imagine a Yeats who had never succeeded in facing the public events of his time other than as a distant and detached viewer; had never confronted the turbulent politics of his homeland nor discovered in his writing the means to embody his feeling about these things in poems and plays; had never become the public spokesman he sometimes was, but had instead wandered off into a kind of versified tourist guide to romantic Ireland adorned with quotations from legends and fairy tales, and with now and then some tantalizing bit of current news thrown in to show that he was after all contemporary. And one knew at the outset that none of it was to be taken seriously, but was intended to be an amusement for people who thought that they might just understand a bit of it and perhaps take home with them a souvenir to show that they had been there.

These impromptu sketches will seem to some to be outrageous, an opposing exaggeration to match that of Bloom's. But are they entirely beside the point? I don't think so.

> We bake a dozen kinds of muffins every day
> yet we are cold and disquieting at heart.
> I fear for his sciatica, though
> we were never lovers.
> Let me memorialize this mattress, M.
> le Comte, . . .
>
> . . .
>
> In the casual track of a zipper my penis
> once got stuck, and it's been like that ever since:

feet stop where no snare lives, the best
is to die down and desist. Perhaps life is better
near the Arctic Circle,

                    ("American Bar")

Could a poetry like this, with its constant shifting of images and view-
points, have been written before the age of television? This seems to me to
be a question worth asking, for reading these poems is uncannily like
watching a series of sound bites, of news images projected and then withdrawn, to be immediately replaced by others totally unrelated to what one
had just been watching and listening to. Anything resembling a potential
depth is dispersed in a moment; little remains but a sense of having been
provoked into an expectation destined to remain unfulfilled.

If one were to concede that an age dominated by TV, by the public media and the constant distraction it provides, would produce a representative talent in poetry, one that for certain readers and critics would mimic
what the media provides the general public, then perhaps an Ashbery, or
someone like him, would be that poet.

Think of it as some god-liberating whimsy
that heaven and the emperor's mice detain
in the province of boredom. The signor's wrath
is cold at these times, to nail the fizzle,

                    ("Joy")

Another possibility occurs to me, and that is the impression to be
gained (though *gain* does not seem to be the right word) from looking at
the cultural landscape, at the fields and houses and people, while driving
at speed through the countryside and the towns. And this fleetingness is
further transposed to a nearly global scale, so that glimpses of architecture, episodes in history, names and events, are telescoped into a kind of
weird and distorted travelogue, an international shopping spree, and with
perhaps some trivial comment or moral at the end of it.

. . . Look, I have a vacuum cleaner.
In the janitor's hand some prurient
fun must be planned and I'll go where the washer decides me

---

into small dovecot openings that are for the birds. Please,
accept kindly the running board of my road . . .
("The Wind Talking")

Only it does not end. Turn the page, and it continues with a new title. And into this hectic, driven journey with no destination are blown up from moment to moment scraps of newsprint, discarded announcements and ripped posters, to accompany, to illustrate and emphasize, the pop culture of our time, with its neon-lit totems that crowd the highways and litter the malls: Buns, Tacos, Video Rentals, Used Cars, Cinema, Travel, Banking, Nintendo, etc. . . . And all of it with no visible center, no perceptible order, and nearly without end. But here and there, through the blur of traffic signals, some fleeting sign of what was once a well-ordered street or neighborhood, with houses worth looking at and living in; now and then some barely visible clue that another and finer culture once dominated the scene.

Another day he likened it to the roar
of Paris traffic, how expensive it all seemed at first;
later, a sparrow.
("Alborada")

It may be that the key to reading these poems with some minimum enjoyment lies in seeing them as a kind of collage, of fairy tales combined with bits of news and gossip, arcane facts culled at random from whatever sources; and all of which when mixed together blow into the poems like grit on the wind. And for a moment, perhaps, when the wind slackens, a kind of clarity prevails before the cloud of dust, of bits and pieces, closes off the view once more.

And when an elf
sits on a golf tee before you, and someone
behind you asks to play through: then, then
it doesn't matter much which of the old gypsy crones is
really a princess in disguise, with flowing
chocolate braids, and olive-dusted complexion!
("Irresolutions on a Theme
of La Rochefoucauld")

One might say that what Ashbery does he does skillfully. Perhaps. But my impression is that what he does must be relatively easy to do, and this accounts for the abundance of it, for the number of books, and the length of so many of the poems. There are no ideas to struggle with, no central vision to attempt to clarify. All that this writing requires is a certain facility with words, a handy catalogue, a map or two, some names, and a dictionary.

> Some time later, in Provence,
> you waxed enthusiastic about the tail
> piece of a book, gosh how they
> don't make them like that in this century any more.
> ("Baked Alaska")

In our time and place license is carried to an extreme of absurdity. There are, however, other versions of reality. Could a poetry like Ashbery's have been written under conditions of political constraint, of dire threat, conditions that prevail at present, say, in Bosnia? Unlikely. My guess is that the poetry would more closely resemble the sinister nonsense of an untitled poem by Aleksandar Ristović, with its concluding stanza:

> Time of fools is coming,
> time of the know-nothing teacher
> and the book that can't be opened
> at either end.
> (Trans. by Charles Simic)

There are, on the other hand, books that *can* be opened, and we are condemned to read them.

Nowhere in these poems do I find anything resembling the intellectual focus of a Stevens, that steady attention to an idea and to all that the idea embodies and leads to when faced with the problem of poetry and the world in which poetry must justify its existence. Characteristically, Ashbery in the better part of his work simply stands Stevens's rage for order on its head.

Nor is there anything like the personal quest of an Eliot, with its tormented vision of an intellectual and spiritual continuity always on the point of being lost; that search for which an entire life must be risked. One need not be an Ivy League critic to appreciate the utter seriousness of these things.

If you can believe that the late and increasingly realized purpose of this society is to popularize and trivialize the better part of the artistic and intellectual inheritance of Western civilization, then by an inverted logic an overpaid sports hero becomes a genius, an Andy Warhol becomes a great artist, and a John Ashbery becomes the foremost poet of the day.

What is most apparent to me in reading these poems is a facility that seldom comes to rest on anything; an incoherence to match the incoherence of our time. But let me quote from a nearly forgotten essay by Robinson Jeffers: ". . . it is not necessary, because an epoch is confused, that its poet should share its confusions." ("Poetry, Gongorism and a Thousand Years," 1949) On the contrary, rather than imitating the disorder of his time, the greater artist will seek to impose on it, on the material it presents to us, another and preferable order. It seems to me that this is what the representative poets of our time, whether we are speaking of Stevens, of Eliot, of Rilke, of Yeats, or of innumerable other poets, managed to do, each in his own way; and it seems to me further that it is the first responsibility of the serious writer to do so.

Hotel Lautréamont numbers 157 pages, and is an attractive book to look at. It contains eighty-two poems, many of them several pages long. Reading through them has been for me a rather tedious business, and I would have to say much the same for the other books by Ashbery I have looked into. This review is not the occasion for an extended assessment of Ashbery's work, nor would I be tempted to undertake it. Doubtless there are others more eager to do so, and who will find things in that work to celebrate. There are in fact moments in Ashbery that hint of something finer and more satisfying than we are mostly permitted to enjoy here. The third stanza of "Still Life with Stranger" seems to me to be one of those moments:

> Call these phenomena or pinpoints,
> remote as the glittering trash of heaven,
> yet the monstrous frame remains,
> filling up with regret, with straw,
> or on another level with the quick grace
> of the singing, falling snow.

The brilliance of that central image, "the glittering trash of heaven," is arresting. If only there was more of it. The opening poem of this collection, "Light Turnouts," a matter of four brief stanzas, is also compelling in its own way. And from an earlier book, *The Tennis Court Oath,* there is that lovely little poem, "Thoughts of a Young Girl." For me, Ashbery is best when briefest, in those poems where his talent for unexpected combinations and weird juxtapositions is concentrated and exposed to best effect.

Is this enough for a major poetry, for a representative poetry of this age? An answer to that depends on what you expect from poetry, on what, ideally, you want it to be. Those of us who look to poetry for something more than a versified equivalent of the public media will look elsewhere.

1993

Less than Holy

Review of Philip Levine's The Bread of Time: Toward an Autobiography

The appearance of this book, *The Bread of Time,* a loosely organized collection of autobiographical essays by Philip Levine, marks one more contribution to the history of American poetry in the past three or four
decades. Though uneven in its writing, often distracting in its self-focus,
it is on the whole an absorbing and valuable book, at its best honest and
revealing of character. Whether it is, as the publishers claim, "essential
reading," will depend on your view of poetry at this time.

Levine's has been a distinctive voice in our poetry. Unlike many
present-day poets, he has never lacked for a theme — mainly his personal
growth as a poet from his Detroit working-class background. It is a theme
that, with its repeatedly emphasized identification with the poor and dispossessed of the world, he has made effective use of in his poems, even
when at times he appears to have converted it into a pose.

Briefly described, the essays take the reader by a circular route from
Levine's apprenticeship as a student of writing at Iowa in the 1950s, back
through his years of schooling and wage earning in his by now mythical
Detroit, and bringing him more or less up to date as a professor of writing
at Fresno State University. Along the way he traces his early adherence to
the principles of anarchy, and which he later connects with a period of

43

residence in Francoist Spain. Through it all we are afforded detailed studies of his teachers and mentors like John Berryman, Robert Lowell, and Yvor Winters, together with impressions of his family and friends, with passing glimpses of individuals whom for one reason or another he rejected or despised. The style is discontinuous and episodic, at moments breathless and boyish, at other times considered and eloquent.

The opening essay describes Levine's early years at Iowa where he had the good fortune to find as classmates such young and promising people as Donald Justice, W. D. Snodgrass, Jane Cooper, and Henri Coulette. The classroom scenes in which Berryman and Lowell figure so prominently are in themselves excellent, and convey a strong sense of the excitement and companionship present at the time. One must envy Levine that rare convergence. It was a heady atmosphere, and he renders it with passion and loyalty.

At the same time, we see here the signs of something less agreeable: a premonition of the poet as celebrity, and a portent of more dubious things to come. At the outset, Levine is reminded of the ordeal and circumstances from which poets in the past have made their art. And he goes on to question what he calls here "the amazing growth-industry" that poetry and creative writing have become: "Today anyone can be a poet; all he or she need do is to travel to the nearest college and enroll. . . ." To his credit, Levine expresses skepticism regarding this development. What may have been fresh and exemplary with Levine and his classmates, has become unreflected habit in many subsequent candidates.

In Levine's account of class sessions under the guidance of his various instructors, something additional makes its appearance: a reliance on the judgment of a poet-teacher, someone who may, often enough, be less than a master of the craft, and with the added consequence, all too common now, of a preferential system among graduates.

Contrast this, if you will, with the lonely apprenticeship of an Eliot during his difficult early years in London; with the solitude of a Stevens on his long, meditative walks while the poet in him was slowly maturing, and you have a useful measure of a certain decline, of the absorption of independent creative effort into an institutional system. Anyone entering our time from an earlier epoch might view this academic growth with a certain wonder and mistrust. Was it really necessary? Did the art of poetry in an age of mass media, confirming Wordsworth's intuition of 1800, really need to become, not a hobby but an industry?

For a satisfactory answer we must look to society at large, to the growth of a corporate mentality that would overturn every human value, converting the whole into a bureaucratic instrument of absolute control. With all due appreciation for the many advantages—the companionship and, ideally, the creation of a congenial atmosphere among students and instructors—I do not think you can separate the growth of "creative writing" from the larger social problem.

Throughout this book there occur passages that illustrate both the virtues and shortcomings of Levine's prose, as well as the working of his self-mythology. Early in his story we find this:

> That autumn I found poetry. After dark, ambling the deserted streets, I would speak out to the moon and stars about the emotional revolution that was raging within me . . . I sang out to the city and the larger world beyond . . .

I must admit that this bit of self-conscious romanticism aroused in me a certain skepticism. Then, much later in his life, following a strenuous class session at Amherst, comes this quiet and lovely passage:

> Somewhere bells sound the noon hour. The students file out in silence and, once released from this odd encounter, resume their usual lives. Now their good-natured chatter echoes down the halls . . .

Nothing could be more natural than the cadence of these simple sentences.

Elsewhere, in an otherwise scathing description of a wealthy family by whom he was employed as a tutor, Levine recalls a scene of domestic quiet in which all antagonisms have for the moment abated:

> Outside the window behind Mr. Chase the late light is dwindling or perhaps an early darkness is falling from the air. I hear the door to the back porch open and close. The black cook and Gwen are no doubt beginning their trek to Livernois Avenue and the long wait for the evening bus. Their muffled voices fade.

In his exploration of a suitable background for his personal history, Levine repeatedly identifies his heroes: the writers and individuals he has at one time or another admired or compared himself with, whether they are the Lorca of *The Poet in New York,* the Mexican painter Diego Rivera, or the anarchist Francisco Ascaso. A problem with this emerges early in the essay titled "Holy Cities," in which Levine combines his own Detroit with the Byzantium of Yeats and the Barcelona of the Spanish Civil War. In doing this he deliberately places himself in compelling company. But Yeats's self-dramatization had the full weight of Irish history behind it—a matter of inheritance, an identification borne of events and intensified by his participation in those events. This cannot be said to be the case with Levine, and the difference illustrates one prominent failing in contemporary American writing: the absence of a meaningful dialogue between the poets and their nation. The poet, typically, is left with an isolated self, to be exploited in a space dominated by mirrors and echoes.

It can be said, too, in reference to the Spanish Civil War, that the Barcelona of George Orwell, so memorably evoked in *Homage to Catalonia,* of the Spanish poets and anarchists whom Levine so ardently admires, was not merely a literary convenience, but a true place in which they fought, wrote and, often enough, died. Levine's situation is of another kind entirely. In a poem of his own quoted here, "Francisco, I'll Bring You Red Carnations," he adopts the fallen Spaniards of his choice:

> Here in the great cemetery
> behind the fortress of Barcelona
> I have come once more to see
> the graves of my fallen.

It is a strategy that in this case, and despite an initial and lingering sense of a false note, can be said to work.

In Levine's defense, it can be argued that this self-conscious association, exaggerated as in his case it can be, is no more than we might expect of an ambitious American poet who, in a fundamentally indifferent society, must seek to identify and claim a place for himself, however he is led to do this. It can be said that Whitman did no less, though he spoke from another age, a more hopeful and innocent time, when it was still possible to believe in the human potential of American democracy; when many people read and referred to poetry as a matter of ordinary social discourse; and when one could speak not only as a poet and private citizen, but on occasion in that finally necessary public voice, a voice still possible for Auden in his time, and which continues to be on occasion for a writer like Wendell Berry in our own.

There are a number of memorable episodes in this book, and among them I would mention the prolonged search by Levine and his wife for the anarchist graves in the Barcelona cemetery. Both as gesture and as narrative I found this exceptional.

For me, many of the best parts of the book remain the glimpses of people, the individuals encountered throughout the poet's life, in Detroit and California, in Spain and elsewhere. And not always nor necessarily the *names*—celebrities like Lowell, Berryman, and Yvor Winters, as important as these may have been to his development. But also the ordinary people and the less well known: two members of the Spanish Civil Guard whom he meets in a bar on a wet day on the Spanish coast; Sr. Rusiñol, his Barcelona Spanish tutor; the translator Hardie St. Martin; family members like Aunt Trish and Uncle Clem, and the numerous individuals in transit like Florence Hickok and Eugene Watkins, whom he calls on from his youth and later years.

Perhaps because they recalled for me my own reading in Spanish poetry, I found some of the finer pages in a lengthy essay centered on the poet Antonio Machado and the countryside from which so many of his poems emerged. Levine's affectionate regard for this man and poet transcends the bothersome self-attention otherwise so evident in this book. At the end of the essay, while recalling the Spanish countryside and imagining Machado on one of his evening walks, he says this:

> The world comes to him whether he is on the cold roads of Soria or in a mountain town of Andalusia. A river comes into view curved like a crossbow, the boughs of the plane trees bend to the weight of bees, the wind stirs in the long grasses at the edges of sight where a few travelers appear over the green mounds of the distant hills. The air deepens and stills in the fields; time stops.

Toward the end of the book, and in an entirely different vein, Levine quotes from a conversation with a friend named Jonathan this stunning description of a butterfly:

Consider this creature, it has a brain smaller than the head of a pin, yet it can walk, swim, fly, it can hunt, sleep on the wing, shit in various colors, change its own shape from grotesque and stumbling to dazzling and soaring. It can re-birth itself. It is millions of years older than we and has not changed in all that time because it is already far closer to per-fection than we'll ever be, and it is beautiful to behold.

Finally we have the poignant story of a young woman named Dorothy who began early as a gifted poet, and then disappeared from the writer's life and from poetry itself, to be recalled at an affectionate and inquiring distance.

It is for such things that I am most likely to return to this book; for these, and for the look it gives us into the problem, never entirely re-solved, of the poet in our time and place. Whether honored or not, we are here, every one of us devoted to the written and spoken word, and we need all the help we can get. *1994*

Less than Holy

Introduction to
The Estate of Poetry
by Edwin Muir

It is good to have this book in print again. As I recall, I first read *The Estate of Poetry* when I was teaching at the University of Washington in 1974. I was impressed with it then, with its essential decency and its broadness of outlook, and I have returned to it many times in the years since. From time to time I have assigned it to graduate classes, and have seldom failed to meet among students a grateful reception for what Muir has to say. Reading him once again, I find in myself renewed respect for the man and his thought.

This is the second of Muir's works that I have been privileged to introduce, the other being *The Story and the Fable,* an early version of his *Autobiography* reprinted by Rowan Tree Press in 1989. That volume particularly, together with the present work, would be enough to assure Muir a lasting reputation even if we did not have his poems. But all of Muir's critical work that I am familiar with can bear rereading, for its intelligence and integrity, even when the immediate occasions for his reviews and essays have passed and become part of the history of literature in our time. Criticism of the kind that Muir wrote, and this can be said of Eliot also, remains active, useful to both poets and readers; it does not date.

In this regard it is well to keep in mind that Muir wrote during the high days of modernism, when the great works were being written or had recently been published and, where necessary, were being translated from other languages. Muir was very much a part of that time with his journalistic work and the translations from Kafka, from Hermann Broch and other European writers, undertaken with his wife, Willa. Their translations of Kafka can be said to have established that writer's voice in English, and the Muirs' edition of Broch's major novel, *The Sleepwalkers*, first published in 1932, is still the standard text.

There have been many studies of poetry in recent years, overwhelmingly aimed at an academic audience, but none so thoughtful, informed, and generous as Muir's. It is particularly useful now to read *The Estate of Poetry* in context with more recent comment on literature and intellectual life. I am thinking, for example, of books like Russell Jacoby's *The Last Intellectuals,* and of Alvin Kernan's *The Death of Literature.* To compare the substance of books like these to Muir — their emphasis on the professionalization of letters and the decline of an independent intellectual life as Muir himself lived it — is to appreciate how much we have lost in the four decades since Muir gave his lectures; how far we have come from a time when a writer of stature might presume to speak to and for the society in which he or she lived, to an attentive and significant audience within it.

I can think of one other text, not widely quoted, that has the seriousness and corresponding absence of self-concern that we find in Muir, and that is Robinson Jeffers's brief essay, "Poetry, Gongorism and a Thousand Years," published in a limited edition in 1949. However much one might disagree with some of what Jeffers has to say there, expressed as well in his letters and his poems, one does not question the utter honesty and conviction, nor the humane sensibility that lie behind his statements. Poetry for men like Muir and Jeffers, as it was for Wordsworth and Yeats, had in the end little to do with celebrity and professional cheek, and everything to do with an attitude that, as Muir well knew, lies close to the religious spirit. Those for whom poetry is something more than a career will know what I mean by this.

It is worthwhile, too, to consider *The Estate of Poetry* in the light of Dana Gioia's essay, "Can Poetry Matter?" published last year in the *Atlantic.* Of all recent discussions of poetry and its audience, Gioia's can be said to come closest to Muir in spirit. And by that I mean, among other things, the concern that poetry might one day escape its current institutional dependence and regain, not only a depleted vitality, but something of the authority it once enjoyed in the general life of people.

The *Foreword* contributed to the original edition by Archibald MacLeish and reprinted here, seems to me still to be as admirable an introduction to the man and his work as any that might be written today, and in some respects more in touch with what Muir stood for. I would like merely to reaffirm at this time two or three of the ideas raised by Muir in the course of his lectures.

One of these, already referred to by MacLeish, concerns Muir's emphasis on the tendency of poets to turn inward into poetry and away from society and a potential audience within it. Surely few would now deny that Muir's description has become even truer than it was when he wrote; a situation indicative of more than the condition of poetry, and which Octavio Paz has recently likened to the retreat of the arts and intellectual life into the monastery during the Middle Ages.

A second and striking point raised by Muir lies in his remarks on the nature of the poetic forms that have come down to us, and that have in some way become, through repeated and masterly use, organic. Muir's remarks on the subject are among the wisest and least polemical I have read, and of special interest now in view of a contemporary debate concerning *form* as opposed to free verse. We have heard much in our time on the merits and defects of a prevailing habit of verse assumed to speak more directly and adequately to our modern sensibility. Yet there is the alternative possibility suggested by Muir, and which I would frame as a question: Is there not, after all, something *organic* in Dante's three-line stanza, whether rhymed or not, something true and eternally useful to poets?

And I would reaffirm one additional idea among Muir's closing remarks, again cited by MacLeish, and that is the idea of a "great theme greatly stated." We forget all too easily, in these days of a diminished public role for poetry, that it is *thought,* the capacity for conceptual thought, together with one's ideal intuition of what the art can be, that allows poetry on occasion to emerge from our all too common private preoccupations into those universal statements that, one can fairly say, compose the art's final justification.

I recommend *The Estate of Poetry* for its wisdom, its clarity and generosity, for its quiet and embracing passion that offers a balanced and effective reply to all current and perennial wars among poets. What it has to tell us can never grow old, for it is the very ground of poetry.

1992

JOHN HAINES   51

On Robinson Jeffers

Robinson Jeffers. What to say of him now after all these years? I had not reread his poems until lately, had not gone to a bookshelf in search of him. But for a number of years this poet was among those who stood behind my own verses—not in his case as a model, for so far as I know I never learned anything directly from him. But as one more example of the variety and power of poetry in English in the first half of this century, Jeffers for me held, and still holds, a unique place.

I don't recall when I first read him; it must have been early, at an uncritical stage in my own development. In 1949, following a long winter as a student under the GI Bill, I was working in the Navy Department in Washington, D.C. Jeffers's *Medea* was then the hit of the theatrical season. One or two of the people I worked with in the department had seen the production and spoke of it with enthusiasm, but for some reason I did not go to see the play. If I had read Jeffers at all, it seems clear that his name and his poetry did not yet mean very much to me.

But a year later I was living in New York, and things had changed. I have a very clear impression now of reading aloud to someone, on a cold, gray afternoon, one or more of the longer poems of Jeffers, and of being caught up in admiration. And that winter in New York we went to see a production of *The Tower Beyond Tragedy* with Judith Anderson in the role of Clytemnestra. My impressions of that performance have faded, other than for the somewhat strained atmosphere of the production, as if the people onstage had to some extent misread the poem and were overdoing the passion.

In 1952 my first wife and I left New York and moved to California. The Big Sur coast was much in the air then as a place to live; one or two of our New York acquaintances had gone to live there, and about that time Weldon Kees, whom I had known briefly had moved from there to San Francisco.

We found out very quickly that we could not afford to live in Big Sur, and we had to look elsewhere. For two years we lived in an old redwood barn a few miles up Carmel Valley, close to the river. The valley was still mostly rural then, and there was a lot of country to explore in the headwaters. The summer fogs came up the valley from the sea, the countryside was quiet, and the living cheap. Jeffers was still alive, and very much a legend in the area. More than once we drove around the Carmel shoreline in the Model A truck we had, and looked with awe at what we could see of the stone house and tower bulking over the foreland. But not a sign of human life did we see there; Jeffers and his family kept well out of sight. We were astonished and disappointed by the thoroughly developed character of the shoreline, so different from the descriptions given in the poems. It seemed to us that there was hardly a quarter acre of land left open, so densely had it been built up. We chugged on by, taking with us a lasting impression of the crowded yet lonely appearance of that house and tower, the only things, other than the sea rocks, that seemed as if they belonged there.

In the situation in which I lived and wrote then, an older poet whom I admired was to me like a spring in the desert. I wanted very much to meet the man and talk with him; but as a still young and unformed poet I never had the courage to attempt to visit him, and I do not know what I would have found to say to him had I by some chance met him. I respected his solitude. At the same time, his spirit was everywhere in that countryside, so much so that already it was unthinkable that I, or anyone, should attempt to write anything about that coast, its ranges and valleys, so fully had the man and his poetry seized upon it and changed it forever.

Many years later, after Jeffers died, I was able to visit the house and the tower, guided by the poet's son, Donnan, who still lived there with his family. I had in the meantime read the beautiful edition of Jeffers's letters with the photographs that accompanied the text, so I was to some extent prepared for what I was to see. Strongly moved by that long-delayed visitation, I wrote a brief description of it that seems to me now to convey my impressions as well as anything I might invent at this time:

> I was shown through the rooms of Tor House, their spaces and objects still saturated with the intelligence that had summoned them from the darkness. I felt there the deeply rooted quality of the man's life and work, evident not only in the house itself, but in the poems, in their hold on that place, full of insight and passion. This house was built, the poems written, by a man who had discovered while still young who he was and what he would do. . . . As we sometimes say, "He knew his mind. . . ."[1]

Among the things I was shown was a photograph of the first small house he had built on that shore, with nothing but space and ocean around it. Standing at the top of the tower with Donnan Jeffers, I compared that photograph with the densely settled scene before me, and I felt acutely how discouraging and embittering that intrusion on his solitude might have been to him, taking from him finally all but a piece of land not much larger than a normal city lot. It was a lesson in how relentless and cynical in its regard for the intrinsic nature of a place our society has always been. In the face of that encroachment, fulfilling his own prophecies, Jeffers's patience (or resignation) seems exemplary. I have lived long enough to have seen a part of my own neck of the woods radically changed by a sprawling frontier settlement, the roads extended and bearing more traffic yearly, but nothing so drastic, cluttered, and pretentious as that shoreline in Carmel.

My feeling for Jeffers and his poetry remained constant for as long as I lived in his country. When I returned to Alaska my thoughts turned eventually to other poets and to other kinds of poetry. But a long ways from that fog-lit coast I kept a warm affection for the man and his poetry, so remote in its style and content from that of his major contemporaries, and very different from what was to become my own way of writing. I retained, laid by and half-forgotten, a kindred sense, of a thing like and unlike, and yet to me supportive in that firm decision to remain himself in his own place.

I may have imagined more than once, in New York and California, that I would one day return to my own symbolic rock (though it was not a rock but a high shoulder of wooded hillside above a cold, gray glacial river) and there live out my life, separate and perceiving. This was not, I was to discover, an entirely true conception, and I had much to learn about myself. In spite of the intensity of my attachment to that given place, I have since come to understand that there is more than one way to growth; a man is not a tree, however much he may admire in trees and stones their immobility. The life of our time is not necessarily to be lived at its most intense in a single place. But in season and out, coping with the difficulties of weather and isolation, I dreamed the country and filled it with spirits and voices of my own. To what extent Jeffers provided me with an example of that possibility, I would find hard to say now with any exactness. But it seems to me that of all things a poet might do, to live deeply in a certain place and, through voice and imagery and story, make it a permanent part of our heritage, is a thing most admirable. And Jeffers did this so thoroughly that never again, I suspect, will a poet be able to approach that coastal landscape without paying his respects to the man's spirit and the remarkable power of his evocation of the land and its inhabitants.

For reasons not entirely clear to me, contemporary criticism has not done well by Jeffers. Perhaps this says something about the nature of literary criticism in our time, honed on the subtleties and hiatuses of Eliot and Pound and whole schools of lesser people—those, we have been taught, who constitute the modern tradition. In the case of a poet like Jeffers, whose content is expressed with such force and clarity, and whose means are always adequate but never displayed for their own sake, criticism may find little to do but to carp or dismiss.

And there's little doubt that Jeffers has suffered from a good deal of partisan and mediocre interpretation. When I went to a library shelf in search of material for this essay I found, along with the bulk of his own works, a number of books on the man and his poetry. One or two of these I read long ago, and to little purpose. There were several that were new to me, and which, from the brief look I had of them, I am unlikely to read. The best commentary on Jeffers known to me is an essay by Horace Gregory, "Poet Without Critics," which appeared in an issue of *New World Writing* sometime late in the 1950s. It can still be found among

Gregory's collected essays, and on rereading it I find that for me its interest has not diminished. I would not be surprised to learn that it is still the most balanced comment on Jeffers to date.[2]

Apparently it is all too easy to misjudge this poet. The editors of *The Princeton Encyclopedia of Poetry and Poetics*, for example, place Jeffers among contemporary lyric poets, but they are mistaken. He is a narrative, a dramatic, a meditative poet, who sometimes soars into lyricism. In a time when the lyric voice, or often enough something that only weakly resembles it, is the prevailing mode, it is easy to lose sight of these distinctions. Moreover, in any sense that might be critically useful, Jeffers is not a private poet. His poems can be read, often enough, as addresses, speeches to the people. He had the public voice and, as Radcliffe Squires remarked to me once, something of the common touch. He was not afraid of the large, the general statement, he did not shrink from the employment of ideas, nor did he draw back from the risk of cliché. Like Neruda in another language, he took the chance of writing badly at times in order to write greatly. We hear all too much these days about "risk" in poetry. As employed in discussions of writing, it is a misunderstood and misused word, more apt to refer to some minor verbal particularity than to anything fundamental in life and letters. Jeffers, on the other hand, took the real risk of assuming that he had something of importance to say and, like Yeats under very different circumstances, could imagine both himself and his audience.

In his mature work, Jeffers is a long way from any popular current conception of a poem as, more or less, a found thing, its form and substance to be discovered in process. In this view, typically, we do not know what we have to say until we have said it. This happens to be the way I myself have written often enough. But it is not the only way to write, and I suspect it is not the way most poetry was written in the past. But in order to write another way you must know what you wish to say and know how to say it.

When we read a poem these days we take it for granted that the poet is speaking to himself, to another poet, or to an audience of poetry readers or teachers of poetry. I don't say this is necessarily wrong, but it does place very definite limitations on the poetry. We have, for one thing, forgotten how to write in any voice but our own. We miss, I think, the dramatic voice that can only be used in the presence of an audience, actual or imagined. It would be difficult to name a major poet in whom this dramatic voice was entirely absent. It is certainly present in Eliot, and in his own way Williams had it also. For Jeffers this sense of the audience was not only instinctive, it was, I think, essential to his poetry. We can never forget while reading him that he is speaking to a certain largeness in us, as to a congregation; his voice, at once personal and public, has that authority.

A wonderful thing about Jeffers, as with all true poets, is that personality, in the ordinary sense of it, is transcended, transformed into something else, additional to and greater than the person. Out of this changed condition the voice of the poet speaks as if from a hidden source; speaks, as it were, *through* the poet. This is a mysterious and little discussed matter, but I believe it accounts for what we call "greatness" in art. And Jeffers certainly possessed it — or was possessed by it.

I myself am no longer as sympathetic to Jeffers's philosophical outlook, his "inhumanism," as I once was, and portions of his longer poems in particular I now find hard to accept for their excess of passion, even while I admire otherwise the energy, the narrative drive, and the accuracy and resonance of his imagery. But as I can overlook in Yeats some foolishness, and pardon Eliot his loyalties, I can forgive Jeffers a point of view I do not entirely share, and forgive also the crudity and arrogance of voice in which his truths are sometimes uttered.

He was rough-hewn in his way, homemade as so many Americans of genius are, putting together from odds and ends of the classics, from European culture and Eastern thought, combined perhaps with an indigenous American experience, some reasonably coherent attitude with which to face a disintegrating world. In this, Jeffers was more successful than most of us. By present-day standards he was very well educated, and in the matter of verse writing particularly he knew well enough what he was doing. His rare remarks on poetry, to be found in his prefaces and his letters, are refreshing to read for their common sense, are never dogmatic, but stated with matter-of-factness and a modest authority. The brief essay called "Poetry, Gongorism and a Thousand Years," which he published as a chapbook in 1949, is characteristic in its spareness and directness, and utterly clear — if anyone needed proof that clear statement is the inevitable partner of true content, he can find it here. No deviousness, no jargon, no gossip, just some good, sound advice to the aspiring poet, and for the reader of poetry profound insight into the nature of poetry. I can't think of another essay that in less than a dozen pages manages to say so much that is sound and helpful.

On consideration I would say that the best of Jeffers's poems are as good, as strong, as likely to last, as anything written in our time. Not long ago I reread the poem, "Night," and felt again its power and eloquence. One of Jeffers's most moving poems, it is built on a scale to match its subject, and gains moreover from its familiarity with the great English poems of the past. Contained within its stanzas of alternating long and short lines, the poem moves with a grave and resonant music from beginning to end.

Jeffers's poems remind us that there was a time when words and things were not separated, but joined together in the body of the world. This is clear enough in the uncanny way in which his poems, simply from their appearance on the page—in the shape of the stanzas, the movement of the lines, and the weight of the imagery—seem to embody almost physically the very substance of his thought and feeling.

Equally impressive in Jeffers is the way his narratives, his dramas and persons, are confirmed in their relation to a greater and more inclusive world, and gain thereby in scope and significance. His elements of rock and water, of night and dawn, fire and storm, have something of the vitality of the ancient personifications of the natural world. The old gods have been replaced by the impersonal forces of the universe, but nothing much else has changed in a thousand years or so. People continue to love and hate, to live and die, with a driven finality reminiscent of persons in classical drama in contest with powers greater than themselves. We now know (or think we know) that these forces are very much within us and not in the world without; but we are not always so sure. A health and sanity may be found in the placing of human fate and action within the larger field of nature, where the elements at least wear familiar faces and can still be named and spoken to. Humankind has always needed symbolic representations of light and dark, good and evil, and these cannot be adequately provided by abstractions and theories.

Even with so much that is positive to say of Jeffers, I still have no satisfactory explanation for the neglect of his poetry. It may be that the whole drift of modernism, with its truncations and interruptions, its increasingly scattered attention, finds something alien and unsympathetic in Jeffers, as if he were in some way an anachronism, a throwback to an older tradition in which it was possible to entertain some large and general assumptions concerning poetry and its place in the world. It may be also that we feel in some way challenged by him, secretly accused for our prevailing subjectivity, for the narrowness of our poetic world, and for the absence of an ability to write for, or even imagine, any audience other than the specialized and mainly academic one we do have. Given the limitations of talent, and a fatal disposition in the age itself, there may be little more to be said about this; but I would insist all the same that the attitude of the poet—toward his time and place, and toward the art itself—is the first problem, and the place to begin.

I intended to conclude this essay be asking if we had anything to learn now from Jeffers, but I think an answer to that has been given in what I have already said. I would add, in summation, that we have in Jeffers the example of a certain clarity and integrity, of a conviction concerning the poet as one compelled to speak out, to tell the truth, even at the cost of becoming unpopular and unread. And, further, that the poet, as witness and prophet, is one entitled to speak directly to the people, and who asserts that right even when he knows that for the moment no one may be listening. And with these virtues, a certain temper of mind, with the long perspective of poetry as a mode of truth and verification in human life—an art that is finally beyond fashionable notions of craft and reputation, and has its source in the mysterious circumstance of the universe.

The sense of grandeur and of largeness remains. If the very rocks of the shoreline disappear and the cypresses are displaced by the restless engineers of our world, the words, and the verse lines that contain them— steady and monotonous as the beat of the ocean, or soaring at times like one of his memorable hawks—will survive.   *1986*

Formal Objections

Review of Expansive Poetry: Essays on the New Narrative &
the New Formalism, *edited by Frederick Feirstein*

Invited to review this book I have wondered what to say of it, wondered
what might be worth adding to an already overextended and preemptive
argument. Some of us have by now heard quite enough about the new
formalism and its so far questionable achievement.

I will begin by saying that I have read through these essays with considerable impatience and annoyance. For relief and a renewed perspective
I have meanwhile turned elsewhere, to the literary essays of Edwin Muir,
especially to that luminous book *The Estate of Poetry,* and refreshed myself in the open and spacious intelligence of his pages, in his unfailing
ability to place poetry in a context beyond promotion, above faction and
self-interest. Among Wallace Stevens's rare remarks on poetry one finds
on occasion a similar disinterested authority, an attention to the thing itself and its increasingly scarce excellence.

With the generous and inclusive spirit of Muir's criticism in mind, it is
all the more disconcerting to turn back to the promotional style of the
majority of these essays with their characteristically narrowed, contentious, and self-justifying tone of voice. One's initial impression is that
we have a disproportionate number of piddling Pounds who, despite their

rejection of the master's work, would like to emulate Ezra and once more set poetry on a new course, but in reverse.

Among the poets and critics included in this book are some, like Dana Gioia, Mark Jarman, and Robert McDowell, whom I have on occasion read with attention and respect. Others here have impressed me more for the crudity of their opinions and for their rude dismissal of poets far better than themselves. There are in fact some worthwhile pages in this collection of essays, and not all of the arguments are contemptible. Yet the overall impression is of something negative and disagreeable. One essay after another opens on a similar programmatic and self-nominative note: "One of the most remarkable developments . . . to revitalize American poetry. . . ." (Paul Lake); "The reflorescence of formal poetry . . ." (Robert McPhillips); "The return to form . . . the boldest and most unexpected innovation. . . ." (McDowell), etc.

It is not difficult to appreciate the frustration and exasperation of many people when faced with the prevailing mediocrity of current poetry, the trivialization of verse forms, the utterly substanceless claims for attention on one book jacket or another. I too share a certain impatience with these things, and with the general condition of what has come to be called, and perhaps too conveniently, *postmodernism*. One looks at the recent past, at the accomplishments of the prominent moderns, and inevitably asks: What else is there to do? What can we add? There may be good reasons for a revival of metrical forms, for a renewed interest in verse narrative, if only to relearn how certain things were done, and to refresh our understanding of what modernism actually did, what it departed from in its break with tradition. There are for me no reasons sufficient to justify the accusative voice characteristic of these essays, none that excuse the indiscriminate use of terms like "poseurs" or "the comfortably tenured corps" in reference to people who happen to teach and who also write in free verse. Nor do I see any justification for the outright misrepresentation of what a given poet has said or done or intended, nor for the wholly dubious way in which certain older poets are called upon in support of an attack on other poets, especially when we know how little, in the case of someone like Frost, the poet would have approved his reputation being misused or himself in any way called upon in support of a group or a school.

If one had the patience and the critical disposition to do so, it might be useful, if damned tedious, to go through these essays and provide a page by page and point by point correction of many of the claims presented here, the numerous mistakes in judgment, the carelessness in comparison and quotation, and the all-too-evident impulse in some of these critics to discount an achievement of the past in order to make room for something a little meaner, duller, and more recent.

An assertion by Richard Moore that Williams, of all people, refused "to consider the virtues of conventional American life" is so preposterous that it is difficult to believe the writer had any purpose in mind beyond glib provocation. Nor do I see any justification for suggesting, as Timothy Steele seems to do, that neither Pound nor Eliot understood verse, or that they were somehow responsible for an "abandonment of meter." The notion is too absurd to be taken seriously and entirely refuted by both poets in their poems and in their criticism. Elsewhere, Moore devotes time and space to a wholly frivolous devaluation of Eliot's "Prufrock," while dismissing an early, classic imagist poem by Pound as merely "notorious." Actually, for things of this kind and for its generally dismissive tone, Moore's essay is probably the cheapest advertisement for a fictional self I have read in some time. But it is not alone. Wyatt Prunty's academically corrective discussion of minor poems by Creeley and Ammons trails off into absurdity, and his essay otherwise is mainly contemptible.

The promotional element in these essays is at times subtle. An essay on narrative poetry by Mark Jarman opens on a moderately promising note with particular reference to E. A. Robinson, Robert Frost, and Robinson Jeffers. It is when he quotes narrative samples from poets now writing that I begin to question the direction of his essay. There is something intellectually shabby in comparing favorably, as Jarman seems to do, lines from poems by T. R. Hummer, Andrew Hudgins, and Garrett Hongo, with the work of Robinson and Frost. Not only are the lines quoted inferior as poetry, it is as if Jarman means to say that a certain real importance can be gained through this easy association. Further on in his essay Jarman refers pointedly to poets "working on Jeffers's scale." Whether intentionally or not, a remark like that is misleading. *No one* is working on the *scale* of Jeffers for the simple reason that no one writing at this time has the conviction, the passion, or the skill to write that way. And if such a poet *were* writing today he would do exactly what Jeffers did and invent his own idiom and his own forms. This is what good poets have always done, and the reason why an important generation of poets is always individual and distinctive. Anyone attempting now to write in the Jeffers manner will be automatically doomed to empty imitation.

So much seems to me to be basic. But to continue in this vein, calling attention to the more obvious excesses, the half-baked opinions and borderline slander, is for me a dispiriting business. It is possible that what I most object to here is the result of naiveté and an excess of zeal. At other times the arguments seem to me not simply mistaken but fraudulent.

A frequent complaint in these essays is that until recently there has been no acceptance of, no place for, poems written in metrical form. Yet these same critics will admit that right along with the free verse majority a few older poets like Richard Wilbur and Donald Justice have continued to write in those forms and with measurable success. The lesson I draw from this confusion of arguments is that the older poets referred to managed in some years of effort to write a few memorable poems, while these more recent poets so far have not.

I would feel much better about the intentions of these formalist poets if they simply wrote their poems and let us dispense with the programming and the self-advertising. Whatever there may be of a reforming character in their poems would sooner or later speak for itself and far more persuasively than all the dubious rehearsals of the lapses and failures of modernism. How impressed would we be by Jeffers, for example, if he had announced in print beforehand that he intended to write a new kind of poem about California, and had proceeded to explain and to diagram the ways in which he planned to do this? The idea is, of course, ridiculous, but no more so than the many untimely revelations we find in these essays.

Dana Gioia, at least, seems to understand that it is not the form in which one writes that finally matters, but the way in which the individual sensibility works within, fills out, and exemplifies that form. Some remarks by Stevens are helpful here:

> ... Poetic form in its proper sense is a question of what appears within the poem itself. It seems worth while to isolate this because it is always form in its inimical senses that destroys poetry. By inimical senses one means the trivialities. By appearance within the poem one means the things created and existing there. The trivialities matter little today, and most people concede that poetic form is not a matter of literary modes.[1]

These remarks were written forty years ago, but I see no reason to believe that the problem of poetic form has changed appreciably in the meantime.

The announced intentions of these formalists have on occasion been compared with a more extreme conservative temper in the country. It is true that at times one senses an eerie correspondence between the assertions in a book like this and the current political environment with its mood of empty forecasting based on little more than a popular poll-taking. Whether the comparison is justified or not, it does seem likely that the revival of traditional verse forms arises from more than a discontent with existing poetry; that it is symptomatic of a deeper discontent in society itself and of which the quarrel of poets is but one visible sign. To put it another way, the return to metrical form can be seen as another means of imposing on an incoherent society some form or order it does not have. And perhaps no one would object to that were it not for the inflated claims for an achievement where none so far exists.

Dana Gioia's "Notes on the New Formalism" is perhaps the most useful essay in the book, intelligent and informative, speculative without being dogmatic. On one or two counts only do I find myself in disagreement. The concern with an audience voiced here by Gioia, and repeatedly by others of these poets and critics, seems to me misplaced, as does a concern with the length of a poem. Neither goes to the heart of the matter. I would say that if poetry is to regain vitality and authority it can only do so by resuming a rigorous criticism of society; in this lies its most potent power. Anything less than this criticism amounts to a kind of complicity in the criminal enterprise this society has in great part become. If this is true, I do not see how the cultivation of "a broader popular audience" can be consistent with it. But here we come back to the situation of the poet in society, to his ordinary citizen duties and capacities, his loyalties, persuasions, and so forth. Each of us must resolve these things as we feel individually compelled to do, with all the reservations and potential losses that are implied. Only perhaps when one has nothing to lose can one speak openly and directly, without fear of either failure or reprisal. I suspect that if poetry were true to this idea in principle it would find an appropriate audience when the time comes.

The isolation of the poet in American society has its consequences, some obvious, some not. The position of poets and writers in the university is one sign of this isolation and embodies a certain contradiction. Those of us who teach, whether occasionally or as permanent faculty, are driven to be here, I would say, by a particularly acute sense of that isolation. Yet our very being here is a way of solving the loneliness on society's terms, in becoming a more or less honorary servant of the bureaucracy. From the point of view of poetry having any substantial effect in the world, any potential audience in society itself, the solution can only deepen and intensify the isolation. Among related and less obvious consequences, I would point to the mock-scholarly, mock-professional tone of many of these essays and of a good deal of current criticism as well. It is as if poetry might save its soul by becoming as nearly as possible a respectable activity, a member in good standing of the business and professional community—surely the most grotesque solution of all.

But poetry is not in any useful sense a profession, and it is certainly not a competition, no matter what the behavior of individual poets might at times seem to indicate. It is something else: a complication of reality, a questioning of values and appearances, subversive to the extent that it asks necessary questions; a surrender, a dedication, as well as being at certain times and in certain instances a sacrifice—in which situation all questions as to career and professionalism become irrelevant.

There remains the problem of the long poem, whether it is still possible, whether it is even necessary. In a brief introductory essay on narrative and epic form, its tradition and apparent demise, Gioia asks whether Milton could have succeeded so well without the example of Homer, Virgil, and Dante behind him. The question is reasonable and the answer is obvious. But if one is going to ask a question like that it seems to me that one ought to continue and to ask whether Eliot could have succeeded as he did with his *Quartets* if he had not had certain older poets, Dante among them, to draw on. And perhaps one would recognize at the same time that, whatever past examples he may have had in view, the form that Eliot's poem took was substantially a new thing.

I make a point of this because some hard words have been written here, by Gioia and others, in reference to the "sequence." Against all current argument and malpractice I will defend the poetic sequence, that ruminative form not invented by modernism, surely, and which goes back through Yeats to Wordsworth, and perhaps even to Dante himself. I am speaking of thought that moves in considered periods, through one formal variation to another, and which says that we do not always nor necessarily think in a straight line. But in this context, as in most human undertakings, it is thought itself, the ability to think, to discriminate among particulars and shades of meaning, that makes the difference. In the *Quartets,* for example, it is clear that the sequential intelligence—an ability to incorporate, to combine and articulate, a number of modes of expression, narrative as well as dramatic, verse paragraph as well as lyric stanza, and all within a thematic, musical structure for which no adequate prose equivalent seems to exist—is the outcome not only of superior talent, but also of a certain maturity. It cannot be taught, and is not now common among poets, to say the best for the situation.

The final essay, by Frederick Turner and Ernst Pöppel, seeks in a wholly mistaken manner, and in part through a demonstration of recent brain theory, to place the new formalism on a sound scientific basis. There is a good deal that is merely silly in this essay, but to suggest, as the writers do in their conclusion, that free verse has somehow conditioned us to a totalitarian state of mind, is not simply preposterous, it is irresponsible and dishonest as well. I will leave to a more energetic reader than myself the deciphering of such passages as this: "The brain possesses built-in sites for the reception of oipoid peptides such as enkephalin—the endorphins—and also other pleasure-associated neurohumors such as the catacholomines. . . ." Leaving aside its grammatical clumsiness, you would think that any intelligent, literate person would immediately recognize the inappropriateness of such language when applied to anything as fundamentally darkened and mysterious as artistic expression. At this point we are about as far from poetry as we can get and still find our way back— a long way from anything humane and helpful to us in the social and spiritual isolation in which we find ourselves, and from which poetry on occasion offers one of the few means of rescue.

The revision of modernism attempted by many of these poets and critics contains, along with a good deal that is merely assertive and obvious, at times ethically dubious, a few helpful insights, and for these I am grateful. Having set the book aside, I can think of no more balanced and useful way to end this review than to quote a remark made by the poet William Stafford at a long-ago reading: "A poem is anything said in such a way, set down on the page in such a way, as to invite a certain kind of attention." Our formalists will surely balk at such modesty and apparent inexactness. Yet in whatever mode one chooses to write, at whatever moment, and in whatever place or circumstance we find ourselves, it is exactly that attention, the quality and intensity of it, that makes all the difference.

1990

Something for Our Poetry

I am sitting at a table in a small restaurant on the outskirts of Fairbanks. Outside, the sun of another subarctic summer warms the earth, and the newly unfolded leaves of willows and birches toss and shimmer in the windy light. One block down College Road noontime traffic is moving through the dusty intersection below University Hill.

And across the table from me someone with a skeptical edge to her voice is saying something about a recent book of poems.

"Oh, I don't know . . . I don't think they are really *her* politics, she's just using them in her poetry."

The book referred to is Carolyn Forché's *The Country Between Us,*[1] much talked about here in the spring of 1983, and apparently seen by some as a kind of breakthrough for "political" poetry in our time and country. It is a book I was prepared to dislike when I picked it off a bookstore shelf not long ago. I was suspicious not only of the heated claims for the poetry that were displayed on the book jacket, but of the passions I felt were bound to be recorded in the text at a time when the boundary wars of distant small, noisy, and ungrateful nations are once more disturbing our complacencies and upsetting the normal and peaceful conduct of economic empire.

Here in Alaska, where one speaks slyly of moose looking into the cabin windows at night, of berry-picking and woodcutting, and of the going price for an acre of swampland; and where nearly all talk about poetry seems to center on the matter of getting published or on teaching the "craft" of writing—in this provincial setting the mention of politics in conjunction with poetry brings a momentary pause in the conversation. Almost imperceptibly the attention at our table shifts onto some plane of distraction where we all sit in mute incomprehension.

The meal continues, and in a moment the conversation picks up again, having left the silence behind. At the outer edge of my attention I become aware of a blankness in the atmosphere, of a certain opaqueness of mind, though I would not until recently have thought of calling it that. For in that brief interval in the conversation a number of mislaid or discarded images arose, images that grouped themselves around a common enough suspicion: that under this very sun, and while we sit here in indulgent ease, people elsewhere are shot and mutilated, die and are left to rot in a tropical rain, to be buried with no more ceremony than the sound of a spade forced into the sandy earth.

These last mentioned are not original perceptions, nor do they represent events without precedence. But it would be a mistake to assume that they do not occur in the minds of people who may otherwise behave as if the images and the news they carry did not exist, and who by one means or another will submerge the images in a strangely stricken conscience.

What follows here is an interrupted rumination on poetry and politics carried on during the past several months by someone who, often enough, will prefer to avoid the combined subjects as being confused and intractable, but who knows nonetheless that each of us who writes and thinks about that writing must come to a self-understanding of the relation between these two human activities if he or she hopes to preserve in their poems and prose something of this age and its meaning.

There is a particular form of knowledge in our century; or, more exactly, an experience whose content is translated into knowledge: of endlessly repeated interrogations and mass arrests, of disappearing borders and the wholesale displacement of peoples—of changes so drastic and final the mind has difficulty in finding a place for them within what is understood and accepted in normal life. A few pages from Edwin Muir's *Autobiography*, recording his experience in Prague following World War II, offer us an early and soberly modest account of a condition that seemed destined to become universal:

> We were living in the midst of these changes, without any clear notion of what was happening, but aware of a constant invisible pressure, which seemed more dangerous than the isolated acts of intimidation or terror that came to our ears. The pressure produced, as by an exactly calculated process, a deepening of the apprehension which already anticipated the future. . . .

Taken together, these dislocations and disappearances constitute what is possibly *the* experience of our time. And of this vast trouble we here know little, other than in its materialization as *news*, as if the world were to be a kind of entertainment for us, an unbroken rehearsal of happenings far-off in unsafe lands.

The somber weight of this knowledge is stamped on much of the significant poetry of our time, whether it comes to us from Poland, from Russia, from Germany, from Italy or Greece—from almost anywhere in Europe, even as it appears in the poetry of countries like Sweden, not directly affected by these events. If this knowledge reveals itself as no more than a certain tone of voice, it is enough, and unmistakable to serious attention. It is as if underneath all possible speech can be heard something that resonates through the bedrock of the modern world. Steeped though it may be in horror and dread, this something—sound, arrangement of syllables, tone of voice—brings with it at the same time the terrible liberation that accompanies all profound experience: that which burns and strips away all encrustation, that the human soul be laid bare to its essential element.

This knowledge, the experience of which it is the fruit, would seem to have no root or counterpart in American poetry. Its absence, I believe, contributes as much as anything does to the relative inconsequence of the better part of writing in this country. A kind of willful innocence preserves us, for which we pay a price in the loss of intensity, and in a persistent suspicion that there is little of consequence in what we do.

One may do many things in life and art, depending on the available circumstances and on the individual fortune. Any one of many situations and resolutions may provide a satisfaction, personal and esthetic. But it seems to me worth considering whether or not an experience of this magnitude can be bypassed without serious harm to the spirit. If it is true that the better part of the central and searing experience of this century has so far passed us by, it follows that our behavior may be marked by an unacknowledged and pervasive guilt, that we will think, speak, and act from the inner poverty of those who through no superior virtue have been spared.

In the voice that articulates any part of the experience of the past six or seven decades can be heard an authority derived not simply from personal choice or inclination, but through absolute necessity. A single brief statement by Hermann Broch in commenting on his novel *The Guiltless* makes this clear:

> Political indifference is ethical indifference.

Given the circumstances under which Broch wrote, no other statement was possible for him. The greatness of the man and artist in his case brings to the statement a convincing rightness. Were the atmosphere in an American university at all favorable, I can imagine a seminar devoted to this statement alone.

An unequivocal conviction speaks also in a statement made by the artist George Grosz while on trial in Germany in the 1920s:

> If the times are uneasy, if the foundation of society is under
> attack, then the artist cannot merely stand aside, especially
> not the talented artist with his finer sense of history. There-
> fore he becomes, whether he wants to or not, political.

The tone of voice in each of these statements, the sober conviction that rings there, seems to come from some center in the age where whatever constitutes its essence can be found, and where men like Broch, Robert Musil, and others, staring out of the debris of a culture confronted the features of an awakening beast.

If we examine briefly political poetry written in English, for example that written out of the period of the Spanish Civil War, (by Auden and others,) it's clear that a similar conviction is lacking. That war, and the political condition it arose from and led into was part of the scene in which Broch, Musil, and others were destined to write; but something in the

English poets never came adequately into focus on the time and place, never surrendered itself, not to a cause, but to whatever the experience held in terms of human passion, outrage, and essential justice. What came, then, of the poems by Auden, Spender, and others was a kind of pseudo-content possible for young English intellectuals at the time, for whom the Spanish war was an adventure, a lark to be withdrawn from whenever the game became too dangerous and the politics too serious.

Something similar, perhaps, can be said of the "committed" poetry written in this country during the past two or three decades, and surely of that from which so much was hoped at one time or another, that of the Beat generation. There all, or nearly all, was fuzzy declamation where it was not simply adolescent protest and histrionics. Nothing, or almost nothing, was thought out, felt deeply enough to come to any mature utterance. By now it seems reasonable to say of Allen Ginsberg that a public image has long since replaced any possible substance.

No real definition of politics, as it presents itself in the modern world, has yet been undertaken by Americans; at best only on a local or regional level, and nationally on what appear to be grounds of nostalgia alone. And few poets so far have succeeded in making a convincing poetry from the political content of contemporary American experience. And it is not difficult to see why this should be so: that which has not been lived cannot effectively be written of. Words alone will not replace experience, nor will easy sympathies and pseudo-convictions made up overnight for whatever occasion or program. The true content will come out of blood and bone, out of metal and rubble, or it will not be much.

Neither Yeats's politics, nor Brecht's, where these took form in poetry and drama, were imported, nor were they solely a matter of personal choice. On the contrary, they were given, a part of the time and place. In such a situation the artist takes up the more or less imposed position, and the resolution in terms of art becomes a matter of individual genius.

In the poems of Czeslaw Milosz I hear, from moment to moment, a voice:

> We learned so much, this you know well:
> how, gradually, what could not be taken away
> is taken. People, countrysides.
> And the heart does not die when one thinks it should,
> we smile, there is tea and bread on the table.

And only remorse that we did not love
the poor ashes in Sachsenhausen
with absolute love, beyond human power.[2]

What is it that resonates here, that seems to speak, not for the poet alone, but for a generation? The self somehow defined by its being enlarged and multiplied, and the experience lived through not once but a thousand, a million times.

In place of this understated and universal anguish we American modernists have, characteristically, something else, something more personal and limited in its frame of reference, more limited finally in its significance: the exaggerated, self-tortured sensibility of the modern soul caught up in a world it does not like, and that does not understand it or have any genuine place for it. This so-called existential agony of the isolated individual whose self-laceration in search of intensity and meaning must by now be boring even to itself.

In Milosz's volume of essays, *The Captive Mind,* (1951) there is a paragraph much to the point:

> . . . I am not in favor of an art that is too subjective. My poetry has always been a means of checking on myself. Through it I could ascertain the limit beyond which falseness of style testifies to the falseness of the artist's position; and I have not tried to cross that line. The war years taught me that a man should not take a pen in his hand merely to communicate to others his own despair and defeat. This is too cheap a commodity; it takes too little to produce it for a man to pride himself on having done so. Whoever saw, as many did, a whole city reduced to rubble—kilometers of streets on which there remained no trace of life, not even a cat, not even a homeless dog—emerged with a rather ironic attitude toward descriptions of the hell of the big city, descriptions of the hell in their own souls. A real "wasteland" is so much more terrible than any imaginary one. Whoever has not dwelt in the midst of horror and dread cannot know how strongly a witness protests against himself, against his own neglect and egoism. Destruction and suffering are the school of social thought.

This paragraph impressed me strongly when I first read it. Employing it as one more useful point of view, I have been able to see American poetry in a much clearer light and place it, I think, in juster circumstances than is customary nowadays among those who assign the credits and write the reviews.

In writing the foregoing paragraphs, I have been aware of the risk I may run in being unjust to any number of admirable people, poets and critics alike. Yet, in any worthwhile attempt to make the subject, poetry and politics, clearer, one would want to know to what extent the present situation of the literary arts in this country contributes to that opaqueness of mind I referred to at the beginning of my essay. Can a situation in which nearly every poet, every writer of note, is in some way beholden to a system that supports, condones, and participates in the wrongs done by society, the political and economic structure of which it is part, ever give rise to that questioning of values that might alone justify poetry and the teaching of it? Or is it not just as likely to sustain an atmosphere in which *talk* comes to stand for serious thought? Talk, I think it would be fair to say, under certain conditions becomes a kind of silence. And what we have learned to do, as anyone who has taught for a while in university programs must know, is to talk at length about things—values, principles, where these are talked about at all—without ever committing the naive error of belief and practice. We have learned to discourse without conviction, without feeling any obligation to have lived first these things we talk of. And talk itself encourages, almost imperceptibly, a distance, a kind of superior isolation in which it is assumed that because one has some command of words one has also, by natural right, the knowledge and experience the words ought to convey.

Projecting this supposition further, could we not assume from the above description that where literary commentary emerges from people who are in one way or another part of an institutional system, the commentary would almost automatically have imposed on it certain limitations of thought and speech? Which writer among us, secure in a university position, would be ready to renounce his or her tenure and salary when faced with gross injustice and tyranny, or even with subtler and more mysterious modes of oppression and self-interest? I do not ask this merely to be cantankerous, since I ask it of myself first of all.

Turning briefly to *The Country Between Us,* my impression is that Carolyn Forché may have demonstrated more forcibly than anyone else at this time just how inevitable and necessary is the intrusion of politics into poetry. It would be easy, it might even be appropriate, to criticize the simplification of viewpoint in these poems, the at times crude association of imagery and events, the ready use of foreign words and phrases guaranteed to catch the attention and enlist the sympathies. Yet overall the range of her attention and the intensity of her concern are impressive. What redeems this poetry from its defects is the passion, and for the time being, the conviction of voice. Without passion poetry is not much. It is passion that has kept many of Yeats's poems alive long after the opinions in them have become irrelevant and the politics have disappeared — or if they have not disappeared altogether, have changed into something else, and so far as Ireland is concerned, something more murderous and without a saving idealism.

Having set this slim book of poems aside, what remains in my mind is a certain shape that I find convincing and true, and that I can place securely in my own time. The shape is composed of a connected sequence of images: a broken imagery of the missing and the erased, of entire towns and countries deleted from the maps, of exodus, and of exile in one's own land. Where these poems speak most convincingly, ironic distance is annulled in the sound of one person speaking to another; so the private anguish returns to and amplifies the general grief, and all that is false and extraneous is cancelled.

And this is no small achievement. Whatever might be its flaws in content and expression, *The Country Between Us* points in one direction for poetry: beyond craft, beyond provincialism, beyond self-absorption, into that universal human territory we must sooner or later enter.

It is another summer, after a winter of personal doubt, of confusion and change. Where I am sitting on a bluff above the Tanana River, the sun is bright on the hills, the wind comes off the river, now warm, now chilled from the snowfields in the foothills across the valley.

Faced with this vast and purposeful disinterest of nature, one instinctively recoils from opening a newspaper, not only because of the *news* one is apt to find there, but for the plain lack of intelligence displayed by commentators and public men alike. And the news as it comes to us from Salvador, from Baghdad, Washington, and elsewhere isn't exactly promising. Perhaps the news from such places has never been promising, but only tentative at best where it is not downright discouraging. It speaks now of dishonesty for hire, of a determined and malicious misapprehension of reality; it speaks also of a continuing anguish of spirit in unsheltered and less fortunate lands.

MX, *Pershing,* and *Triton* are names that surface in the news with a metallic shudder. As I write, a U.S. fleet is patrolling the North Pacific in an idiotic show of force refloated from the 1940s. Earlier this spring I watched a convoy of trucks and personnel carriers roll past the house, returning from an army "exercise" in the Alaska Range to the south of us. Across the valley one night I saw a pattern of bright yellow flares floating to earth, lighting the wilderness below.

It is unlikely that poetry, no matter how well it may be made or how major its impact, has the power to affect the world directly, though it can often change the life of an individual. But the shape that it can give to things and events—the emotional force it embodies, the exactness of insight as signified by its apparent structures—tells us as well as anything can where we have been, who we have been, and how full or depleted was that measure of verisimilitude by which we lived our time on this planet. And the poetry will be true and just to the extent that we do not lie for hire or fashionable advantage, nor falsify what we have seen and learned. We do not know the extent to which a single creative act may strengthen a positive force in the universe. It does seem believable, however, that any creative work in itself partly redeems us from the wrong we otherwise do.

In some prominent place of instruction I would like to post the following remarks by Octavio Paz:

> In our epoch poetry cannot live within what capitalistic society calls its ideals. . . . Today all poetic activity, if it is truly poetic, must oppose that society. It is not strange that for certain sensitive souls the only possible vocation is solitude or suicide; neither is it strange that for others, beautiful and passionate, the only imaginable poetic activities are dynamite, political assassination, or the gratuitous crime. In certain cases, at least, one must have the courage to say that one sympathizes with these explosions, which are testimony of the desperation to which a social system based solely upon

the conservation of the status quo, and especially economic gain, leads us.[3]

Nothing at this moment seems truer to me than this, be it ever so often said, and nowhere more clearly said than here. Probably there are any number of people who would acknowledge the general truth in this statement, and yet not fully understand its meaning or see any reason to apply it to their lives.

It may be that in what I have written here I have exposed a few of my own uncertainties. If so, that exposure is needed, for only the most rigorous examination of conscience and conduct are likely to preserve us from repeating the mistakes and miseries of revolution and social renovation so evident in this century. It is unlikely that we will prove to be any wiser or more temperate than other peoples when faced with events asking of us restraint and humane understanding. Yet, where it can be identified, we are bound to oppose evil, and if in that opposition we are sometimes led to excess, in language and act, we can at least hope that another generation will understand and forgive us. *1983*

You and I and the World:
Some Notes on Poetic Form

Modernity is precisely this transitory, fleeting, contingent factor.
BAUDELAIRE

The subject of form, in poetry as in art generally, can be argued on the ground of availability and convenience alone. As most of us know, a suitable form can sometimes make all the difference. At the outset we would have in mind what sort of movement, pace, or measure should be introduced into the poem, what kind of urgency we would want to suggest to the reader. The cadence of a meditative poem would not be that of a lyric, the form of an address, or an exhortation not that of a narrative. The practice of free verse, as we mostly know it, leaves little choice as to a suitable form, and consequently our poems all tend to look alike and sound alike.

That there are outstanding precedents for a certain number of three-line stanzas in sequence; that a pairing together, in a poem of some length, of two lines that will rhyme and in which there can be no more than a given number of syllables; or that a certain kind of thought or emotion can be expressed in a specific form of fourteen lines—that these modes represent a significant past accomplishment is somehow reassuring. Even if one never makes direct use of the models, it is good to know that, yes, great poems have been written in these forms.

But when the spirit of things changes, and the inner substance of thought undergoes a transformation, it may turn out that the form is no longer adequate; it ceases to act for us in a vital way and becomes mere formality. And this, of course, is pretty much what happened in the early decades of this century with the rise of modernism. The true form thereafter would be one realized in the act of creation — the form in process, to be discovered in the language we speak, in which we express our thought and our passion. This speech, carrying with it what elements of traditional form and usage we might feel to be still useful and satisfying, would more nearly express for us the truth of our life and time. Or so would seem to have been the argument once, and for some of us at least it remains a valid premise.

Direct comparisons of kinds of verse writing can be useful. This is not what we ordinarily find in a review of a book of poems these days, where a few lines from a poem will be quoted in support of one opinion or another, and from which we learn almost nothing apart from the critic's personal bias. Partly for my own instruction, but in the hope also that it will prove to be of some interest to others, I have chosen four examples of verse. (I would prefer to let these stand alone and speak for themselves, but for the sake of clarification I have added a brief commentary.) The verses should not be merely looked at on the page, but should be read aloud.

My first example is taken from a poetry journal that came my way not long ago:

> Staring out at rapids and ice
> I think of Michigan and us
> buying beer from Eddie and Doc,
> the oldest boys in town,
> and going to the dump to shoot rats.

My second example is from a poem by Monroe K. Spears in a recent issue of the *Hudson Review*:

> Unlike many a genius, Hayden was beloved;
> Generous to his rivals, faithful to his wife,
> Religious, hard-working, charitable and kind,
> A great artist and a truly good man.

My third example is a brief poem by Walter de la Mare, called "Napoleon":

> What is the world, O Soldiers?
>   It is I:
> I, this incessant snow,
>   This northern sky;
> Soldiers, this solitude
>   Through which we go
>   Is I.

And my fourth example is taken from one of Pound's last Cantos:

> Time, space,
>   neither life nor death is the answer.
> And of man seeking good,
>   doing evil.
> In meiner Heimat,
>   where the dead walked
>   and the living were made of cardboard.

The lines quoted in my first example may be taken as one extreme, and fairly typical of much verse writing these days. By no means of emphasis in reading them can I get these lines to sound like poetry. With effort, an approximate verse can be gotten from them, but the content, in keeping with the technique, remains trivial.

In my second example the verse is more sophisticated, and there is an obvious intelligence at work. I note a certain metrical regularity, though it is not pronounced. The lines are from a poem I rather liked—liked for what it had to say, while I admit that no single line or group of lines remained with me after I had read the poem; only a sense of having read something that I found agreeable for the information it gave me. What I find missing is some element that would finally distinguish the verse from prose: an intensification of pace and phrasing, the information concentrated as imagery in place of statement—or simply that indispensable ingredient in human speech: passion. The language throughout the poem is intelligent, pleasant to read, but with little emotional force. And in fact the thought expressed in the poem is not particularly original.

What the two preceding examples lack, in the sheer immediacy of poetic speech, de la Mare's poem, as brief as it is, has in abundance. It is a small masterpiece, a lesson on how to get the most into the least, and worth many pages of biography and historical commentary. The poem gives us the impression of complete freedom while confined within the bounds of seven short lines.

In my fourth example, in the lines I have quoted from Pound, once again, though in a completely different mode, we have something distinguished from prose by an emotional and intellectual concentration. The distinction is evident in the precision and lightness of the language, in the acute sense of physical movement. As in de la Mare's poem, it is not difficult to feel in Pound's verse an underlying musical figure, made all the clearer in this case by the way the lines are arranged visually on the page.

More than is the case with de la Mare's poem, Pound's lines have a contemporary ring to them, as of a familiar note being struck. In the gaps, leaps, and hesitancies of Pound's verse, in its swiftness of reference, there is something not only characteristic of good poetry generally, but immediately contemporary in its altered, expanded sense of time.

Even if you don't know that the German phrase means "my homeland," the sound alone conveys a good part of its meaning. Among its other virtues, Pound's verse assumes a certain level of intelligence and information in the reader; this in itself, whether or not the reader is aware of it, makes of the poem a lasting gift.

So far as I am able to tell from my reading of current poetry journals, little that approaches the skill and authority of these lines is being written in this country today. By which I don't mean that I think there is no good poetry being written; but that a certain intelligence, a perspective at once personal and historical, seems not to be much in evidence.

It might be asked, in view of the obvious discrepancy between my first and last examples, are comparisons like this fair? I think they are. They represent what any honest and aspiring poet, wishing to learn the art, will do instinctively, much as a young painter will spend hours in a gallery or museum, studying a few good works, comparing, and learning to make distinctions.

The truest impulse in art and literature in our time has taken the form of a questioning of appearance and reality. In recent years this impulse, in poetry, has fallen into a shallow scholasticism, into autobiography and trivial states of mind all but emptied of any transpersonal content. This development (to call it something) has kept pace with what I take to be a standardization of free verse and a radical reduction of vocabulary and metrical resource. In view of the probable accuracy of this description, it might be worth asking whether yet another argument as to the validity of free verse, another exchange of opinion on the "poetic line" will leave us with any better options than we now have, any clearer sense of our present circumstances. It seems to me that the inquiry might begin elsewhere.

The motivation in art is always the same: to renew contact with the world, to maintain a creative flow between the inner and the outer worlds—to have them, in fact, *one*. This ancient dialogue can be illustrated in the following way. Among the Dogon in West Africa, an individual gifted in divination will go outside the village in the evening, and on a space of clean, raked sand will draw certain signs in a more or less geometrical pattern. When he is done, he will carefully and strategically scatter peanuts or other food scraps over his table of signs. During the night a jackal, lured from the nearby bush, will come out to eat the food. At sunrise the diviner will return, and by noting where the tracks of the jackal enter, cross, or seem to communicate between the signs, he will read and interpret their meaning.

What I have just introduced may for a moment seem obscure in reference to a discussion on poetic form; but it speaks to me of the profound relatedness that lies at the heart of all genuine experience with the world—how all things hinge on each other. As in any significant dialogue, the relation between art and life is not a thing we can subdivide. In taking up and renewing in some way an old form, in making, or suggesting, if only to a limited degree, the possibility of a new form, we renew not only the art, but life itself.

Great poetry has been written in formal measures and strict forms, in "free" verse, and sometimes as intensified prose. I see no reason why this should not continue to be the case, unless we are going to insist on one or more kinds of orthodoxy and turn the entire thing into a subdivision of politics.

Poetry, the making of a poem, is an act whose significance we can only grasp through the force of a great example; without that we have no true measure. Finally, the only adequate argument is a poem or a poetry that justifies its forms and its impulse, and establishes in some way a precedent—in our time perhaps no more than a fleeting instance—for what a poem can be. And this, it seems to me, is what the great poems, past and present, offer us, each in its own way. It is up to us to choose and to make the best possible use of these.

A further, and more complete, account of modern art and literature has still to be written, and will not be written until we have a criticism as broadly familiar with the content of contemporary experience in all of its phases as it is with the history of literary movements, so that it can dispose of the significance of trends and fashions with an assurance that these are not necessarily in themselves things of first importance.

A more satisfying explanation than is usually given for the appearance of "free verse" as a dominant form in poetry, as well as for the rise of abstraction in art—the impulse evident in these toward a new, organic shape, or image of reality—may lie somewhere in the field embraced by psychology. I don't mean this in a pathological sense, but in the much broader sense that all of modern art and literature can be seen as an attempt to come to grips with, to define and make visible, forces we can all sense within us, and often in the world at large, but that are too intrusive, wayward, and demonic, to be at home either in the traditional, naturalistic images of art, or in those inherited forms on which poetry has depended and from which it has drawn much of its strength and coherence in the past.

That a specific, resident spirit seeks its voice, form, and definition in a given age can be demonstrated in the case of a number of poets and artists in our own time as in the past. The uprooted and dispersed character of this age, the restlessness and formlessness so typical of the modern spirit, is familiar enough, and produces, in art as in life, a pervasive if unacknowleged fear—of chaos, of dissolution and death. And the prime example of this circumstance in English and American poetry is Eliot, in whose career the opposing forces of creativity and dissolution can be seen at work. To look, with an attention free from academic cant, is to see in "Prufrock," in "Gerontion," in "The Waste Land" and "The Hollow Men"—in these poems as well as many of his others—a thing strange and disturbing, but unmistakably modern, assuming its outlines, seeking its resolution, and almost in spite of the man and his personal welfare. What we know of biography and composition in Eliot's life make it clear that poetry is not always nor necessarily a personal affair. Individual talent and ambition account for only so much, and then something else assumes control that acts at no man's bidding.

And at this distance in time it is understandable that he should have taken up the conservative position he did in regard to tradition, to rescue himself from the very real threat of incoherence, and to establish, if only for a moment, a balance and order: a point of rest, one poised between a past and accomplished form and a still-to-be-realized new form that would justify itself, its time and place. According to this notion, and in keeping with the present discussion, this *form* would seem still to be mainly a matter of individual questioning and search, and not of secure and general possession.

There is a form that exists, independent of our will and invention, and one need not believe in either God or Plato to acknowledge a truth in this claim. To the extent that a poem corresponds in some degree to this living, timeless, but never more than partly revealed form, the poem will justify itself and outlive its moment of conception. We will call it apt, or fitting, or beautiful, like a house to be lived in.

All things have a life of their own. It is not we who have invented this life and assigned a meaning to it, nor do we in the creative act set in motion a process that did not exist up to that moment. This thought can be verified in the feeling we often have that the form and substance of a poem are somehow *given*—not precisely, of course, but essentially—and from that moment it is up to the individual to bring that form and substance to their fullest realization.

Anything—a thought, a phrase, a speck of matter—once set in motion, seeks its potential and specific form. In this sense, a line of poetry is no different from anything else in nature, an *idea* not essentially different from a seed dropped into a furrow and that germinates and grows into a shrub, a tree, or an entire thicket, with its own distinctive outlines. There are types and mutations, as we know, and nothing is fixed forever.

We should keep in mind that everything by which we know ourselves and define our being, in life as in art, has its root and model in nature—not only in the outward forms of polished rock and spreading tree, of mottled insect and singing bird, of physical body and airy cloud—but in what we choose to call *spirit,* that all but invisible, dynamic source from which spring not only our insights and inspirations, but every possible form, sound, color, and variation. I recall with particular force a remark somewhere in one of Jung's essays that what we call creative ideas have their own timeless existence. Whether these are actually ideas in the abstract sense, or take the form of specific structures, the meaning is the same. We do not discover them so much as we are discovered by them. We do not create them; they create us.

One final example, a poem by the Swedish poet Werner Aspenstrom:

> *You and I and the World*
>
> Don't ask who you are and who I am
> or why everything is.
> Let the professors solve that,
> they get paid.
> Put the kitchen scale on the table
> and let reality weigh itself.
> Put on your coat.
> Turn off the light in the hall.
> Close the door.
> Let the dead bury the dead.
>
> We are walking here now.
> You are the one who is wearing
> white rubber boots.
> I am the one who is wearing
> black rubber boots.
> And the rain that falls over us both
> is the rain.
> (Trans. Siv Cedering)

I cannot be certain whether in Swedish this poem is *free,* or by what rule or measure it achieves its effect. But I know that its effect on me is unmistakably that of poetry, of art; that through some magic in its choice of images, in the relation of its few and inevitable details, and because of the unique sensibility that, having composed its structure, shines through the words of this poem, I am convinced and released from words into the world.

And perhaps we should leave it at that. In the end, the only acceptable attitude toward art, as toward existence itself, is that of openness, of an inborn susceptibility that can otherwise be described as a capacity to see and to listen.

And to see with eyes closed, if it comes to that.   *1985–86*

Reply to Mississippi Review

This brief comment was written in response to a question asked by an editor of the Mississippi Review *in 1990. Specifically, I was asked to reply to the following: "It has sometimes been said that contemporary poetry, however technically brilliant, is without a 'statement' or 'vision.'"*

The question as it is phrased seems to me both vague and simplistic; it immediately suggests any number of additional questions. What, for example, is implied here by "statement," or "vision?" I am equally uncertain of what is meant by the phrase "technically brilliant." The question arises whether such an assumed brilliance is even possible in the absence of significant content. If we mean by it that many people have been taught to write, have come to the making of verses without any compelling reason to write—anything that could not just as well have been left unsaid— then the statement makes some sense, even if a better way might be found to say it.

It might be more useful, and accurate, to refer to the absence of an informed social and political criticism in present poetry; to the dominance of that ubiquitous, autobiographical "I" for whom the world has no more interesting fact than its very limited connection with an equally limited "I."

But how many of us, however gifted, have a self that deserves a book of poems every two or three years? How many of us could even begin to define that self in relation to the world that surrounds it and of which it is in some way a part, tenuous and conditional though that may be? People will write and publish as they please, but to expect of hundreds (or thousands) of aspiring poets that they have some vital thing to tell us, something that might constitute a major addition to, or revision of, literary history, is an absurdity.

What we call *vision* in a poet is more likely to be recognized by others, and often long after the event. But what if the one possible vision now must take into account the progressive economic and political deterioration of society? What kind of vision would that be? Artists and writers in Europe today will contend with a new vision of that continent, one bound to present both difficulties and, doubtless, new combinations. For Americans at this time the situation appears to be radically different, and the outlook is for further deterioration of the social bonds, with a corresponding increase of instability, violence, and oppression. Faced with this possibility, what position, what attitude, is the creative writer to take? Can, for example, an adequate critique be voiced from within the establishment, from within the university?

Meanwhile, the institutionalization of literature and intellectual life has proceeded, bearing out a prediction made by Max Weber many years ago regarding what he saw as "the total domination of the bureaucratic ideal."

As for poetry, there are, here and there, more hopeful signs. A recent anthology from the *Amicus Journal* contains a number of poems of considerable merit, marked by an intensity of regard for this world we inhabit and abuse. Here, and in a recent collection of writings on the Valdez oil spill, I see evidence that, given so immediate and drastic an event, many of us possess the talent to make of the occasion, if not great poems, poems at least that do not shame us. Perhaps, gifted with a certain modesty and affection for truth, we can learn from the example.

Reflections on the Nature *of Writing*

This brief 1992 essay originated as a contribution to a symposium sponsored by the editors of Mānoa, *and devoted to the question, proposed in a brief essay by John A. Murray, as to whether or not nature writing was becoming the genre of importance in American literature. At one point in his essay Murray referred to* Walden *as a "deeply flawed book."*

The question asked is a provocative one, and with much of what Murray has to say I can agree.

Poetry and fiction may, as Murray and others suggest, have diminished in importance and imaginative appeal. That diminishment may or may not be due to exhaustion of a particular genre. It is just as likely due to the limitations of individual writers and to the concentration of writing, in all forms, in the university. If nature writing is also to make its headquarters in the English department, is there any reason to believe that it too will not, sooner or later, be affected and diminished by this institutional association with its resident demon of specialization?

One thing can be said about it: the potential subject, Nature, is so vast and inclusive that it is not easy to imagine it being exhausted by any amount of study and writing. Nonetheless, the capacity of this society to seize upon, promote, and trivialize, any and every enthusiasm should not be discounted. Few people really know Nature in any depth or detail, whereas many would write about it, if for no other reason than that they have read some of the books and because it is now the thing to do.

We are to some extent handicapped in this discussion because we are prone to think of Nature as something outside of us and therefore subject to control and exploitation if only we can find the means for it. It becomes possible, therefore, to speak of "the death of Nature." This phrase is by now almost a popular formulation, one that tends to diminish understanding. We are unable to see Nature for the inclusive force that it is. It is about us and within us, a necessary part of everything we are and can do, of everything we make, even the books we produce. It is in the dust of our carpets, in the spiders and roaches that seek whatever household crack or crevice exists for them, and in the shifting foundations of our buildings. It is in the squalor of the streets and neighborhoods of our cities, where Nature, shunned otherwise, returns in the form of random violence and deliberate criminality. It is in the decay of our political systems, and in the confusion and incoherence of our public discourse. Strictly speaking, there is no life apart from Nature.

I am not certain what to make of Murray's remarks on *Walden*. I wish he had expanded on them, because as they stand they appear to be an insinuation without substance. I would say, rather, that Thoreau succeeded as he did in *Walden* because he was, among other things, a poet, and was able to see and to feel as a poet. His language as a consequence has a concentration lacking in most nature writing. Additionally, the language itself was, in his day, still an instrument of some precision and clarity in the hands of writers and thinkers like himself and Emerson. The public statements of scholars and politicians had substance and conviction as is seldom the case today. Much of the American continent was still fresh and new, or appeared to be. Moreover, people generally lived then much closer to Nature, simply as a matter of everyday necessity. These facts in themselves seem to me of considerable importance.

Familiarity with the natural world informed great writing of the past, as any sample from Dante, Chaucer, and Shakespeare can demonstrate. If attention to the world—to the ants and the sparrows, to the stone and the dust at our feet—can return us to the human predicament with renewed insight, then so much the better. But let us insist on veracity, on real knowledge, on *truth*, as it can only be discovered by men and women as they go about their lives from hour to hour, from day to day, and from season to season.

As the novels and tales of Chekhov, Tolstoy, and Giono, to name three exemplary figures, make abundantly clear, fiction can include Nature and human character in such a way that the two of them enhance and clarify each other, become in fact representative of this single world we all share.

But these writers are from another world than ours. Perhaps, then, the problem lies not so much in the genre as in our lives and the way we live them. The poetry will improve when poets have again entered the world as most of humanity must experience it. But, as in most things that really matter, there are no rules, only a certain ground on which to stand and from which to observe whatever is of most importance to us.

I remarked once, in a symposium devoted to contemporary poetry, on the virtual disappearance of the love poem, and with it a closely related affection for the world, its creatures, persons, and objects. If that affection must now become the province of nature writers, then so much the worse for poetry, but for us also. For poetry is still the primal utterance, whether conceived in verse stanza or in prose paragraph. There is no final reason why poetry cannot, in the right hands and arising from the right motives, include whatever of nature study is appropriate to its means and mission. If contemplation of Nature, and the attention it demands of us, can restore to poetry, and to fiction too, something of the old intensity of desire and affection, then by all means let us embrace it.

III

Selected Letters

Isn't it the function of every poet, instead of repeating what has been said before, however skillfully he may be able to do that, to take his station in the midst of the circumstances in which people actually live and to endeavor to give them, as well as himself, the poetry that they need in those very circumstances?
WALLACE STEVENS

A Letter

To the editors of AWP Chronicle, *June 1989:*

I would like to thank the editors of *AWP Chronicle* for reprinting Joseph Epstein's essay "Who Killed Poetry?" I happen to agree essentially with everything he has to say; but even if one does not agree with all that he says, nor especially like the way that he says it, it is important that he has brought into the open, and more prominently than anyone heretofore, a good deal that many of us have felt and thought at one time or another, even when we have not said so aloud. And it seems to me all the more valuable that this has been said by someone who, though he obviously cares about poetry, is not himself a poet.

Nor is it purely a matter of the state of poetry. Far more has happened, it seems to me, than we know or can readily admit: a qualitative loss of relation and fellowship, of that spontaneous flow of feeling for, of delight in, another person or another creature. The disappearance of the love poem alone should have warned us. If there is no place in poetry now for this most immediate of human situations—the intense regard of one individual for another, a regard that does not preclude the possibility of that *other* being something besides, or in addition to, a man or a woman—if there is no place in poetry for this, then what essentially is left to us, since all other relationships can be said to derive from this one primary affection? Who now would write a poem to daffodils, to a rose, to a nightingale or a lark? Who now feels the unclouded affection for the world that allowed a poet in the past to write such poems? An affection, moreover, that would, not so long ago, have sprung spontaneously into song, into verse? We have put the world under glass, studied it nearly to death, asked of it what further material profit it can bring us. As a consequence we know a great deal about the world, and we can talk and write at length and in detail about it; but we are no longer, in our inmost self, a part of it. Despite the means for material satisfaction increasingly available to us, potential life for the individual, if one is to believe the evidence in the representative contemporary poem, and in much fiction too, is reduced to this intensely narrowed, ungiving, and unreceiving concentration on the smallest possible self.

For all of that, I learn more of contemporary life from reading a story by Ray Carver or Richard Ford, more about society and its political arrangements from an interview with Noam Chomsky, than I do from reading any poet I can name at the moment. The reasons for this are probably complex, but may owe something to the perceived position of the poet within society, and which might be stated: "Society behaves as if I did not exist. Therefore I will write as if society did not exist."

It may be true that poetry, as it appears in verse form, is the more easily trivialized of literary forms. It *looks* easier to write, a matter of lines arranged in a more or less interesting pattern, rather than pages and paragraphs; narrative, character, and argument can be dispensed with in favor of a few random impressions, etc. It is apparently more susceptible to abuse by the personal pronoun; the better part of it fits in very well with Milan Kundera's definition of *Graphomania*: an attempt "not to create a form, but to impose oneself on others."

The problem of poetry and its audience was stated with clarity and intelligence thirty years ago by Edwin Muir in *The Estate of Poetry*. To my mind, nothing written since has added anything essential to the discussion. Given the state of society at this time the problem may be intractable, and any solution achieved at the expense of poetry. But if there is, finally, no apparent audience for poetry, the serious person has one remaining option, and that is to follow Robinson Jeffers's example and write *as if* there were an audience. With integrity and luck, one day there will be.

I have mentioned Chomsky, and the example is instructive. Here is an individual whose work in the field of linguistics is respected, commented on and, I'm sure, disputed. Accomplishment enough, one would suppose. But he has done something else, what few people in academic life ever do, and stepped outside his special field. He has taken his intelligence, his gift for analysis, for clear thought and expression, and applied it to politics and to government, and with notable results. I would like to ask why do not more of us—poets, writers, and professors—do the same? Were we to do so, not only literature and "creative writing," but university instruction and public life generally might gain significantly.

The enduring vitality of Chaucer, of Shakespeare and Dante—of the great classical poets and writers whom we continue to study and admire—comes not from superior talent, though that is there also, but is as much the fruit of their participation in the world, a commerce with people and events. It is hardly incidental that two of modern Europe's greatest writers, Hermann Broch and Robert Musil, were, individually and to one degree or another, successful in business and engineering, steeped in philosophy and psychology, experienced in military life and in journalism. When, with enormous patience and following a period of search and hesitation, they became, finally, *writers,* they were ready to write. Only very great talent, of the kind that knows how to wait, could have succeeded in transforming so much experience into art. But then greatness is precisely what is asked of us. It has been said before, but seems worth repeating here, that Yeats would likely have remained a good though minor poet had he not been forced by circumstances and events into Irish public life, its theater and its politics. The world does indeed feed its poets; sometimes, not always, the poets give something back.

In any discussion of poetry, its past and present merit and importance, we may keep one additional thing in mind: this life, yours and mine, will never be lived again; and therefore everything seen, heard, felt, and re-membered, has this universal potential of being made into something—a poem, a song, a story—that will speak to us in a voice never to be heard again. Whoever understands this and can conduct himself or herself ac-cordingly, in both life and art, may be reasonably assured of immortality.

A Letter

To the editor of Northwest Review, *April 1989:*

In response to Greg Kuzma's review of Dana Gioia's *Daily Horoscope,* and to the letters it has provoked, I would add the following remarks.

Were it not for the heat it appears to have generated, it might be best to dismiss Kuzma's attack as simply another rotten review and let it go at that. If he had stopped with his first four or five paragraphs he might even be complimented on having said a few useful things. But his subsequent misuse of Gioia to further his argument strikes me as lamentable. I have great respect for Mr. Gioia as a critic, and I am grateful to him for the many thoughtful essays he has contributed to the discussion of poetry in recent years. Even when I do not fully agree with him, I admire the energy and intelligence of the writing; often enough his comments have clarified for me problems I have considered at one time or another but have not found the occasion to write about. This criticism, what I have read of it, seems to me among the few freshening things to be found nowadays.

My copy of *Daily Horoscope* is packed away somewhere, but I have read enough of Gioia's poems otherwise to feel confident that if they are not yet great poetry, neither are they as inept, as inconsequential, as Kuzma makes them out to be. It is enough for me at this moment that Gioia is attempting with honesty and skill to write the poems he feels it necessary to write. If the iambic beat occasionally intrudes, and to my ear it does, I am willing for the time being to suspend judgment and listen; something may be happening that I do not understand.

Is something wrong with American poetry? Apparently, since so many seem to think so and find ways to express their dissatisfaction. Many of the complaints—such as the characteristic self-absorption of much of the poetry, its lack of significant content, the poverty of metrical resource— are justified, and they are not new to me. In more than one critical essay published in the 1960s and 1970s I called attention to these things, but few were listening. Meanwhile, a system of patronage and self-interest has prevailed in the proliferation of programs and conferences, as a result of which the quality of the poetry would appear to decline in proportion to the number of claimants.

It is true, I think, that the better part of the commentary and reviewing of poetry, as well as the teaching of it, originates with people who are in no way exceptional. They have merely been licensed to talk and to write *as if* they had something to say; their numbers comprise a dominant mediocrity that insists on its own marginal standards and unfailingly praises its own reflection in many school mirrors.

Let us add also the confused and irritable defensiveness of many poets now, their touchy territorial instincts, and their cruelty toward one another. Not unrelated to this is the sense one has, often enough, of a deliberately exasperated sensibility, as if out of some undefined and unadmitted guilt a false suffering must be introduced in place of a true suffering in common with a universal humanity. This false anguish, combined with an inevitable inflation of content, may be one more indication of the price we pay for submitting to the seductive humiliation of this society.

My impression of the better part of the poetry now being written, in whatever mode, is of too many words; too many words and too much talk. And by talk I mean mainly a chattiness disguised as verse, and gossip pretending to be art. It is difficult for me to see how any "Expansionist" program is going to improve this. My reading of a recent issue of *Crosscurrents* together with an anthology of metered verse edited by Robert Richman, has not been reassuring. That is to say, the talk has not been visibly improved by being set to meter, nor has the self-concern become less prevalent.

The word "gentility" has been invoked here, and perhaps unfairly. Yet, despite a handful of interesting poems—by Bishop, Warren, Gioia, Fred Morgan, Andrew Hudgins—it is hard to think of a better term for most of the poems in Richman's anthology. There is grace, pleasantness, skill of a sort, to be sure. But one may read this anthology forward and backward, and find little direct evidence of the century we have lived through. Other than for a certain attenuated sensibility, we would hardly know that two world wars had occurred, one of them within living memory, nor that subsequent conflicts have involved us in ways not fully acknowledged; that we live still with the legacy of a totalitarian mentality unprecedented in the scope and violence of its effect on the world; that such things as death camps and mass deportations had taken place—that none of these events, whose consequences have by no means spent themselves—now matter; nor that we inhabit, and partly as a result of these events, an increasingly poisoned and threatened planet.

It is as if the modern age, with all of its disasters and dislocations, had disappeared. In place of that disturbing memory we find a catalogue of cheeses, a rhymed discourse on the amorous effect of a good martini; we find word games, and we find lost marbles. The people in these poems do a lot of eating. There is insomnia, to be sure, but there is no hunger, and no one is homeless. If warfare is mentioned, it took place long ago and is now an occasion for nostalgia. Hiroshima has become a curiosity of tourism.

Perhaps a word that best describes the effect of this poetry is *boredom*. It is largely the poetry of people who have lived no life apart from the suburbs, the classroom, and the bookshelf; if they have ventured elsewhere, the experience has left little trace in their writing. Reading the better part of Richman's anthology is rather like shopping for cosmetics, stuffed animals, and fine knickknacks, while outside in the streets and barrios the poor and displaced of the earth hunt for a scrap to eat and a place of shelter from the night.

This is not to say that a typical free verse anthology, minus the rhymes and the elevated diction, might not yield pretty much the same impression, and with a talky slackness of its own. In fact, once the refinements are dispensed with, I suspect one would discover little essential difference in the two modes of writing.

The essence of modernism, in poetry, as in literature and art generally, has been identified with a clearing away of historical debris and cultural baggage, that the spirit of the age—mutilated, skeptical of inherited values, but determined in any event to seize from the wreckage something it can hold up as truth—might find adequate expression and at least a partial fulfillment. And this expression must have at its command a means and potential effect not dispersed or deflected by traditional consolations, whether in terms of an agreeable music or of familiar structures, at least where these would seem to support the illusion of a harmony that no longer exists. Though poetry now seems to have lost much of that decisive energy and purpose, I do not believe that the need for it has diminished, whatever trends or appearances may suggest otherwise. If poetry has become irrelevant in the world, as many feel it has, it may be because it has forgotten its mission and no longer questions our thinking.

As much as we might wish for it, would it be necessarily a good thing to have poetry a more general possession? It would all depend, and perhaps only if that poetry constituted a genuine criticism of society and was not merely a somewhat elevated form of entertainment for certain of its members. But here, it seems to me, the thing tends to cancel itself; for if the poetry *were* a true criticism, society, in its present state of moral and intellectual torpor, would have nothing to do with it, but turn away to other pastimes, to other, less demanding, forms of criticism.

Kuzma thinks that the current argument will be good for poetry. Maybe so, but I am skeptical. The irritable tone of the dialogue, to the extent that it can be called a dialogue, the mean-spiritedness that at times shows itself, is not encouraging. The premises seem inadequate to account for the vehemence of feeling displayed in one opinion or another, and that must arise from a deeper discontent. The atmosphere is very far from that generous and open spirit characteristic of modernism in its best days. In keeping with that spirit, one may respect a true formalist like Louise Bogan while admiring the innovative energy, the free verse mastery of Pound, Williams, and others; and respect, too, the work of poets who, like Roethke and Carruth, have done good work in both free and metrical forms. To ignore the mutual tolerance and respect that prevailed among many of these poets, and to square off, say, with Stevens against Williams, as some would like to do, is to place a false emphasis on the whole thing.

Finally, it is not a matter of mode, of forms free or formal, but of one's attitude toward the world; of the extent and the quality of one's relation to and participation in that world. Which is not to say that *form* is unimportant. It becomes important, it seems to me, mainly under two conditions: when it is justified by the content, by the inner substance of the writing; and when it is raised arbitrarily into prominence by people who have otherwise little reason to write at all.

The condition of poetry is also the condition of society, and a more thorough discussion would take us some distance beyond the quarrel of poets. But I do not intend to attempt here a comprehensive critique of the "new" poetry. Mainly, I wish for us all a measure of generosity, a little less rancor and peevishness.

A Letter

To the editors of the Hudson Review *in response to a letter from a teacher and writer at Bowdoin College who raised objections to my review, "Formal Objections" (see page 60):*

Denis Corish has written an interesting response to my review of *Expansive Poetry,* and I thank him for it.

I think most of his points are answered in my review. It ought to be clear that what I object to in part is not a return to metrical verse and/or narrative forms as such, but to the so far unproven claims for achievement. One would like to think that a decent modesty might prevail, and that a poet, or group of poets, would be willing to wait until a more substantial and mature body of work was available before the critical ranking was in place and the promotional machinery began working.

I am unable to see the situation, as Mr. Corish seems to, in terms of an endowed clique. What does dismay me is a mentality, all too prevalent now, that insists on the choosing of sides. According to this, if I respect Eliot I am somehow disqualified from also respecting Williams. Or if I cherish the poems of Wallace Stevens I must consign Robinson Jeffers to the dustbin. And so forth. But why must I choose among the poets whose work I love? Why can't I have them all, each for the sake of his or her own excellence? In fact, I do have them all, and so does any reader who cares about the art and not some petty jurisdiction adjacent to it.

Perhaps confusion arises in the use of the term "tradition." For the sake not of argument but of clarification, let me say that I regard the preeminent moderns, whether by this is meant Eliot and Yeats, Pound and Williams, or whomever, as being well within the tradition—the only tradition that matters, that of the individual writer attempting to clarify and give form to some fundamental content in the age in which we must live. And I suppose further that what we call modernism had its beginning at least as long ago as Wordsworth. What is "modern" in the end but a restatement of essential content in a form that renews not only the art but the material of life and the language it must make use of? Thus, for me the tradition includes, besides the more prominent names already cited, Edward Thomas as well as Edwin Muir; it includes Thomas Hardy, D. H. Lawrence, Hugh MacDiarmid, Kenneth Rexroth, and H. Phelps Putnam, as well as any number of poets who for one reason or another have fallen into an undeserved obscurity.

One would like to know more exactly what is meant by a "popular audience." I would not, for example, expect the poems of Louis Simpson to become popular. Not only are they far too intelligent to attract a wide public, they contain, and at times exemplify, that criticism I refer to in my review. I believe this criticism to be absolutely essential, unless one assumes that the function of poetry is to confirm a consensus view of reality, or that it is meant to entertain a middle-class audience and flatter its opinions.

If one looks at what is generally called modern poetry, in English as well as elsewhere, one sees a wide variety of forms, poems of many different kinds, and the fact is that modernism had room for these. The question is what happened to that generous and adventurous spirit that it has declined into faction and clique, into program and petty careerism?

The institutionalization of intellectual life far exceeds that small corner occupied by poetry, as I'm sure Mr. Corish must realize. But if certain effects of modernism have become the property of university departments, I am not going to make the mistake of blaming individual poets who were, after all and as usual, making the best of a difficult time. One notices in this connection, despite invidious references to the "tenured corps," that nearly all of our formalists teach. One suspects from this that the "revolution" anticipated by Mr. Corish may end in becoming merely another orthodoxy, surely a dismal prospect.

Well, I am for an open and creative disagreement. It might interest Mr. Corish to know that one prominent spokesman for the new formalism read my review and remarked that he agreed with *most* of it. That is rather more of an agreement than I expected, and more than enough.

According to Mr. Corish, "poetry will rise again." I for one hope so, though it would be helpful to know more precisely from where it might rise and into what. It seems altogether possible that it may do so in ways not anticipated by Mr. Corish nor, for that matter, myself.

A Letter

To the editors of the New Criterion, *November 1988:*

I would like to comment on Bruce Bawer's review of William Carlos Williams in your September issue.

Bawer has a few useful things to say, but taken as a whole his article struck me as an almost willful misrepresentation of the man and his work. Is it really necessary to subtract from Williams in order to add to Eliot? And if so, why? Eliot was, if you like, the greater poet, and Williams's quarrel with him had its unfortunate side; but it was at least consistent with the direction of his thought, expressed throughout his life in verse and prose: that there is (or was) in the New World a true theme, a new idea, a freshness, waiting to be discovered and given artistic form. In all phases of his career Williams remained true to that as he saw it. If he was, or seemed at times to be, incoherent, that was in part the price of his originality.

If you choose the right details and are clever enough in arranging them, you might make anyone's life and work look pathetic or ridiculous. A more generous estimate of Williams would be to place him, along with Walt Whitman, Charles Ives, and Emily Dickinson, among the instinctively innovative American spirits. Bawer's reduction of him to a kind of bumbling amateur is a disservice. Without perhaps intending to, Bawer perpetuates the odd notion that Williams lacked both intellect and sophistication. By implication he, Bawer, has both, and is thereby authorized to put Williams in his place.

Among the more glaring of Bawer's errors is his slighting reference to *In the American Grain,* one of the profound and resonant American books. This passion and insight brought to bear on a nation's history is not to be so casually dismissed. Contrary to the impression given by Bawer, much of it is brilliantly written, a fact I have confirmed recently in rereading parts of it. Whatever it may owe to Lawrence's *Studies in Classic American Literature,* it is utterly unlike that book.

With what seems to be condescending approval, Bawer quotes from *Spring and All,* one of Williams's most engaging poems. He does so without sufficiently noticing that the movement of the poem follows with precision the poet's attention to the details he presents. Williams's avoidance of transitional devices is deliberate and successful. The same might be said for many of Williams's more memorable poems — "To Elsie," "These," "The Yachts," etc. — poems that could have been written in no other form, could hardly be imagined in anything like traditional measures. Moreover, such poems have, and notably, what most present-day poems lack: a certain largeness and thingness of involvement with the world and with people; a largeness in which there is room for astute social comment, as well as for the minute particulars of ordinary life.

As for Bawer's discussion of Williams's "The Red Wheelbarrow," my impression, here as elsewhere, is that Bawer simply cannot read the poem for what it is, and must discount it for not being something else. The poem, however, speaks for itself. As any moderately intelligent reader can discover, it is precisely Williams's placing of a few essential details in isolation and in a certain order, that makes all the difference. To explain or belittle it, following either Perloff or Bawer (take your choice), is nothing else than pedantry.

The modernist revolution may be over and, typical of revolutions, has left in its wake mainly confusion and the petty tyranny of factions. But what remains most important is the astonishing variety and richness of American poetry in the first half of the century; an achievement that includes Eliot *and* Williams, includes Pound, Jeffers, Stevens, Crane, Moore, Cummings, and a number of other people, none of whom resemble each other in either manner or substance. Williams's contribution to that achievement was substantial and unique, and to diminish it as Bawer does seems to me to serve no useful purpose.

In passing, Bawer makes approving reference to the new formalism. While wishing all good fortune to those by whom this work is done, and some of them are friends of mine, I doubt that the rescue of poetry from the prosaic mediocrity that afflicts it lies much in that direction. The typical poem of today will be just as lacking in substance whether written in free verse, plain prose, or formal measures. In all too many cases, form only incidentally enhances an otherwise trivial content.

Poetry is born of a certain attention paid to the world, to events, things, and persons. This attention has a way of placing objects and events in some hitherto unrealized relation to each other, a relationship that results in something for which we have no better word than *truth*. How this is done is the question, and the secret. The decisive fact seems to be just what it is, precisely, that one finds most significant in the world, of all that might otherwise seem important. Questions as to verse form are not irrelevant to this attention, even when the explicit form is not entirely a matter of individual choice. The single justification for choosing one form over another is the accomplished poem.

Bawer's article raises far more than it resolves, and a letter such as this is an inadequate form in which to respond to it. One thing that emerges inadvertently is that we no longer look to poetry (or to the novel) itself for what we most need to know, but rather to commentaries on it. The reputation of a critic like Helen Vendler appears to rest partly on this fact, and in its own way Bawer's essay confirms it. Without fully realizing it, we have entered an age of biography and explanation.

In reference to another of Bawer's remarks, one final note: fundamentally speaking, there *are* no ideas but in things. It is this fact that has always sent artists and thinkers back to nature—to the visible, tangible, physical world—for confirmation and a fresh insight. In his understanding of this, as in much else, Williams was more intelligent and consistent than Bawer gives him credit for being.

A Letter

To Mark Jarman, February 1991:

Thanks for your long letter and for the thoughts on my review of *Expansive Poetry*. It seems to me that in this current dispute over meter and form, between new formalists and writers of free verse, an important thing has been overlooked, and it is that few poets in our time have been able to assimilate the lessons of modernism and go on to make something new of what that period and its major works have left to us. A number of people have taken over some mark of style or manner from, say, Pound or Williams, exploited it with less than mastery, but without adding much that was new, not already there in the original work. And then, of course, hordes of additional talents have appeared and imitated or learned from *their* work; and with all of this we get farther and farther from the thing itself. Any walk through a museum these days leaves a similar impression in painting, and as we get closer to the present the work is shoddier and emptier, with few exceptions.

I don't find this any more edifying than the next person. A question I put to another writer not long ago, in reference to modernism and all that it represents in a lasting achievement, "What happened to that generous and adventurous spirit . . .?" is for me the real question to ask. To look for scapegoats, individuals or schools, to blame for the current situation of poetry, as tempting as that is, doesn't help us much.

In looking through one or two anthologies of current formalist work, and without for the moment naming names, I have yet to see anything that impresses me as being essentially new. To be sure, a kind of ambition comes through the work and the various commentaries attached to it, but it is not ambition as I understand the term, nor as I think Keats would have understood it. And so far as their insistence on the example of certain past models is concerned, I would remind them of a remark in one of Eliot's essays, that no good poet would seek to do over again what had already been done well.

As for Jeffers, it may well be that I have my personal view, though how I could have anything other than that I don't quite understand. Is there an acceptable view, generally available? But what impresses me about Jeffers is precisely his making something fresh and original from his reading of English poetry and the great classical poems he also read and absorbed; a poetry so unexpected that no one could have predicted it nor the place of its origin on the California coast at that time. He's not, for some people, an easy poet to like, not easy to teach, either — at least not in Cambridge, to judge from Helen Vendler's dismissal of him.

No discussion of Jeffers's work can be separated from his vision of life and human history, his understanding of classical drama, etc. As I tried to make clear in my review, the new thing is born of life lived and lessons learned, is never predictable, and certainly not by publicists . . .

A Letter

To the editors of Poetry Flash, *June 1988:*

Dawn Kolokithas's "Slippery Terms" review of *Poetics Journal #7*, in the May issue of *Poetry Flash*, virtually defies transcription into anything humanly intelligible. She seems to have understood little of what she attempts to discuss; the vocabulary she relies on for communication might in itself be sufficient testimony to what "postmodernism" in one of its phases has come to signify: namely, confusion.

Whatever her intentions may have been, and I will assume that they were worthy enough at the outset, the truth is that Ms. Kolokithas's article, together with its quotations from the text in review, is a stunning digest of ill-chosen, misapplied words and phrases, a catalogue of clichés, some original, some not. A short listing of these would range from the merely inappropriate to the opaque and the outrageous; from a simple misuse of "differentiate" to any number of the following: "shared concerns," "define its constituents," "full spectrum," "future arbiters of dissemination," "strove to rectify," "fracturing the unified," "political praxis," "central spread," "elevates behaviorism," etc. And—one minor point— just how does one "erect a border?"

That Dawn Kolokithas is not alone in this parodic usage is shown by, among other instances, Steve Abbott's review of Kathleen Fraser's work, a self-conscious effort that echoes the terminology and in which we find such monstrosities as "binary opposition," etc.

It strikes me that the use of this language is a way of appearing to have something important to say when in fact one's head is empty. Something very much like it can be found elsewhere, in almost any issue of *Artweek*, for example: a similar attempt to supply, in a totally inappropriate language, what the work itself so evidently lacks. The people quoted by Ms. Kolokithas seem deafened by their own talk; nothing can get through to them, bemused in their jargon with its air of consecrated self-importance—an importance completely misunderstood and belied by its non-effect on events.

". . . partially premised" in its "range and tenor. . . ." Is this language borrowed from economics, perhaps? From biology, sociology, or psychiatry? Or is it derived in some way from an electronics instruction manual? It is not easy to decide which, but it is deadly enough in its inappropriateness and incompetence. That it shows up here in its present form so abundantly is one more indication of the extremes to which intellectual life in this society is increasingly driven.

It is not alone the prevalence of these words and phrases, empty in themselves, that is most disturbing, but the entire tone of the discourse, the meaning of which seems to be that the less influence poetry and serious literature have in the world the more preposterous and self-serving becomes the discussion of them.

Rather than being a true criticism, writing like this is really a surrender to forces that have nothing in common with art and literature and are hostile to them. This mock-professional tone, so common now, this "processing" of what until fairly recently was a subtle and resourceful means of expression, sounds to me like nothing else than the death of poetry. The question is how long can this phase of things last, and what will come next.

A Letter

This letter of July 1988 was addressed to a young woman who was mentioned in an article in the New York Times Magazine *as having a keen interest in poetry, in becoming a poet. Her apparent emphasis on being a "success" prompted me to write.*

In an article in the *New York Times Magazine* last month, I read a brief paragraph in which you are quoted as having an interest in becoming a poet. I feel that someone should say something to you about wanting to be a "success" as a poet.

That is the wrong way to go about it. In poetry, as in the fine arts generally, there is no "it" to make in the professional, careerist sense of the term; I think you need to understand this before you take another step in life.

Poetry is a life-dedication or it is nothing. Either you love it, or you should leave it alone. There are people now who think otherwise, and who do not balk at cheapening and trivializing something that has moved and instructed people for thousands of years. But they are mistaken, and they are not the people you should be listening to.

Learn first to be an intelligent and passionate reader. If you must be "successful," then find an occupation that will allow you that; and write, if you must, when you can and what you can.

At age thirteen, you have plenty of time.

A Letter

To the editor of the Anchorage Daily News, *August 1990:*

Briefly, in regard to the discussion on federal funding for the arts (Sunday, July 22), it seems worthwhile to attempt a few clarifications.

I can see no compelling reason why the public should be obligated to pay for artwork it does not understand, does not like or see the need for, and does not want. Admittedly, this statement is incomplete as it stands. Public money (my money, your money) does pay for any number of items and services that few of us would approve of if we were asked for an opinion — including the salaries of certain public officials one finds it difficult to respect.

But censorship as such is not necessarily implied in the present case; the individual artist remains free to work and produce as he or she wishes to do — is freer, in fact, if one considers that an articulate criticism of society is and has been one of the marks of most serious work in our time.

Ours is a conglomerate, commercial society that has never held high art in much esteem and does not do so now, even while it pays a kind of guilty, abstract respect to the idea of it in principle. In such a society we should not expect government funding of the arts to remain indefinitely free from interference, persuasion and/or coercion; sooner or later administrative attitudes and expediencies may justify that interference.

There are at least two questions we should ask in the dispute. (1) What did artists and writers do before the NEA? (2) Has the incidence of good art and good writing increased significantly as a result of NEA funding? Depending on your answers to these, you may or may not agree that federal support for the arts is a good thing and worth continuing.

A Letter

The following letter was written in reply to a student at the University of Oregon, who had written me in regard to a book he was editing. Specifically, he had asked a number of people—writers, scholars, individuals in public life, and others—to respond to a single question: What, given the times we are living in, would be your most concerned advice to the young? In reply, I invited him to choose from my letter whatever seemed to him of most value for his project.

Thank you for writing to me. You have an interesting, if intimidating, project in hand and I wish you well with it. Frankly, I am not certain that I or anyone else can sum up the difficulties we face in "one piece of advice"; I have besides at the back of my mind what Thomas Edison once replied to a similar question: "Youth does not take advice." All the same, I must take your question seriously.

Yes, we are living in scary times, and they are likely to become even scarier. But even if the worst fears and predictions turn out to be exaggerated, the consequence in part of a universal hysteria, there is every possibility that society as we have known it has approached certain limits beyond which we can persist in our present course at a cost greater than any advantage to be gained. It is hardly conceivable, for example, that some billions of people can subsist on this planet at anything like an American or Western European standard of living; yet that is the direction in which government and corporate policies seem to be driving us.

Faced with this situation one has, it seems to me, the choice of two attitudes. One can avoid thinking, become more or less mindless, since to think at all constructively about the mess we are in, other than in a specialized way—proposing technical solutions to specific problems—for

114

most of us may seem insuperably difficult. Human thought, despite what we are prone to believe, may have final limits in its ability to affect the world, to manipulate nature, or to alter the direction of history. Not to think, to dull one's intelligence, whether with drugs, with work, or with entertainments, will not make the problems go away, but one can live from day to day in this nonthought and get by—for a while.

It seems to me, however, that we have at best no alternative but to think, no choice but to understand as well as we can, not only the physical world that sustains us, but ourselves and the origin and meaning of our history—not for the sake of any imaginable "breakthrough" in whatever field, nor for any immediate material advantage in it—but for the sake of existence itself and our own continued relation to it; a relation that, though often enough baffled and mistaken in its motives, still has an underlying vitality and a potential apprehension of reality that is as much spiritual as it is material.

The last place we should look for help and guidance is to our appointed leaders and managers, for the simple reason that they are only too well indoctrinated, too deeply immersed, in thought and in professional advantage, in the very systems that have brought us where we are. Beware, then, of "world leaders," of statesmen and policymakers, of business spokesmen and established thinkers. View with a critical skepticism their proposals and solutions, while not rejecting any of them outright.

What all of this means, finally, is that one must educate oneself, in the deepest and truest sense; and having acquired a certain, always limited, understanding of events and consequences, be willing to apply that understanding in the best way possible, with all due regard for the general interest. And if this seems too difficult an assignment, remember that we all do this, most of us much of the time, and in one way or another, or we would by now be truly a race of puppets.

In several thousand years human nature has changed very little. Despite all current claims and distractions—the absurdities and superficialities that command our daily attention—that nature is not likely to change fundamentally. Hence the eternal appeal to us in a thing as apparently useless as poetry.

It is possible, certainly, to become stupider, and very difficult to behave wisely. Yet wherever one is, in whatever field or circumstance, one can do good in the face of evil. I was reminded of this when I was in California last year and read in the San Jose newspaper of a group of local citizens—

wage earners, carpenters, retired teachers, and Vietnam Vets—who had gotten together, bought a used truck large enough for their needs, had stocked it with canned goods, clothing, tools, and medical supplies, and had driven the truckload from San Jose to Nicaragua and distributed the supplies where they were most needed. And this was not the first time that these people—a neighborhood group needing no official authorization or public support—had done this. I must say that I have a deep respect for those individuals whose act seems to me both humane and poetic; a respect that exceeds by many times my regard for the majority of professional people—poets, writers, and professors among them—with their self-concern, their careers, and their petty allegiances.

IV

A Certain Attention

When we look out on that high and open tundra with its scattered ponds and grassy mounds, I think our attention to it has little to do with an ideal, but rather with a memory, so embedded in our consciousness that we respond to it without quite understanding why. If, as I think, that landscape corresponds to an original setting for humanity, and if in some part of ourselves we have remained open to it, then our response to the land has a sensible explanation; and imagination, released by those contours and details, awakens, and the mind finds a true home for a moment . . .
JOHN HAINES

On a Certain Attention to the World

It's some time now since the river,
the nightingale, the paths through the fields,
have disappeared from man's mind.
No one needs them now. When nature disappears
from the planet tomorrow, who will notice? . . .
There may be nothing so quiet as the end.[1]
MILAN KUNDERA, The Art of the Novel

I am looking at a photograph of the Milky Way, at an arrow pointing to our Sun, a microdot in all of that interstellar dust; and attached to the Sun, though we cannot see it, a small planet we call Earth. YOU ARE HERE reads a caption fixed at the top of the arrow.

And this is nature, so much of it that we will never know but the tiniest fraction of it. The star closest to our sun is 4.5 million light-years away. Our sun is 30,000 light-years from the center of the Milky Way. Each galaxy contains at least 100 billion stars, and the universe contains at least 100 billion additional galaxies. To speak, then, as some do now, of the "death of nature" is merely, in the context, but another instance of our unrepentant arrogance.

This small item in the universe called Earth, with all of its manifestations and seasons: the flowering and dying away of species, the shifting of continents, prevailing dynasties, wars and decimations—so important, and yet they are nothing. Nothing and everything.

I think of the poet Robinson Jeffers, of some of his more passionate evocations of the night sky; of the stars and planets as he watched them wheel and pass over the western ocean; and of his instinctive placing of human crimes and passions in that context—one poet among us who felt deeply and actually the immensity of things, of our own relative insignificance, and who found a place for this in his poems.

I think too of the painter Richard Poussette-Dart, some of whose later paintings, abstract as they may appear, have in them something of the substance and impression of this photograph I am looking at—myriad points of colored light, swirls, and galaxies—a reflection, whether intended or not, of that immense ring of light in the sky; as on another scale, some of his later work seems in its black-and-white simplicity a reflection of a snowy field marked with stubble.

Last spring, while in Washington, D.C., I spent some time in the Museum of American Art. And there, among other impressions, I was once again struck by the consistent accuracy of those towering landscapes of the early American frontier and the Far West, with their complexity of details, their space and solidity, their record of things seen and felt: water and woodland, soaring peak and quiet pool. Hardly modernism, yet in its own way the art is compelling, and gives rise to the thought: how close and necessary was that relation then to the physical world, and which the observation that went into the work bears witness to? Clearly, on the evidence, something has been lost in the art of nature study in this century; not simply curiosity, or even excitement, but a better word: *rapture.* It is an emotion that comes, not merely from looking at things, but from seeing them with a kind of veneration, as if within these objects, these vistas of water and mountain, something of the impenetrable mystery might be sensed and named, and before which one might be, not designing or dominating, but quietly attentive.

While it would seem that enormous attention is being given to the world, to nature, in recent decades, as witnessed in numerous studies and reports, and by the many calls for action to rescue what is left of wild nature from the abuses of humankind, few of us now see the world as they who painted these works must have looked at it, long and patiently, and with the utmost affection—that which alone sees to the heart of things. It is there in the ordered details of their work, down to the last feather of a loon or a duck, to the last wave-break on the shore of a mountain lake.

For this art one needed, at the least, a conception of reality, of light and shadow, distance and detail, depth and rising plain, that could only have come from having lived acutely in a physical world, and from which one might escape only at great cost. Today, with all the technical means

On a Certain Attention to the World

available, that escape is possible on all fronts, but again at a cost and only for a time.

I am thinking too of a book I have recently looked into, Priya Mookerjee's *The Wayside Art of India,* and which evokes in its carved stones and painted objects, its abundant folkloric imagery, something of the incredible richness of ancient religions, with their manifold deities; the gods and demons, male or female, principle and manifestation—and which answered in the most apparent and profound way to the variety of nature in the outside world. Here, as in all of the old religions, each of the elements, or what we now call by that name, are represented by actual beings. In the heavenly bodies could be seen, and sometimes spoken to, actual people, gods and heroes, all of whom might figure in a symbolic and instructive story, or who ruled in some significant way a part of the cosmos. And this view of things, animated and filled with human drama, can be said to have been as true as any of our later explanations of phenomena, whether scientific or otherwise.

The images shown in this small book are referred to as "pathway icons"—images that accompany and make easier for the pilgrim his path from village to village and through life itself; as once similar images performed a like purpose for devout Christians on their way to a shrine or holy place.

A few phrases and descriptions from the introduction to this book seem to me to illuminate the nature of our subject, and I would like to quote or paraphrase a few of them here.

"Trees are anointed and worshipped, for they symbolize the cycle of growth and regeneration. Each tree has a spirit, and a large tree is always revered by the village community." We are told that "nature is a mirror reflecting the divine. . . . ," and we learn that artistic creation is "a means to carry the individual consciousness into the universal." "The artist invoking the images gives form to the formless. . . ." And of particular importance here: "images are not made as art objects, but as channels of communication with the divine, generating a power not often felt in images placed in a museum."

Here, as in all of that memorable art of the past, life, art, and religion are one. "The creation of a work of art is an act of worship in the true sense, in which the invisible becomes visible."

Nature and Art: forms and objects, representations that are the embodiment of emotions, of will and personality, in the things of nature, its plants, insects and creatures, wind and water. To turn to art, to make art of this, is "an act of discovery that unites the human spirit with the divine."

Life, art, and religion are one. Behind the art forms and within nature stand the gods, the forest deities and indwelling spirits; the divine embodiment of earth and its weather, stars and planets—all of it, and without which it is impossible to imagine *art* in any form. The true sign and proof of this is to be found in the artifacts of the past, in those richly articulated representations in stone, metal, and wood, of reptiles and insects, animals, fish, and birds; and in the intimacy these display, and which is so far removed from our own semidetached curiosity and sentimental descriptiveness. These objects, but they are more than mere objects, were alive in ways that we have all but forgotten, and the voices within them are seldom heard now.

Here as nowhere else we encounter the varied personality of the world, and which embodies, among other things, the principle of conflict in nature, in the opposing forces of good and evil, light and dark. "Duality is intrinsic to nature. Creation and destruction are two faces of the same coin."

Much of our problem, I feel, lies here, in this difference between the attitude of worship with its implied humility toward the resident spirits; a humility that encouraged at once a confident familiarity with those spirits, together with a necessary respect for their evident powers and in which the art participated; and our own modern attitude and practice of reducing everything to its particular function and direct usefulness to us. In this difference lies a whole world of time and loss.

To turn from that ancient sensibility to its characteristic modern counterpart is to measure the abstraction and dissociation we have fallen into. This subtle change, whose effects and full significance have in many respects gone unnoticed, can be verified in a late remark by C. G. Jung that "the gods have become neuroses." The import in this remark can be compared with a comment by the psychoanalyst James Hillman: "In the absence of the gods everything becomes huge." These observations, as brief as they are, give us, among other things, insight into our obsession with power and bigness; and to which we can add the universal use of the word "super" to preface or describe nearly everything from games to markets.

We are involved here with a subtle and ancient paradox: while we talk at greater and greater length about *nature,* nature itself, in its assumed sense, has retreated from us and before our very eyes. Meanwhile, nature in other and less attractive forms reasserts itself: violence, irrationality, aberrant forms of social behavior—aren't these also nature, returned with a particular force?

In this context, and as beguiling as it may seem, the idea that we can somehow "fix" the planet, repair what we think has gone wrong with it, is so absurd and self-referential as to resemble one of those panic periods in history, when all kinds of normally sane people begin to see signs and omens in every manifestation of nature and human behavior, and to believe in radical remedies, seeking scapegoats and sacrificial victims.

It is worth remarking on, too, in respect to the loss of that ancient richness of the many gods and companionable spirits, each ruling some manifestation of nature, that all of this multiplicity, and the art that came of it, should have degenerated into the *One,* the all-demanding, righteous and vengeful Father, with the withering injunction to "subdue the earth"; that in this idea of the one god lies the origin of the totalitarian spirit, or at least its final justification.

If we turn for a moment to the English literary landscape, to the descriptions of the countryside to be found in Wordsworth and Clare, in Keats, Hardy, Lawrence, and others, we find again this vital and affectionate closeness to things, as from a deep historical past, and which has only recently lost its hold on imagination. What I refer to can be felt, for example, in a few characteristic lines, from William Collins's "Ode to Evening":

> Or where the beetle winds
> His small but sullen horn,
> As oft he rises 'midst the twilight path,
> Against the pilgrim borne in heedless hum:

There is little that resembles this fluent familiarity now in English and American poetry.

But how potent was that influence, that familiarity and affection in the past, from Chaucer on to Edward Thomas; and even in Eliot, whose subtle evocations of places in England have not been equaled in subsequent poetry. In contrast, much verse in recent years has been almost entirely concerned with subjective states of mind. We are given, characteristically, little more than a kind of baffled personality, intent on imposing itself on the reader. The words, rather than revealing the world, tend to obscure it and become an end in themselves.

It would follow from this impression that poets now do not see things clearly, or see them, perhaps, through a screen of words and books. A lack of precision and appropriateness shows itself in the use of that ubiquitous term "like," where the likeness, more often than not, is forced and unconvincing, as if mere use of the word were enough. The simile, that ancient device of comparison, has lost the better part of its accuracy.

But not only have we stopped looking, we have stopped listening also, if the lines I have quoted from Collins can be said to be representative of a certain acuteness of sensibility. It is apparent to me, at least, that the cadence of such verses, and of innumerable poems from the tradition to which they belong, must have derived from centuries of foot travel, from walking in the land, not driving through it or flying over it. Once more, it seems to me, we are faced with that indivisible connection between the way we live and the art we must make of that living.

It is just here, I think, that Kundera's insight, in the passage I quoted at the beginning, becomes tangible and can be verified. That is, even while we talk more heatedly about nature and wilderness, and about saving the planet, and about all related topics, as necessary as that attention is, nature in its ancient and spiritually flourishing sense is passing from our lives. We are, as Kundera remarks in a closely related text, already looking elsewhere.

Reality has assumed a form we hadn't anticipated. But it is always so; as when the conduct of empire has lurched onto a downward track, and society begins to show unmistakable signs of instability, statesmen and political people continue to talk as if matters were still as they were just yesterday. Meanwhile, nature, that baffled and refuted thing, has taken up residence within us, in our very household, and we become, not the masters of nature, but its prey.

The relation between art and nature can be demonstrated in so oblique and mundane an instance as the behavior of the stock market, in the surges and rallies, deficits, and episodes of panic buying and selling, etc. And the point here, surely, is that once a system, whether economic or political, is put into place, it soon assumes a life, a vitality and direction of its own; becomes in fact a natural force only slightly and erratically subject to control. The illusion of control, of course, is much a part of the attending problem. Hence the eternal surprise of investors and experts over market behavior, its ups and downs. Nothing is more obvious in reading the business page of a newspaper than the fact that no one, in a moment of crisis, is really in charge, or has, typically, much understanding of what is happening. And the greater the illusion of control, the more drastic the consequences when matters really begin to deteriorate.

But a real artist, and there are such in the economic and political spheres, will comprehend the energies at work, and be able at times to make of the situation a more positive and creative force. Such an art, in the field of politics, in business and warfare, is not after all so far removed from the field of art itself. The principles of selection and imitation, of precedents and their usefulness, are in many ways alike. Which is to say that human creativity can be understood in a much broader sense than we mostly admit.

Are these things of which I have been speaking in any direct or essential way related to our assigned topic, Art and Nature? I believe so. They are, after all, a sign of the way we see the world, of the kind of attention we bestow on nature, on the things of nature, and on people. For all of this too is nature, is a part of nature and its processes, if the corruption and decay of societies and civilizations tell us anything beyond being a lasting and dismal chronicle, and from which we seem to learn almost nothing.

I am thinking here of the cattle trucks I passed or which passed by me on the interstate last summer: those horrendous metal cells, boxes on wheels, whether empty or filled with captive beasts, going to market or returning from it. And it occurs to me that this passion for capture and imprisonment, for what must seem at times to be a total domestication of the world, must pursue humankind with its consequences forever. For it is not far from the stockyard, with its animals penned and waiting for slaughter, to cattle cars and death camps for people. We may think otherwise, but history, that relentless ghost, tells us it is so.

The way we see and experience the world is inescapably determined by our attitude toward it, by the use to which we put nature and the things of nature, whether this means diverting the flow of a river, removing a hillside to make room for a highway, or otherwise converting land, bird, and beast to our specialized purposes. With increased technological means, and the sense of power and mastery that these seem to instill in us, the world has become radically changed. A field or a woodland, a rose or a lark, with all of their gloom and light, their vibrancy and color, are not for us what they were for Wordsworth, for Keats, for Yeats or Thomas Hardy, emblematic of more than mere stem and leaf, feather and petal. From being places and creatures of mystery and fear, of myth and local tale, they become something else: objects of concern, of examination and analysis, perhaps, but not of enchantment.

What is missing, and for some time now, is delight, that sense of delight in discovery that renews everything and keeps the world fresh. Without it, poetry dies, art dies; the heart and the spirit die, and in the end we die. Which is to say, perhaps, that the more we know the less we truly know. And in our terrible world the original beauty, the instinctive awe and mystery, become in time a matter for nostalgia and of scenic views.

I think of the blackbirds I saw this past spring in downtown Minneapolis, hopping up from the pavement and the nearby benches with straws in their bills, and flying off to a nest they were building somewhere close by; making for themselves a life in all of that street noise, among shops, walls, and windows. The city may disappear one day, but these will go on, picking straws for a nest from the debris of an empty street.

A sudden flight of birds, rising from a tree in alarm, scattering and reforming in a flock; and I know in that image the scattering of my own thoughts disturbed by a sudden interruption, and then once more composed. And with that image in mind, it occurs to me to say: we have no thoughts that do not come from nature.

It should be obvious to us by now that we have invented nothing. Of all that can be pointed to as human accomplishment—whether it be an electronic contrivance, the wheel as a mode of transport, a dance figure, a composition in line and color, or even a line of poetry—it can be said that the model exists in nature. The same can be asserted in reference to any field of human thought and action, no matter how apparently abstract, if we were able to trace it back to its source. And to use the figure, "field of thought" in itself evokes a certain truth.

One can say further that there is nothing in this *mind*, this imagination, this capacity for thought, that does not find its source, its example and inspiration, in the natural world. To forget this is to account for the confusion and chaos that every society is prone to sooner or later, as is surely the case with our own at this time.

To Nature, writ large, we owe every art and skill. It is, to say it yet another way, the great book we have been reading, and writing, from the beginning. Signs, clues, tracks and traces, vocabulary and syntax: it is all there. Yet we do not live solely in nature, but in history also, which is our own story and itself a part of nature. What was said in reference to the Swiss historian Jacob Burckhardt seems appropriate here:

> The significance of history is . . . not the undeniable rise and fall of civilizations, but the enduring and permanent tradition of those values created by men in a thousand situations and carried forward in the collective memory of the race as a guide and inspiration. The "soul" of the Greeks, for example, lives in us. And historical tradition . . . meant especially the body of the aspirations of men, a summation of the intrusions of the eternal into time as delineated in art and literature in every generation. And here, he would say, in this strange land, half reality and half the intimation of an ideal world, is our true home.[2]

It seems to me that the eternal task of the artist and the poet, the historian and the scholar (to use what are inadequate terms) is to find the means to reconcile what are two separate and yet inseparable histories, Nature and Culture. To the extent that we can do this, the "world" makes sense to us and can be lived in.

It would follow, and for many reasons implicit here, that no subsequent art has ever surpassed in power and expression the Paleolithic art of the caves, or that unsigned art of rockfaces and burial artifacts, and little has equaled it or the tribal arts surviving today. In art, certainly, if not elsewhere in human affairs, there is no progress, only change and alteration in the rise and degeneration of forms, techniques, and materials. Picasso understood this; Delacroix and Michelangelo knew it; Arp knew it; Brancusi and Giacometti knew it. All true artists have known it, and in principle and in practice have paid instinctive respect to it, in their reinvention of the very thing that is always about to be lost.

You Are Here. And in the night sky, whether obscured by clouds or brilliant with stars and a full moon, light and shadow come and go on the fields of life and death. On that ground, with its perpetual alternation be-

tween emptiness and depth, are enacted and endlessly repeated the histories of men and beasts, whether they are actual or imagined, and perhaps
the two cannot be finally distinguished. The mind is a replica of what we
see out there, and in its order and disorder, its capacity for expressive
forms and its incapacity for any final understanding, is a reflection of that
world, the only one we have. *1993*

Notes, Letters, and Reflections

It doesn't necessarily follow that the discovery of new worlds results in any gain for the human heart. The true ground remains the inmost being of the individual, as that is revealed in its contact with the world and with other people. It may be that exploration of outer space would one day result in new forms of art; but I would guess that these will always return to the individual experience, and that love, passion, the experience of beauty, of loss and death, would in some form or other continue to furnish the material of art and writing.
JOHN HAINES

I

To look at the world: and when we have learned once more to look, we see the possibility of renewal, of an implied order, in every aspect of the life around us. In the stillness of leaves floating in a forest pool; in the flight pattern of a flock of birds obedient to an invisible current of air; in the twilight folding of a particular hillside ... Sometimes I think that is all we are really here for: to look at the world, and to see as much as we can.

· · ·

We speak of nature, of the natural world, as if that were something distinct from ourselves and the social world we appear to have made, seldom noticing that we are *in* nature and never out of it; that our cultures, our civilizations, for what these may be worth at this moment in time, not only depend directly on nature in a material sense, but are in some way an expression of that nature, a reflection of it in shape and detail—psychologically and esthetically an unintended reproduction of it; at times, almost, a parody of it.

· · ·

Beyond any elitism regarding *nature,* any current vogue for it and its managerial manifestations, we sense a truth to which we pay a certain involuntary respect, as a source to which we return, in the truest sense, and for which we must periodically attempt a definition.

. . .

Wilderness is not a separate and isolated department of life. That notion is a part of our modern splitting of everything into pieces. It is not a matter of one or the other, but of both, of nature *and* culture, and all that these imply. Strictly speaking, we are never out of nature. Psychologically, spiritually, wilderness (as fundamental state, not merely as topographical preserve) is *the* condition of life, now and always.

. . .

We began by reading the world around us, of necessity and as a matter of survival. It would seem inevitable to have discovered in the sequence of natural events a narrative and foretelling—in the advent of the seasons, in the coming and going of creatures, in the brightening and fading of the constellations. And we are still, in our deafened and defective way, through weather map and telecast, reading signs in the heavens, noting the pattern of earth movements, of rainfall and snow cover—in a thousand occurrences. Perhaps all we have done is to shift the range of attention, narrowed our focus here and broadened it there, invented science in place of magic; but the fundamental activity remains the same.

. . .

We read every day the signs of the social and cultural world we inhabit: traffic signals, the layout of streets and housing, motions and gestures in a crowd, the lights and allurements in shop windows, the winking of advertising displays, and so forth.

It is strange how the language of commercial advertising, for example, with its lettering, its lights and colors, shapes and motions, takes advantage of the residual store of natural signs and exploits them—unconsciously, perhaps, but uses them all the same—and it is not difficult to appreciate its effectiveness. It plays along the circuitry of an ancient and half-remembered imagery, with all of its still latent power to arouse desires, fears, and antagonisms. So far has the language of nature, enhanced, trivialized, driven to extremes of expression, evolved among us.

. . .

The model for what we attempt exists in nature, and without it—the example of how a thing can be or ought to be —we lose our sense of relation and proportion, of a suitable fitness. And somewhere here we find the reason why, when the process has gone beyond a certain point, dissolution becomes inevitable, headlong and irreversible; all false order must collapse, and a new order, going back once more to a primary example, begins to assert itself. Revolutions in art and literature, and in society too, take this course and have a similar outcome.

．　．　．

Domestication is, unavoidably, a part of our human problem. When we observe cattle or sheep grazing in a pasture, we are looking at a fallen species. Compared to the alertness of the wild creature, a steer or a sheep is changed, into something less, even while we sense in the dulled gaze of the domestic beast a wildness that is merely slumbering and is never completely converted. And it seems all too likely that as we have tamed and reduced these creatures according to their utility, we have at the same time deformed something in ourselves.

．　．　．

At times, even in our present urban mode of life with its mass-produced abundance, we may catch sight of the haunted, displaced hunter and gatherer seeking among the bins and aisles his lost tribal self, of which he is informed by newscast and magazine advertisement that it still exists somewhere if only he could find it. But of course, this is what people in the malls and supermarkets are doing: reading brands and labels in place of animal signs and vegetable seasons.

II

One can say what one likes about the present time, its terrible spiritual emptiness, its reliance on an ever-increasing material possession. But when one has understood the true situation of the peasantry, of the mass of people in Europe and elsewhere in the past, I think few of us would wish to return to that life, to be at the mercy of landlords, the church, and the governing classes, indentured and bound to a place with little hope of escape. No wonder so many came to America when they could find the means to get away. And yet, in regard to that old village and country life, bound as it was to soil and locality, how rich in human character it was, and how poor in that we seem to be now.

．　．　．

The world and its people are what they are and can hardly be "improved." For, fundamentally, what could be changed? At any moment in time, in history, whatever was possible in human achievement and satisfaction has been known. Adding to that a surplus of materiality increases nothing essential. Perhaps a real evil in the world comes of people who would raise false hopes as to improvement and progress; since there can be no end to that, no goal except *more,* the entire thing becomes a chimera. Or, to put it more directly, "human engineering" is a concept that can only become despotic.

· · ·

Human nature is always in conflict. In order to realize that higher being that is the fundamental substance of religion, it must depart from, rise from, its animal nature. But this animal nature is always calling humankind back to itself, and it is the rare individual who escapes the consequences of this mortal conflict. Yet the "soul" surely exists, and is perhaps the potential realization of what our nature might be if we were ever to succeed in reconciling the oppositions in our character.

· · ·

Observing people in the stores, shopping, intent on something or other; or at a certain predictable hour, riding the Metro home from work, standing with their briefcases, staring over the heads of the other riders: one thinks that no matter how driven and spiritless their lives may at times appear to be, it is far better for them to have a job from nine to five than to be sitting at home, in house or apartment, watching television, and with nothing to think about. For many of us there is an enviable certainty in knowing that one must get to work at a definite time, and that the next day and week will be the same. It makes sense that beyond this most people cannot and will not go.

· · ·

What strange, substanceless rites and celebrations society is prone to now—hometown parades, football events, and flower festivals—and which have no apparently deeper significance than their relation to business interests and tourism. And then, at intervals, our political campaigns with their balloons, placards, and plastic effigies . . .

In memorable contrast to what I have just remarked on, I recall the Feast of Corpus Christi I witnessed once in Toledo, Spain. The narrow, winding streets of the old city were strewn with twigs of rosemary gathered from the surrounding hills. The odor of the trampled herbs, the flowers and bright banners hanging from the balconies where people stood and watched, dressed in their finest clothes; the procession of priests and attendants, full of color and motion, the chanted litany—all spoke of an immensely old and deeply symbolic presence. And I wonder at what expense to the spirit this latter conventionality of ours has been contrived, and to what problematic future it may be aimed, when some darker and more violent drama will compel us as audience?

. . .

The survival of winter bonfires in places in Europe as a symbolic rite of renewal, reminds us that periodically in many old societies life was believed to have been used up; the world had grown old and had to be renewed: the sun had to be encouraged to rise, to return from its winter decline and death. And so the old huts and houses were burned, old clothing discarded and burned, the old pots were broken, and all the old things were thrown away or destroyed. Then, new housing was built, new clothing made, and new implements; and life, refreshed by this symbolic act, could begin again.

These beliefs, their embodiment in some intelligible act, have mostly been lost to us in any conscious sense. And yet the force itself, the spirit in which it manifests itself, doesn't simply disappear. And it might well be, as a consequence, that a society, modern in all outward respects, yet unable to renew itself effectively, would in some strange and disproportionate way become self-destructive. People, without knowing why, would turn into assassins and terrorists, and other forms of destructiveness would appear. Much that occurs in modern societies might be explained along these lines.

. . .

Considering the disappearance of a divine presence in the world, the original source of fear, of wrath and dread, and in the arts an intelligible representation of irrational, demonic forces at work: would this mean that an inability to locate, or imagine, a source for these things in the outer world—in nature or the cosmos—might, so far as society is concerned, result in each individual discovering in himself a counterpart, an unreasoning fear and anger, depression, neurosis, paranoia, and so forth?

The disappearance of a mythological or religious framework, in which the passions had not only a figurative form, but their place and purpose, might mean also that in the arts expression of these emotions would lose intensity and conviction, and become at first mere sentiment, and then simply an empty gesture, a style, a vague expression of something for which one had long since lost the meaning. And overall a cruder, more violent replacement might sooner or later appear and assert itself . . . An attempt, perhaps, of which surrealism was a type, to revive the irrational and the sacred.

III

You can interpret your dreams in one or more ways. They are clues, gifts. And if you have the instincts of a writer or an artist, then your job is to take those clues and build on them, make them into something. Or you can see them as hints toward a deeper life and understanding. Once the problems connected with them have been resolved or outgrown, they will disappear, and you will go on to live with a clearer mind.

Animal images in dreams particularly can be read as expressions of a fuller, more intense, life. There are very old and deep reasons why this is so. They can be fearful and threatening, but only from the point of view of the person disposed to see them that way: i.e., the conventional person. The open and creative individual will see them for what they are: friendly and encouraging images. As I have said, when you no longer need them, they will go away. You will miss them, but they will have served their purpose in your life. I suspect that if you refused them they would take another form in your life and exact a penalty for that refusal.

. . .

If the essential human predicament in the present time can be described as one of conflict, of doubt and contradiction, of dislocation and a kind of orphanhood on earth—a situation only temporarily resolved for the poet and artist in terms of art—then I think the tension inherent in that condition must show through and in the art. For me this means, among other things, that we can never be too sure of our truths, and that the writing will be fundamentally a search.

. . .

Contemporary poetry and theory are like a head without a body. A poetry without roots in the commonality of life is not likely to survive beyond the classroom, which is its main refuge these days. The gathering of poets and writers into the university is a symptom and cannot be a cure.

· · ·

In one of his dialogues on the novel, Milan Kundera remarks that the novel exists to say what only the novel can say. Perhaps we can adapt this to poetry as well: that the poem exists to say what only the poem can say. Given a command of verse and something of substance to write about, what finally counts in a poem is the passion and conviction of voice. This in itself constitutes a kind of truth, one that can be found nowhere else.

· · ·

It seems not too much to say that virtually no one writes love poems anymore. Any survey of contemporary verse would confirm one's feeling that this form of the poem has practically disappeared. There are plenty of poems about sex, for example; far too many poems expressing resentment against an individual of the opposite gender, and far too many borne of old grudges and renewed antagonisms, all of which add up mainly to some form of power. But that poem borne of passionate attention to the loved object, and which places that object or being on a plane approaching adoration—that poem seems nearly lost to us now. And it is difficult to avoid the feeling that in losing that poem we are losing something near to the heart of poetry itself. For in that attention, that open gaze into another's being, or what of that being can be disclosed to us—that attention which precedes and outlasts mere attachment or possession—the entire significance of art is revealed. There is a certain power in this also, but it is not the negative and often destructive power of possession. On the contrary, the attention I speak of raises and makes beautiful the commonest thing in the world.

· · ·

It may be that the only adequate role for poetry now is that of prophecy. All else, no matter how it is praised and rewarded, amounts to gossip and entertainment. To see into the future, or to clearly discern the present moment and its probable outcome—this effort alone is worthy to stand with the great works of the modern spirit. Lacking this power, the only course for poetry now is to become an occupation of academic interest. Among the prominent moderns, though he wrote in prose, Hermann Broch understood this; and among American poets, Robinson Jeffers also, though quite differently.

· · ·

There was a time when we looked to these translations—from German, from Polish and Czech—as having the qualities we most missed in our own poetry: political awareness, sense of historic moment, spiritual insight, and so forth. But reading them now, years later, how flat many of them seem in English, lacking in resonance, in music and verbal resource. In many cases, these translations have bred a writing in which there is hardly a trace of true poetic energy . . .

. . .

I think work of this kind, and there has been a great deal of it in recent years, may exemplify the limits of translation, as useful as that area of the art has been and can be. But poetry lives in, has its soul in, the soil of the one language and speech, or it is nothing. To put it another way, I love the poems of Wordsworth, of de la Mare, and Yeats, and I would not like to think that this music has gone for good; for then poetry in English will be dead, no matter what improvisations might seem to resurrect it for a moment's excitement and distraction.

. . .

I think the key to narrative in poetry lies in the impression of physical movement, of journey and action. At any rate, this seems to be the characteristic in Homer, in Virgil, and in Dante. We are on the way to somewhere or to something, or we are engaged in some action, not merely thinking about it. Chaucer's people are on a pilgrimage; Dante descends, and then he climbs. And in a more recent example, Eliot's "Little Gidding," the wonderful passage in which he is walking the streets at dawn and meets his compound ghost: once again the theme is that of movement.

. . .

Perhaps the entire impulse toward narrative, in poetry and fiction, has its source in the primeval journey; in moving from camp to camp, from winter to summer pasture; in having watched, over thousands of years, the companion journey of birds and animals, of fish and insects—and not merely as spectators, but as participants. And it may be that this is what we have since lost: the impression of a continuity of which we are part.

. . .

When belief in the journey, and confidence in effective action dies, then the story must die, and its place be taken by all sorts of maneuvers and improvisations. Narrative ability declines among serious writers, and is continued by the second- and third-rate, by writers of westerns, crime stories, and science fiction.

. . .

With the power out, and no heat or light in the building, it has been like a ghost house here, with no one moving about, and no sound but the rain dripping. Last evening I joined a couple of the residents here in the library room, where there is a large fireplace, and we had enough wood to make a fire for an hour or so. No one spoke for the better part of an hour; we just sat and stared into the flames and the embers. Remember how, in Henry James's "The Turn of the Screw," the story begins with the narrator and another person sitting in front of a fire? I wonder if Dr. Watson would have been moved to tell those wonderful stories of himself and Sherlock Holmes if they had not had a fire to look into in the evenings and on wet, cold days? Maybe the storytelling tradition, the impulse and content of the *one* story, derives from no more than a hearth fire, and from looking into it for thousands of years.

IV

What we see depends on an inner, psychic disposition, so that there can be no final and objective view of anything. The world changes before our eyes, and *mind,* to call it something, is an endless unfolding of many complex relations.

. . .

I refer again to the feeling I had, not long ago, in the Museum of Asian Art in San Francisco, that a well-planned gallery space, one that is quiet and skillfully lighted, and with the old works spaced from room to room— that here is one modern equivalent of a place of worship, free from dogma, available to all, and suffused with a sense of spiritual presence. Though we are aware that this feeling comes to us transformed through centuries of trial and alteration and, finally, of unbelief, what remains in us of a capacity for belief and wonder is to some extent reclaimed and nourished here. We have all known equivalent places in the wilderness, when nature has given us, if only for a few moments, a sense of the sacred, of the meaning and mystery of life.

. . .

When our mind is clear, our attention awake and receptive, it is sometimes possible to hear, or to feel, in a forest clearing, in the clouded height of great oaks and pines, the original murmuring and whispering of the primordial powers. The woodland is haunted, in the most valid sense of the word, with the hurrying shadows and laughter of the gods. Especially when the light is uncertain, in early morning and at dusk, or when a wind is blowing, and the voices and machinery of people are stilled.

.   .   .

A chapel ceiling, carved, painted, and adorned; the soaring gallery and inner dome of a cathedral, with their shifting, mysterious lights and shadows ... Architecture like this could never have evolved in a stone-cropped desert land like Egypt or Sumer, where rock and sand are the elements, and one's gaze asks for something massive, sleeping and solid, like a cliff or a mountain.

.   .   .

The Middle Ages were steeped in the imagery of the northern forests. The soaring columns of the cathedrals were crowned with a spreading and flowering leafery, within which, transformed by vision and nightmare, familiar cats and outcast serpents had their home; and things that would be hawks and owls silently spread their wings. From the carved pillars beaked and grimacing faces peered, and every knot and bole on the stone trunks appeared ready to assume an instantly fearful expression. Overhead, sunlight filtered through the twigs and branches, striking a momentary color in the prevailing shade ... Night in that forest was never far, and with it came the gathering of the dead, and the prowling of awakened, demonic spirits.

.   .   .

The history of Western painting, of art generally, might briefly be described as a slow climb and descent: from an early and intensely religious figuration, a nearly anonymous accompaniment to church ritual, illustrating to the otherwise uncomprehending folk the essential story; and from a gradual loosening of those ties, into a radiant representation of the human, but still illuminated with divine light; and from there into an increasingly secular, worldly preoccupation with style and execution, with here and there a spark, a regained fervor and light; and finally into a nearly complete atomization of reality, a trivialization of appearances—a flat, painted surface, empty of meaning. At which point one might be justified in referring to the death of painting, or the death of art. Or, it may be, the death of a historical phase, but from which the possibility of a new thing might one day reveal itself.

.   .   .

Out of the flatness of the icon and early Christian art generally, slowly distance and perspective emerged: space, and movement into and out of it. And after some centuries that vista became clouded and uncertain; painting began to lose its sense of space, of fullness and distance, until in modern art it disappeared once more into the flatness of the painted surface—into no space at all. It seems reasonable that this process corresponds in some way to a profound change in Western man himself, a gradual uncertainty and unbelief . . .

.   .   .

Painting since the Renaissance can be seen as a sporadic but continuing effort to restore a sense of the sacred, finding it now in landscape, in animal forms, in household spaces, in the human figure, in no more than the play of light and shadow . . .

And perhaps one can say, too, that at least a part of the effort of modernism has been to regain a sense of the sacred, of divine presence in the world; and this meant leaving behind the mundane human figure, abstracting that figure until it became part of the atmosphere, of the landscape, of the furniture in the room. Here and there, in Millet, in van Gogh, in Picasso, and in other subsequent artists, something of the old sense of the extrahuman appears, but fractured, stretched, and distorted. Elsewhere, painting becomes a manipulation of surfaces, a playing with techniques, with ever cruder approximations . . .

.   .   .

When painting detached itself from the walls and ceilings of chapels and cathedrals, when it ceased to be an integral part of a building or a habitation, this was itself an indication, and it may have been seen as such, that art was on its way to becoming an autonomous activity, and would be less and less a part of the common life, with all the meaning that art, without calling attention to itself as art, once had in the life of people. In removing itself from architecture, painting may have gained an illusory freedom; art moved even further from the religious gathering place, the temple, the cave, the grotto, and became a possession, an acquisition—more and more a thing of museums, galleries, and private collections.

.   .   .

The tenderness and sweetness that can be felt in early Christian art, that can be heard at moments in the music that has come down to us, and in the Christian story itself, was an announcement that something new was at hand: a deep psychological change, a *re*-formation of humanity, to counter the legacy of excessive harshness in Roman life, law, and character. So, perhaps, sensing this change, Augustus sent out to number and tax his citizens, and Herod to seek out and destroy every trace of the new thing.

. . .

It is not so much Christ himself, as personality, as historical reality, that is figured in so many representations in the art of the time, and who looks out from countless nativities, but a new soul in a new man. This new soul may never, except in a few individuals, have come to completeness, but it was there, as promise and potential, and of which we have the lasting evidence in the art that survives.

V

No need for sadness. The suffering to which we are all prone on the loss of that unified world or existence we once knew, or remember that we knew, is the more acute for him who remains open to its renewed possibility . . . A loss for which only the creative act offers an adequate compensation. There, perhaps, it can be made whole again.

. . .

The thought that I would like to leave with you is this: that poetry, art, nature, and what we call for want of a better word, culture — but it may be that *poetry* is the inclusive term here, the one that best describes the essential element — are all part of the one process at work. Any truly creative work, whether individual or collective, draws upon and to some extent adds to and restores, the creative energy that is everywhere present. And here, hidden under centuries of cultural baggage and historical terminology, is the real reason why every genuine artist, from, say, Masaccio to Michelangelo, from Rodin and Monet to Brancusi and Henry Moore, has always gone back to nature — not to nature in its scenic picture-book character or cinematic image, but to the essential thing, whether manifested in the cosmos or the human body, in the pattern of coloration in insect and flower, in nothing more than shadow deepened in a pool of water. It is the reason why the earliest occurrences of art, on rocks and in caves, have never been surpassed and seldom equaled. In the shape of a stone, in the filament of web and leaf, in the light reflected through a raindrop: the secret is there, and nowhere else.   *1975–93*

Foreword to
The Story and the Fable
by Edwin Muir

This recovered book by Edwin Muir, so memorable in its substance and its telling, suggests to me several lines of thought. One of these concerns his early years in Orkney, and the meaning of that life, for him and for us. It is an old story, perhaps the oldest we know. To begin life as he did, as it is no longer possible to do now anywhere on earth, in a small and isolated community whose members—immediate family, near and far neighbors—stand out, uniquely individual in their humanity, by virtue of inherited character and assigned tasks; and all of life—land, place, and people—falls together in a perceived rhythm and order, and all the more so, perhaps, if the place happens to be an island. How many of us in our deepest heart have not at times wished for this and would have gone back to it had we ever found the way?

Having once been in Orkney, I can easily imagine the scene—the interplay of land and sea, the sky and the light, the open cloudlit spaces, the brooding fewness of humanity—to this day the essential solitude of an island world. It was, in part, my interest in Muir and his writings that drew me there, an interest that stemmed initially from the likeness of his early environment with my own experience in the wilderness and backwoods of the American North. When I first ventured to Alaska forty years ago, I

142

found something very like the life described here by Muir. Despite the intrusion of a Pacific war and the growing frequency of air travel, it was still pretty much, in habit and outlook, a nineteenth-century life surviving without electricity and with only an intermittent recourse to a commercial center some seventy miles distant by gravel road. When Muir describes members of his family gathered into the kitchen of an evening to hear a story told, I am returned to a familiar circumstance. When he tells of the grain sacks standing at intervals in the field, and of his father striding the ploughed furrows, casting the grain; or when he is witness to a pigsticking and butchering, and describes his own part in the salting down of the meat, I see myself and the old people I first lived among and hunted with engaged in that ancient human activity of gathering, of storing and preserving. It is a story that will always need retelling, for it is the story of ourselves as we once were and may never be again.

Here, set down with clarity and affection, are the island vistas and early insights, the events and retrieved images that surfaced so often later in his poems. Particularly, the observant world of a sensitive child to whom objects and people are seen from a special perspective, reduced or magnified in size and importance. A terrified glimpse of his father's horses treading into the barn at dusk with steam in their nostrils; the poignancy of an island youth come home to die; Muir's cousin, Sutherland, whose success with the island girls was occasion for both amusement and a muttered outrage. A sea-bound world as seen from an island hilltop; a world of distance and longing.

This much of the story takes place, appropriately, within a dramatic alternation of light and dark—the long light of a northern summer, and the long dark of the winter evening. For those of us who have at one time or another known that setting, a mood and a passion are rekindled, such as no other land, sky, or human instance may evoke in us. We recall with affection the old-time neighborly convocations, the morning and evening meals under lamplight. To linger at table and say not a word—not out of awkwardness or obstinacy or blankness of mind, but because of a deeper communion and intuition of silence: the silence in the unlit, sleeping land, and the responding quietness in oneself. And one's dreamlife was rich with an animal imagery, and waking life continued and renewed the substance of dream, for it was all one, the natural and the supernatural, the mundane and the mystical—all that has its source in shadow and, as Padraic Colum has told us, is diminished and done away with when the ancient distinction between night and day is erased by the prolongation of light. This impression is not simply nostalgic; the poetic, imaginative life of humanity draws much of its vitality from darkness and primordial shadow, even while contending with the terror and dread that are also felt to be there.

It was, of its nature, a strongly symbolic life, as in fact life must be so long as it is closely bound to earth and weather, where each event is signified in some way by custom, by word and story, and each event has its meaning in relation to something more that contains the whole. Human life, if it is not cursed with oppression, by real hardship and want, can in such conditions be as good, as satisfying to body and spirit, as any possible to men.

But Muir does not remain there. Through force of circumstance and from natural disposition, he grew out of the island world and its thousand-year piety and custom, as all of us, driven by change and fortune, are in some way fated to do. His story takes us away, into the modern world as he was shortly to know it in all of its turn-of-the-century meanness and squalor and corrosive vitality, a destructive force.

So Muir, at age fifteen or so, leaves Orkney. He arrives in Glasgow with his parents and his sisters, and with his entry to a strange and disturbing new life a second theme emerges from his narrative. Step-by-step, through trial and error, through illness and sorrow, surviving the loss of both his parents and his brothers, in a succession of degrading and repellent jobs, Muir finds his way, escaping from the city into the countryside on weekends, and with at best only an intermittent happiness to sustain him. At times it is as if the circumstances in which he now found himself were to confirm his early and chilling vision of an enormous school building, with all of the world's children filing into it as into an endless factory, never to emerge.

This part of Muir's story is a particularly instructive example of the ordeal of a disadvantaged but intelligent young person seeking to inform and educate himself, trying on ideas and discarding them, taking up this or that position in regard to some argument or problem, guided by intuition alone, or with none but the most accidental and mystifying encounters to aid him—with no guide finally but the example of a few minds who have recorded a few useful thoughts, and who have gone before us by the same or a similar road.

But Muir through all his difficulties succeeds in prevailing, against formidable circumstantial and psychological odds, and his story never loses its coherence and compelling interest. Nor can we easily forget how earnestly he proceeds in his self-instruction. How attractive at this distance is his interest in socialism, his involvement in working-class discussion groups, and the earnestness of his participation in philosophical and political debate. It would be easy to smile at the seriousness with which all of this was taken by Muir and his friends. To many now it must seem almost incomprehensible that intelligent people, young and old, should have taken so intense a part in such things. Yet, even at the time of my own late, postwar entry into affairs I can recall going through a similar phase, consorting with lame-duck technocrats, old-maid socialists, and the like, and I think there was nothing unusual or absurd about it at the time. We forget all too easily that many people, and not necessarily nor even predominately intellectuals, once took these things very seriously indeed: that humane ideas put into practice could change the world; that it was possible to *improve* oneself, not so much in material advantage as in knowledge—that the truth would make you free, as indeed, rightly received, it often can.

In the confusion and search of his years in Glasgow, and with the limited cultural opportunity that was available to him, it was inevitable that Muir should turn to literature, to philosophy and the world of ideas—to the one thing, possibly, that might rescue him from the uncertainty and depression he had fallen into. For it is true, I think, that art, literature, and philosophical inquiry do offer, if only to a few, a way of salvation in an otherwise brutal and incomprehensible world, and do so primarily, perhaps, because of the access they appear to offer to a higher, spiritual value that, in spite of all temporal evidence to the contrary, we persist in believing must lie at the heart of existence.

Not many of us, I suspect, would have survived Muir's drastic initiation into the modern world with so much of himself intact. Despite uncertain health and the personal calamities he endured, Muir seems to have possessed an inner toughness that preserved him. An essential part of his survival may have been his capacity for self-examination. Throughout his narrative we encounter his willingness to review his thought and conduct, and when he found himself in error, revise them. Whatever it may have been in his early life or inherited character that conditioned him to this instinctive self-revision, it seems clear enough that for him it was a natural response to experience.

It is hardly coincidence, I think, that Muir's intellectual growth should have been grounded to a significant degree in the circumstance of his early life, in that relatively uncomplicated visual and social environment in which each person, thing, and event has its clear place and meaning. We know too little of how a mind grows into maturity, but we know enough to believe that the pattern for growth must have its model in some early intuition of a satisfying order. Something like this, at any rate, seems to have been the case with Muir. Following on his marriage and subsequent escape from Glasgow to London, he is already into a process of self-healing; by the time of his departure for Europe in 1921, he is in possession of himself and ready for his main work.

In all that I have to say of Muir I have wanted to locate him in our present time and have him be useful to us, as I feel he can be. If I could point to a single identifying characteristic of Muir, the man and poet, as he emerges from this book, it would be the complete absence in him of envy, of competitiveness and self-seeking. What we find on page after page is a basic decency; in discussing books and ideas, his attention is given, not to personalities, but to the thing itself and to the excellence it calls forth, in the material and in ourselves. Writing of this kind is marked by a spaciousness of mind that in our overspecialized era seems practically to have disappeared.

Muir does not talk about writing, about literature, and the study of literature, as if these were an activity unrelated to ordinary life. As the pages of his diary appended to *The Story and the Fable* consistently show, he thought a good deal about the quality of life generally, and about literature in relation to that life. He has, as a result, many good and useful things to say about society and its workings, together with a steady attention to events then taking place in the world, on the understanding that these things matter to us all, and what we think and say about them (or don't think and say) is of some consequence. In other words, Muir assumed, as we appear no longer to, that all of these activities of mind and spirit — art and literature, science, politics, and so forth — are in some way related. I think it safe to say that much of the achievement of modernism, in all its forms, rested more or less on that assumption. I doubt very much that we can have it otherwise.

Foreword to *The Story and the Fable*

In his universal and humane concern with literature and society Muir seems almost to have come from another age. But that age is not so far back in time as we may think. I remember how, when I was a student in New York in the late forties and early fifties, in that sudden release of spirit following on World War II, we were all *reading*—Proust, Mann, Joyce, Lawrence, Stendhal, Balzac, the letters of van Gogh, and much else—and not only reading, but discussing what we read, and how relevant to the life of art that reading and the keen sense of discovery it conveyed, seemed to us to be. It was all one study and one discipline. And I think now that it may have been that very ambience, shared by painters, critics, and writers alike, that gave New York in those days, and for some time after, its preeminence.

Given his early life in Orkney, with its strong biblical overtones, and the subsequent disastrous removal of his family to the mainland and the modern world, it was inevitable that Muir should have felt so keenly and personally the fall from grace and expulsion from Paradise. For that is, after all, not simply a story from scripture, but a continually relived experience of every human being. Further, Muir's experience in Glasgow, so vividly described here in all its sordidness and appalling dislocation, is of significance in light of what all pastoral or "native" peoples must pass through in becoming modern—in the loss of innocence and the loss of homeland, and equally in the loss of a significant symbolic life. As each of us must learn for himself, the transitions through early life into maturity, the stages of transformation once provided for by the group, by tribe or church, are now mainly an individual affair earned through much pain and confusion. The only alternative to this solitary achievement is a spurious kind of transition marked by diplomas, flags, and business cards.

Muir's story of his childhood, youth, and early manhood, is an exemplary tale, unique as to our common life and unique in its telling. It is written in a prose style true to the man, clear, honest, and with no excess of effect, without a trace of self-pity or self-celebration. Further, his entire narrative, of life and letters, can be read as a kind of parable for the journey of the modern self through time and culture toward a personal understanding and a partial reconciliation. It is this element, along with its intrinsic interest as story, that gives his writing its authority. Conceivably, given a

JOHN HAINES   147

different temperament, and having experienced for a time what we call, for the sake of convenience, "the world," Muir at some point in his career might have returned to Orkney and taken up the old farming life, or something near to it. This is a decision that has been made in our time by others, by Wendell Berry, for example. That it was never a choice for Muir is clear when, in comparing his early life with the disorder that modern society has increasingly become prone to, he says: "Our life was an order . . . competition is the principle of anarchy. The hiker flying from that anarchy to 'nature' is, really, without knowing it, looking for an order. But he will have to look elsewhere for it now." Whether one agrees entirely with that last remark, it is consistent with Muir's life and the lessons he was able to draw from it.

The honesty and wholeness of mind we find so abundantly in the pages of this memoir informs Muir's poetry and his writing on literature as well. I have read most of his criticism and have never failed to find it of lasting interest. Having read his Harvard lectures on poetry, *The Estate of Poetry,* three or four times over the years, I shall read it again whenever I need assurance that poetry once had meaning in the general life of people, and that so long as its possibility is not abandoned completely it may have that meaning again; that there is truth at the heart of it. Muir's reflection at the end of one of his lectures that "a great theme greatly stated might still put poetry back in its old place" can be taken as the statement of faith that it is.

I recommend this book for its wisdom and clarity, for its luminous humanity, and for its unfailing evocation of a time and place. How many of us now can remember what it was like to live before this century of ours? Late in his narrative we find Muir describing a summer walk out from London into the countryside with a friend; they return on foot late in the day, full of excitement from a spirited discussion on literature and philosophy, to see the courting couples walking by in the evening light. Does anyone *walk* out from the city nowadays? Not likely. All of that has long since retreated into the sports van or the cab of a pickup, into a numbness of spirit consoled by tape deck and six-pack. The world may not, after all, have been much better in those days. Didn't those same courting couples (the men, anyway) go on walking, marching, running onto the battlefields of World War I, ". . . eye-deep in Hell," as Ezra Pound phrased it in his "Mauberley" sequence? Maybe so, but I sense all the same in Muir's glimpse, with its slow summer light on the fields and hedgerows, a grace and leisure, a tenderness and sweetness, we are the less for having left behind.

Edwin Muir died in 1959. So far as I can tell he is not much read now, even by people most concerned with contemporary poetry. One young woman poet, with whom I tried to discuss Muir, repeatedly referred to him as *John* Muir! So much for her reading habits, at any rate. But it was not all that long ago, in the late 1950s, that one could find in an issue of *Poetry,* or one of the more prominent quarterlies, a late poem by Muir, or a respectful review of one of his books.

Why some good writers come to be so little read while others continue to claim major attention, is for me something of a mystery. The situation, often enough, has little to do with merit. I have thought about this recently while rereading the novels of Hermann Broch. Broch, that good and deserving man—mention of him in connection with Edwin Muir is not without significance, for it was Muir and his wife, Willa, who first translated Broch's work into English.

In Broch's case, the comparative neglect of a great writer may be due to his being far too original and subtle a mind and talent to find a wide audience at any time. Each of his major works is a significant departure, and his novels and essays require of the reader a more serious and prolonged attention than many people now are willing to give to a book. With Muir the neglect may have other causes. He was a quiet man, not given to assertion, and this fundamental modesty in an age of town criers can be seen as a disadvantage. To the impatient and inattentive reader Muir may appear to be too old-fashioned in his verse and too conservative, too deeply committed to tradition, to be of much interest to a contemporary poet. Whatever the reasons may be, they offer more of a comment on our current state of mind than a criticism of Muir.

I doubt that his not being more widely read and appreciated would have bothered Muir greatly. When he says, as he does at one point in his narrative, that he is not concerned if he has a reputation or not, we can take it that he means just that; it is not being said for effect. On the other hand, it seems certain that during his lifetime he had the attention and respect of the people he himself most respected.

I would like to end by quoting from the last page of *The Story and the*

Fable a passage in which Muir, in summing up his experience so far, with typical grace and good sense, remarks that "the only justification for society is that it should make possible a life of the imagination and the spirit ... but society has not yet solved its most elementary problems, and I do not think it will find it easy to solve them." If these problems, more critical now than when he wrote, are ever solved for us, it will be in part because men like Edwin Muir helped us to think about them.

1987

Foreword to *The Story and the Fable*

On the Writer in a Nuclear Age

This essay was first published in "Writers in the Nuclear Age,"
New England Review / Breadloaf Quarterly, *Summer 1983.*
Contributors to the issue were asked how the possibility of
nuclear annihilation affected them as writers.

My contribution to this forum might be considered a meditation on death. For it seems to me that it is this that lies at the heart of the question we have been asked: Death, and one's attitude toward this elemental event. To attempt an answer to the question asked of us is to answer a question in myself. As I enter my sixtieth year, I am acutely aware that the time is limited, that somewhere before me lies death, and whether it comes in sleep, in the slow wasting of pain, or in a violent form is not primarily a matter of individual choice.

I would like to think, therefore, that a part of my answer might be that the possibility of annihilation does not affect me at all, since it has in a true sense always been there. I would like to say that my perception of life and experience remains the same, that the world of nature has not changed for me, and that the purpose (in part the naming and celebration of a familiar landscape) that has brought me this far remains steady and sustaining.

But I find that this is only partly true. Nuclear threat aside, I am all too aware of changes in the world during my lifetime, changes that make any innocence or optimism regarding the forces at work among us difficult to maintain.

I am old enough to remember the 1930s and the approach of a war in which I took part. It seems to me that my childhood and early youth took place in an interval of truce during which many smaller wars were fought, and people everywhere lived with much inherited misery. The smoke column that was to rise over Hiroshima was a larger version of the clouds that smothered Shanghai, Chungking, and Warsaw. I hope not to see, not even in photographs nor on the screen, the dead and the maimed, the driven homeless of still another major episode. And yet my sense of things tells me that the relative security of our society cannot hold, and that a debt remains to be paid to this century out of the safety we have so far contrived.

The trend toward general disorder and breakdown, the apparent futility of traditional political gestures, the frantic determination to discover and exploit to the utmost every available material resource; the deliberate promotion of appetite, the corrosive competitiveness that leaks into every corner of life—all seem to serve a ferocious will to excess, violence, and extinction of hope, as if what it amounted to was a kind of revenge on life, and in which we are all implicated.

The question asked of us refers to the world's "population." Presumably this means people. But how do I feel about the probability that much of the other life on this planet will suffer enormous losses due to our interference? How does this affect my writing? Or is it that this threat is only a further consequence of the measures we have been putting into effect for thousands of years—is the "logical conclusion" of these?

I tell myself that Earth has seen far greater catastrophes than any we can devise—ages of volcanic fire, of sulphur, of ice, innundation and upheaval—and survived them all. I feel sure that it will again, if that *again* takes the form of human intervention on colossal scale. Whatever humanity may come to, whatever device we may ignite, new forms are possible, new life always, and nothing we can do will cancel this.

Seen from sufficient perspective, it is all right if the volcano blows its top, that villages and cities are buried in ash, mud, and debris; though people die and are scattered, the ash and mud settle, become soil, and sooner or later the land is refreshed, and things flower again. Only wait.

I can be persuaded that Western civilization will one day cease to exist, whether the end comes in the slow attrition of centuries or as a succession of violent blows, and I am not immediately alarmed by the prospect. Fixed in the immobility of its forms, life becomes a museum of itself; any fresh conception must make its way by whatever means, by infiltration or with dynamite, in a sometimes bitter tonic of revival.

There is death in the rigidity of social and political forms, in the fixity of institutional attitudes and practices—all that prolongs the outlived and essentially discarded even while the gestures are repeated in a kind of sleepwalking, a stupor of numbed habit. In the arms statistics, in the repetition of treaty terms and agreements, in the rehearsals of presidents and ministers, already there is the speech of death. This is not the natural death of things that die to restore the living, but a particularly human kind of death: prolonged and tenacious in its repeated crises, and oppressive toward innovation and insight.

I am reminded that we learn to live with terror and dissolution, have done so in the past, and that at other times mass death, whatever the cause—plagues and decimation—was everywhere; men's minds contracted before it, and life became a matter of survival above all in a universal demoralization. The possibility of nuclear annihilation appears on the scene as the most blatant and odious example of a will to dominance and control evident everywhere, unleashed finally to some extreme event here or elsewhere in the universe.

The event may never happen, but as threat it has the power to coerce and demoralize through continual reiteration of the message of retaliation, doom, and extinction, a message in which there is both ignorance and arrogance—the self-glorification of people who mistakenly believe that they have either the power to destroy life entirely, or the means to destroy only half of it and save the other.

Faced with all that seems sheer negativity and opaqueness of mind, I, as a poet, have only an earthbound perception of the energies and principles by which life is made possible for us, and a conviction that the basic terms for existence will not be substantially changed by any conceivable reconstruction of geography or rearrangement of peoples and nations. From whatever perspective, we will always look back on this earthly home and to the wilderness that is its original ground and source of all values.

Perhaps because I am older, I see how essential now is that surrender to the world and to the experience it offers us. If the threat of annihilation impinges on my activity as a writer, it expresses itself in a realization that what is left to me of time and attention must be used with care and not wasted. Faced with the disappearance of my world, I would do the extreme thing and inhabit that world with a greater intensity and affection, recognizing that in this one life, with its related background, lies all the material I could ever wish for, and far more than I will have time to realize.

In times of extreme peril, confusion, and insecurity, there seems to be something irradicable that we can draw on; and one face of that capacity is a belief in the power and sanity to be found in the creative act. That whatever the poem, the painting, the song appears to be saying in any literal sense, it is part of a language, a communication between ourselves and the world, and without which we as a species have not even the sense and dignity of a grasshopper.

Poetry is not a retreat from this century and its appalling news. Rather, it is a means of reconciliation. Life is essentially esthetic in its inclination to order, an innate tendency that is desire. A life given to meditation (which does not imply withdrawal) and of which poetry is representative, offers a steadiness and resistance in the face of all that seems determined to disperse us into incoherence and incomprehension.

Only in this effort to be clear, to seek such meaning as may exist, and to find the appropriate expression, is my life justified. And when I look for instruction, the shadow cast by a tree outside my window may have more to tell me than all the editorials and fictions ever published.

Any reply would be for me unsatisfactory and only a momentary repose. But if, as a consequence of nuclear arms and power, and of all that has come into being as accompaniments of these, my sense of the universe and of our place in it has been added to in some way, then I am to that extent consoled that it is not all as evil as we sometimes think.

I find my images of relief, of grace and hope, in the constant renewal of natural forms, and of which my art is no more than an imitation, imperfect and human. The necessary complement to this is that surprising renewal of perception that from time to time seems to spring out of nothing, though it has its source in all that has gone before. Out of self-created necessity, new thought is possible, new combinations, and there is potential joy in that fresh unfolding.

Finally I don't believe in the extinction of life, not even of human life, no matter what scare stories I am told and can read, no matter what my own fears can sometimes project. And I refuse to be made numb, pliable and obedient by a threat continually exercised by people who intend to use that threat as a weapon in itself, whether their intention be willed or involuntary.

And while I would not be coerced into acceptance of mass death, neither will I refuse to face the fact of death in any false proposition of life versus death maintained by a society whose view of existence provides no comfort beyond the grave nor any effective rite of passage, so that the entire subject cannot be spoken of except with the evasive uneasiness of conventional pieties, or in tones of horror and negation.

Things die, but that is their fate. And whether it is the death of an animal in the field, the collapse of an idea or an illusion, or the slow decrepitude of an entire civilization, is perhaps mainly a matter of degree and perspective, though of course too of immediate self-interest.

The worst may happen, or it may not happen. It may turn out to be an event beyond any effective control, and we will appear as stricken actors in a story written by an invisible author. But I would prefer to be in no hurry about moving the engines onstage; nor would I want to assign to anyone conceivably in power the responsibility for deciding who or what shall live or die.

Meanwhile, there is something for the moment to end on. Quoted from the Acts of the Apostles, it is the closing statement of Hermann Broch's *The Sleepwalkers,* a work of our time, that while it describes with precision the disintegration of a society, does not leave us without hope. Out of darkness, a void into which all recognizable forms are collapsing, the voice of something persuasive and lasting in the ages-long dream of humanity: "Do thyself no harm, for we are all here!"   *1983*

In the Woodland Still

Review of Forests: The Shadow of Civilization *by Robert Pogue Harrison*

One of the enduring images in literature, as in life itself, is that of the "dark wood" to which Dante came, as others have come and will come, in midlife and beyond. It is understandable, even without the testimony available in this book, that this woodland, with its classical companion image, that of the descent into the underworld, should have its psychological counterpart in contemporary life, a place not only of dread but of discovery and renewal.

It is this dark woodland, both as physical habitat and symbolic place, that Robert Harrison sets out to explore. As he states in his preface, "I decided to undertake the labor of writing a comprehensive, if selective, history of forests in Western imagination." To that end, he takes us, page by page and chapter by chapter, back into the old myths, the poems and stories, in which the forest with its emblematic presences has so strongly figured. In doing so, he shows, convincingly, I think, just how complicated with trees and woodland our imaginations and civic habits have been.

Among the texts and figures invoked, from myths and legends, from classical and modern literature, are Dante, Gilgamesh, Dionysus, Artemis and Actaeon, Macbeth and Burnam Wood, Rousseau, Decartes, the Brothers Grimm, Wordsworth, and Joseph Conrad. We begin with Virgil, with a passage from the *Aeneid* in which Aeneas finds himself in a "wondrous forest" at the site of the future imperial Rome; and end with the modern Italian poet, Andrea Zanzotto, whose poems are informed by his close familiarity with a surviving remnant of the ancient forest that once covered much of Italy. The story that unfolds between these two figures is the familiar and still misunderstood one of destruction and enclosure, of the clearing of entire subcontinents, combined with sporadic efforts to manage and preserve what is left.

The forest has from the beginning been a magical and fearsome place, home to gods and heroes, nymphs and thieves. It is inhabited by spirits both benign and vengeful, to be feared and propitiated. There are men who come, literally, from oaks, with gnarled faces and thorny fingers, and whose movements and muttered conversations could be heard in the creaking boughs, in the thrashing and shaking of heavy limbs. Imagination, fed by intimations and by natural signs, was rich in this imagery, and the weight of it can still be felt in the pillars of old churches with their elongated figures of kings and saints, the transformed forest embodied in stone.

But as in all shadowy and darkened places, it is the fear that predominates: of the forest as a place of lawlessness, of danger and abandon, as well as of enchantment—the dual personality it has shown us through the ages, both antagonist and shelter. It has always had its guardians, as represented by the story of Artemis and Actaeon, and the terrible vengeance visited upon one who would look too closely into the secrets of nature.

And this duality is further concentrated in the figure of Gilgamesh, the Sumerian king and hero, whose killing of the forest god Humbaba brought so much grief: the death of his friend Enkidu, and divine retribution. It is the great parable and symbolic story, one that, as Harrison suggests, we seem fated to repeat: of arrogance and pride, of defeat and reconciliation; of the consequences of violence directed against nature and, ultimately, against oneself. As in the example of Gilgamesh's eventual return to his city, sorrowing and wiser, it is at least a minimum consolation that, however damaging one's conduct may be, redemption is eternally possible.

Opposed to this ancient relationship to the forest, developing out of it, is the spirit of enlightenment, with its program, as stated by Descartes, "... the mastery and possession of nature." The forest, with its thickets and uncertain pathways, its unpredictable and potentially dangerous inhabitants, will be domesticated, and with that, presumably, will come a more prevalent sanity in human life. As a clearing in the forest lets in light, so removal of the ancient woodland would diminish the confusion in our mental processes and clarify our view of existence. We will have allotments and fences, useful and productive fields, with a few patches of woodland left over to remind us of the wilderness from which we have been delivered; much as with laws and constitutions, rights and prohibitions, civic order will be installed and a healthful recreation permitted. Defined in this description is the shift, over thousands of years, from a forest filled with dread to one in which we might find solace and a momentary peace. For that to happen, the actual forest had to be made safe, if not marginal.

Something of this age-old conflict is reflected in the current dispute over the spotted owl in the Pacific Northwest. On the one hand, deep concern for the survival of this small representative of the ancient forest spirit in its necessary habitat; on the other, the social and political problem of jobs and products, of an inability on the part of many to see beyond mere utility and profit. In some respects we appear little advanced in our thinking from the days of kings and noble privilege, from a concept of the forest as either a hunting park or a refuge for outlaws.

Throughout Harrison's book we are reminded of how deeply penetrated we are by nature, by the woodland, in our habits of thought and in speech. "The tree of knowledge," for example, is not an idle or fanciful expression. Knowledge, true knowledge, *was* acquired from trees, from the forest, from its fruits that ripened and fell, from the birds, from insects, and other creatures whose patterns, colors, and seasonal behavior constituted a vocabulary in the truest sense. Even now we "browse" among the bookstalls, occasionally become "lost" in a text, or find ourselves confused by a "thorny" argument. Our habitual use of the term "underworld" in reference to the criminal element of society is indicative not only of a source, but of a profound debt. To speak of the "roots" of words, therefore, is to restore things to their rightful place.

Forests is full of thought and food for thought. We learn that the concept of the circle was originally derived from observation of the concentric rings in a felled tree. A long passage quoted from David Attenborough on the cutting of forests and accompanying ecological devastations in Mediterranean Africa during Roman times, and the effect on the conduct of empire, is particularly instructive. Environmental presidents and agricultural wardens should need no more convincing description of our own potential fate were they sufficiently interested to read it.

In this connection, it is perhaps not incidental that a concern for the disappearance of the planet's surviving forests intensifies at a time when our cities become increasingly places of violence and criminality. It might even be worth suggesting that a will toward control of nature inevitably produces in the social body an extreme tendency to its opposite: marked aberrations in social and political behavior. Which is to say that "the mastery and possession of nature" is finally an illusion.

Forests is for the most part admirably written; the opening paragraph of "The Woods of Walden" is particularly eloquent. Additionally, the text is supported by a bibliography and several pages of notes on the works cited. Illustrations from Blake, from John Constable, among other artists, and from Frank Lloyd Wright, not included in my review copy, are certain to add to the published book.

On the other hand, the text is occasionally marred by the intrusion of jargon words, the vocabulary of a technocratic mock-scholarship all too common nowadays. Among examples of this are the following: "triumphalistic," "unviable," "digressionary," "instantiates," "ironizing the irony," "historicity," "pregiveness," "facticity," "forestial," etc. An observant editor ought to have encouraged the author to remove these; there are better ways to say it.

In its densely packed pages *Forests* opens up far more than can be adequately dealt with in the assigned space of a brief review. I have given no space to the ideas of Giambattista Vico to whom Harrison devotes considerable attention; nor to his retelling of one of the forest tales of Grimm; much else must be passed over. I hope, however, that with what I have been able to indicate here of its content and interest, serious readers will be drawn to the book with renewed consideration for a subject the full significance of which we have only begun to comprehend.

As absorbing as it is, the intensity of my own interest in the narrative, in the ideas expressed and their supporting evidence, began to slacken somewhat with its later sections. This is not necessarily Harrison's fault, nor is it proof of a lack of interest in the works he draws on—from Wordsworth and John Clare, from Conrad, Leopardi, and others—but is the consequence of modern sensibility and the problem of nostalgia for what has been lost and can only be partly regained. Early people *were* close to the forest, intimate with the spirit it embodied and the creatures it sheltered; the woodland was not merely a place to which they resorted in a moment of leisure. And that is what makes the difference.

In *Forests* Harrison has given us one considered version of the primordial background to human nature and culture, and a compelling view it is. He has less to say about the influence of another kind of landscape, that of the open grassland—the plain, the steppe, with its spaces and distances, its prevailing light, sudden winds, and oncoming weather—a habitat that would have nourished a very different sensibility than that of the forest with its closed corridors, overhanging canopy, and intermittent sunlight. In my mind, at least, the vista offered by the retreat of the glaciers from the continental slopes and plains, some part of which can still be seen in the interior of the Alaska Range, is a view as stirring in its memory as any on earth, and would seem to have been as significant to imagination as the return of the forests and their eventual predominance over much of our continent.

In one other respect, I question Harrison's suggestion, at the end of his preface, that with the disappearance of the forest, the poet, and with him the memory of the forest, would also disappear. There are other dimensions to human imagination, and as long as a single tree is standing on this earth a poem is possible.

Forests is, among other things, a work of scholarship, and of immense value, it seems to me, one that we have needed. It can be read and reread, added to and commented on for some time to come. Whatever its virtues as a text, for verification, for the *truth*, we must go back to the myths, to the poems and stories, and to the woodland itself, to where in the end Harrison leads us.   *1992*

The Creative Spirit in Art and Literature

In the movement of trees,
I find my own agitation . . .
WALLACE STEVENS,
Opus Posthumous

I asked myself whether the higher forms of the esthetic emotion do not
consist merely in a supreme understanding of creation. A day will come
when men will discover an alphabet in the eyes of chalcedonies, in the
markings of a moth; and will learn in astonishment that every spotted
snail has always been a poem.
ALEJO CARPENTIER, The Lost Steps

Creativity is a continuous and visible process inherent in existence, a capacity latent in all living things, well described in a phrase by the naturalist John Burroughs as "the vitality of connections." What we understand
and appreciate in the creative process originated in a close relation to and
observation of nature and its processes; there is no creative intelligence
apart from that.

Three years ago, while at home in Alaska, I was sitting at the desk in my
small study in the woods one early summer morning, and looking out the
window at a birch tree just beginning to bud. The dark branches mounting at intervals up the trunk were in sharp contrast to the pale, papery
bark. It was a scene I had watched many times in the past. And as I was
watching, I saw a small bird, a warbler, flitting from branch to branch,
from twig to twig, up and down the tree in search of insects. The image of
that bird in relation to the tree and its branches was arresting—in its constant, flitting movements, and then in its sudden significance. For it
struck me that here, in a single and astonishing impression, might be seen
an early stage of musical notation, with the bars and notes ascending and
descending in scale.

For many years I made the better part of my living from the wilderness of the Far North, in Alaska. That is, I hunted and fished, gathered food from the countryside. In doing this over a period of many years I learned, in what I think of as a true sense, to *read* and interpret the country: the ground underfoot, the coming and going of creatures, the arrival and departure of birds, the seasonal flowering and fading of plant life. These things, the physical evidence of them, constitute a language, a grammar, and a syntax; they represent in some way the original perception we may have acquired of a fundamental order in things, in their relationships and significant connections. And I mean by this, among other things, story, narrative, the thread of sequence and consequence.

There is a close connection between reading signs in the snow—the imprint of a bird's wing, or the scattering of leaves and seeds over the surface—and reading words on a page; the same inherent order and process is at work in both of these. And as the spring sun erases the snow and all of its signs and evidence, so do we from time to time find it necessary to erase what we have written and begin over, for the sake of a clearer definition and understanding.

The secret of creativity, of creative imagination, is not to be discovered in a laboratory, nor in abstract theory, nor in any dissection of the brain or the nervous system, nor in computer models of *intelligence*—thinking machines and mechanical pseudopods—but in attention to the world, and for me that means primarily attention to the natural world, to such vital relationships as we may perceive there.

For when we begin looking—and I mean really looking, with an attention cleared of formulations and preconceptions—we begin to see combinations and possibilities, order and beauty, anywhere. Walking, seeing the reflections of trees in standing pools, the light of the sun on leaves and water; the shapes of buildings and houses, the textures of stonework and pavement, the movement of clouds over the landscape: here, under our feet and close at hand, can be found those primary patterns of creative order.

Early in our history we read the course and meaning of events from signs in nature: a prophecy in the flight of birds and the seasonal behavior of animals; in the metamorphosis of insects; in the waning and flaring of the planets. And there was in this first perception, surely, nothing either foolish or merely incidental. The capacity for observation and evaluation on which we depend in so many ways originated in that first attention to natural details.

From looking at the world, the details and events of forest and field, came the sense of balance and fitness—of economy and order, of esthetic rightness—that we value, not only in the arts, but in all activities and pursuits. The model for what we attempt exists in nature, and without it—the example of how a thing can be, or ought to be—we may lose our sense of relation and proportion, and imperceptibly substitute for it some less reliable imitation of our own devising; and by which we lose, little by little, that primary relation to the immediate and original object.

I have been strongly moved to see in Egyptian art-language the images of birds and insects; how hawk and ibis stand not only for themselves, but for a certain concept in thought; how the scarab beetle, in a particular configuration, is born of the lotus under the eye of the sun. Once, long ago, someone watched an insect, warmed by the sun, crawl out of a flower; and to that individual this signified birth and creation. All things were connected in this fertile process, which included water, bird, insect, plant, and light: the great, sun-given cycle of life.

Our sense of order, of proportion, of right relation, of what we call beauty—that which provides us with a certain practical and esthetic satisfaction—must have its source somewhere in an original model given us by natural forms, patterns, and the like. And with natural forms I include the human face and figure, the primary subject of sculpture.

For thousands of years, before high cultures evolved to any extent, people observed nature as a matter of survival, learned and imitated patterns in the world around them. It would follow from this that an imprint has remained, a deep and irradicable understanding that certain arrangements are right and have prevailed, while others are faulty and less satisfying. We may not always be able to say just why this is so, but we do feel it. It is the one principle on which we can base judgment of a given act or piece of work.

Our capacity for wonder, for awe, our sense of the magical and the sacred, too, has its source here—in what we can call a state of grace, and which I take to mean a certain psychic equilibrium. I suppose that what we refer to as the sacred is so because of some primal relation between ourselves and the world. We feel that a part of our being is hallowed or blessed by this, that some acts of ours enhance this feeling, while others violate it.

I suspect that in the interrelatedness of things—by which I mean the world of shapes, colors, forms, patterns, etc.—lies the origin not only of art, but of religious emotion, of what Wordsworth thought of as his "moral being." In this perception of a fundamental order lies the entire notion of an ideal social order that we seem to aspire to but have never attained.

The ordering, the unifying or harmonizing, of scattered and apparently unrelated material is the very essence of the creative impulse. And this activity is everywhere much the same, whether it means ordering the characters and events in a story, the placing of objects and figures upon the ground of a painting, the arranging of objects in a room to make a pleasing and habitable space, or the placing of certain words and sequences of words in a metrical structure we call verse, or in a paragraphic order we know as prose. And one would have to say, too, that this basic description applies to systems of thought, as well as to political and economic systems, and to all systems of social and hierarchical order.

This is what I understand as the creative process. What we refer to as artistic vision is an ability on the part of some individuals—poets, artists, and thinkers—to grasp and present to us in visible form a kind of totality of relationships, which represents in some way the greater totality of existence. We may call this capacity *vision*, and it is that, both in the sense of *seeing* and in what it signifies as *in*sight into the fundamental mystery of life.

Implicit here is the element of play, the delight in fantasy that originates in the play of light and shadow, in the multiplicity of changing forms in the natural world—the interplay of things that suggest infinite combinations. Carpentier, in another passage from *The Lost Steps*, refers vividly to the action of the wind in tall reeds, in a clump of bamboo or slender trees; suggesting that in that waving and tossing, that bending and shaking, can be seen the origin of dance. This perception speaks as well for our delight in ideas, in organizing forms and spaces into a momentary coherence. The writing of a poem, the making of a book, are variations on an essential ability, borne of necessity and latent in the human spirit everywhere.

I referred at the beginning to the restless, fleeting image of a bird in a birch tree. In conclusion, I am led directly to another image, that of the Cumaean Sibyl, the oracle consulted by the hero of Virgil's *Aeneid*, whose replies to the questions put to her were written upon leaves that almost immediately blew away in the wind. This compelling classical figure re-appears in the final canto of Dante's *Paradiso:*

> So is the snow unsealed beneath the sun,
>> And so the Sibyl's prophecy was lost
>> Among the light leaves scattered to the wind.

And the resolution toward which Dante's verse and his vision seems inevitably to be borne finds this concluding figure of eternity:

> Within its depths I saw, bound together
>> By love into one volume,
>> All the open pages of the universe:
> Substance and accident and their functions
>> Seemed intermingled in such a way
> That what I speak of is one simple light.
> I think I saw the universal shape of things,
>> Because in saying this
>> I have the feeling of a greater joy.

It may be that the creative impulse can be defined as an eternal search, both actual and symbolic, for those lost leaves and the answers written upon them.   *1987–94*

V

Days in the Field

This life, now bright blue, now dark—somewhere a bright patch of yellow . . . What does it say and to whom? This thing without a name . . .
ROBERT MUSIL

Notes from an Interrupted Journal

Arrived. All is well. A hard trip from home. Dogs and I are tired out.
It took all day, from daylight to dark.
Diary of F. CAMPBELL, November 1950

July 3, 1980, 6 P.M. We are sitting on a dry hummock of moss near the summit of Buckeye Dome, 3,000 feet in a range of hills that stretches east from Fairbanks toward the Canadian border. As far as we can see, looking north, east, and west, the rounded shoulders of the domes, the forested ridges and deep valleys unfold, bathed in the warm, clear light of early evening.

We take in the view, this incredible expanse of light and wooded earth. Now that we have arrived, we share once again in the strange exhilaration that seems so much a part of the earth's high places: to be able to look so far and see neither city nor settled land, to hear nothing but the wind over the grassy, sunlit ground.

But there is something else to be seen not far from here, not so grand, but given the times in which we live, not surprising. At the bottom of the steep north slope of this dome, in a saddle formed by the heads of two small creeks named Minton and Rosa, there is a rust-colored streak of cleared ground. It is a small but visible section of the Alyeska Pipeline, cut through this back country in the 1970s. With a little squinting from this distance, it might be taken for a highway, but it is strangely silent and without moving traffic. I see it now with neither anger nor resentment, but with a kind of wonder that in my lifetime such a mysterious and drastic change could have come about.

I have written: July 1980. But I could as well have written, August 1954, June 1959, or September 1962. My memory of this dome and its surrounding country goes back over thirty years; farther back than that, if I include what I know of it from the recalled memory of older and vanished neighbors. I can hardly tell now where my own experience and that inherited from others breaks and connects. I am thinking of a hot day in mid-August many years ago, when Peg and I and Fred Campbell stopped here with seven dogs and loaded packs on our way to a small lake hidden now from our view by a long ridge to the northeast. Hot, tired, and thirsty, we were sprawled near this same spot at high noon, resting before the long plunge downslope, and the climb that would take us up that farther ridge, and on to the lake that we would come to late in the day. That summer the shrubs on the tundra around us were heavy with ripe blueberries; we picked and ate them with canned milk sweetened with a little sugar from a jar that Campbell kept here on the dome, hidden in a shallow hole in the brush.

In late September of that year Campbell and I came back to the dome with packs and rifles, hoping to find a fat young bear feeding in the meadows. We saw nothing that day, but once, while we stopped to rest and to glass the frost-browned, sunlit hillsides, we heard far down in Minton Creek the nasal snore of a moose in rut, like a great fly buzzing.

And once again, early in June of the year following Campbell's death, we came over the dome under windy, gray skies on our way to the lake. We found the lake cabin in poor condition; a bear had broken into it, and nearly everything of value—food stuffs, bedding, and clothing—was torn and crushed, and there was daylight showing through the sod roof. We rescued from the sodden floor a few pages of a diary that Campbell kept over the years, written down in pencil on the backs of labels taken from tins of evaporated milk. The next day we made the fourteen-mile hike back to Richardson in a cool, wet wind without stopping.

Roads and pipelines notwithstanding, it is still wild country here. From this round and open hill the wilderness seems to have no end. It will be increasingly rare now on earth to be able to look so far and see only range beyond range, valley after valley, unclaimed and unoccupied. And yet at this moment there is about this land an almost pastoral peace. The higher mountain ranges have their grandeur, their snows, and their glaciers, but the prospect here pleases me more with its gentleness, with its spacious human dimension. And then I think that for so many years this country was the preserve of one man who hunted, trapped, and prospected its creeks and ridges alone until the years compelled him to quit.

From this dome a trail that Fred Campbell kept open for forty years drops steeply to the saddle below us, and climbs that farther ridge we see in the middle distance. And the trail goes on, with many forks and byways, all the way to Campbell's Lake, and beyond that to Mud Creek, McCoy, and Monte Cristo, to be finally lost in the swamps of Flat Creek.

It is remarkable that one individual would claim so much, seeing it all as an extension of his own backyard. And yet, looking down from this place, sensing as I do still the old attraction of the wilderness, I can feel the appropriateness in that claim. In this enormous space and solitude another dimension of life can be felt and grasped by the ready mind—uncramped and unfettered, threatened though it may be ever so little now by that slim, rusty slash to be seen in the saddle below. A cabin on a distant lake, a cache here and a tent site there; water hole, creek, and berry patch: of such native material can a life be made, and the land met on its own terms. A good life on earth, as such things go; difficult and deprived, but keeping at its center an uncommon dignity.

I suppose that with the passing of such individuals a way of life has been dying that we will not see again on earth. The wilderness has been labled and set aside; the vastness has been partitioned, the great American solitude broken for what may be the last time. Now it is refuge, park, or preserve; or it is one more entry on the list of *resources,* in the dubious terminology of our times. Fortunately, the timber on these hills is of little commercial value. It occurs to me that it was considerate of God to make the trees so small; at least our agencies won't come here to make a million in timber sales.

My affection for this landscape has been among the oldest and deepest things in my life. This is where I was born, improbably at the age of twenty-three. Then I had come north to homestead, to till the soil, to pioneer. The years have tempered my zeal for pioneering, though I concede that for Alaska to support a people it must be able to provide them with food, that basic substance of soil and water. And I believe it can do so, with wise practice and understanding, though I suspect with diminished expectations in the years ahead.

Though I am not a farmer, I have cleared my plot of ground, broken up the sod, and planted my seeds, as much as I needed to. And through necessity, nourishing my crops with hoe and watering can, I have learned my lessons with hard labor. I respect the honest man of the soil, even if he works it with a machine. I have seen the cleared fields bordering the road to Chena Hot Springs outside Fairbanks, the crops ripening under the sun. The barley fields in the Clearwater district near Delta have opened the forest and let in the wind and light, and that sight is beautiful to me in its own right.

It is the newness of these things here that confounds us, the swiftness of impending changes, in which we sense more keenly the immediate losses. The intact and roadless wilderness we have known is disappearing, and we will not see it again. Here too in Alaska and the North we will learn to live with diminished horizons; or until, perhaps, those essential vistas reopen for us among the galaxies, and it will again be possible to look out on the unknown, the untrodden, keen on exploration and discovery. For now, we must care for what we have, there is no way to make it larger.

I look west into the light that comes across the hills, toward Banner Dome, four miles away. I have been told that seventy or more years ago, on a summer holiday, the townspeople of Richardson would climb that dome by foot and horseback to picnic in the open meadows. I have imagined them up there, in full skirts, bonnets, and broad hats, picking blueberries, and excited by the view.

Looking out on these hills today one would hardly guess the activity of those years—the numbers of men and animals that the country contained, the creaking sleds and groaning wagons. The trails we walk today were the roads they made through the wilderness, surveyed by eyesight and cleared with an axe. And God knows they did their share of harm in the country, with deliberately set fires, clearcut slopes, and scoured hillsides. They were years of hardship and deprivation, of crudity and innocence, of a thoughtless taking of the land's abundance; of an easy and exuberant companionship, also, if one can believe the written accounts. And now the hills sleep in the sun, and there is not a sound to be heard above the wind.

It is just past 9 P.M. The sun is a long time going, settling in a long north-westerly sweep. While the light is still strong, we decide to take a short walk over the big meadow rising behind us. We want to see something of the country hidden from us by the south ridge of the dome.

The wind sweeps in a big rush across the tundra, pushing us on. There are flowers underfoot: avens, harebells, a small Jacob's ladder, a variety of cinquefoil, others I do not know.

In about twenty minutes of walking we are clear of the south shoulder, and stop to look. A vast panorama of mountain, plain, and riverbed stretches before us: the Tanana with its many islands, its sandbars and gleaming gray channels, and beyond it the irregular, snow-streaked profile of the Alaska Range.

Looking below us, we see the slim, geometrical cut of the Richardson Highway running east toward Delta Junction. And then, in random succession, the Granite Mountains, Donnelly Dome, Isabel Pass, and the sandy, braided wash of the Dry Delta descending from one of the glaciers on Mt. Hays. In the middle distance, the big, blue oval of Quartz Lake, and the level, dark green expanse of Shaw Creek Flats with its countless ponds.

The night shadows are spreading slowly over all that country, deepening the color of lake, river, and sky, though a misty, orange glow still bathes the farther hills toward the Goodpaster River. The view commands a stillness in us. Any steadfast look beyond the arrangements of men can return us to an earlier world, and it is as if no work had ever been done. And for a moment I imagine I understand how it must have been for the gods looking down from heaven or high Olympus, gazing with detachment and concern on a far place of road and township, that strange, disruptive haunt of the tribes of men.

It is all very grand, and if we had time and shelter at hand it might be well to watch through the few short hours of the night until the sun rises. But the edge of the meadow where we are standing offers no shelter from the wind that freshens from time to time, hitting us with a stronger gust. We are tired from the day's walk, and having seen part of what we came for, we return to our camp.

There are times when high in the uncomplicated air of these domes and hills I feel like voicing a loud complaint against the persistent follies of my kind. Damn that fellow, Prometheus, anyway! Why couldn't he have left well enough alone? Why not have left humankind to perish in darkness and cold, as almighty Zeus intended? But no, he had to bring them fire, and stolen fire at that. And look what we've done with it, and all the gifts that followed: the arts, the crafts and sciences, the engineering triumphs, the high achievements—yes. But also the wars and the waste, the compounded vanity and misery, the endless criminality, the destruction of landforms and the decimation of species. And who knows? The gods may win in the end, and a few debased survivors of our kind will perish at last, if not on earth, then in some miserable black hole in frigid space, in that darkness and cold held off for so long.

And would the wilderness have missed us? Not at all, I think. These hills would still have their summers, their winter snows, their profusion of fruit and flowers, and the moose, the caribou, and the bright birds of passage would be part of a wonderful plenty.

And then I think that without that divine arrogance and interference we would not be here. *I* would not be here. And I guess that settles it, for I would not want to have missed being here in this wind and evening light, nor have missed my days in this country.

It is past ten o'clock. And now the sun dips below the farthest domes we can see. The light is soft and golden, suffused over the hills in a prolonged twilight to be found only in these high latitudes.

We unroll our sleeping bags and arrange our bedding on the uneven, spongy tent floor. It is good, finally, to lie down. Light from the sun below the hills in the northwest comes into the tent. The wind billows the blue, translucent walls, and the tent eaves occasionally tug and strain.

I lie awake for a short while. Images, voices from past years spring into my mind, released from the day's attention:

> July 10. Very hot today. 80 in the shade. I done a wash. Picked blueberries. Swallows make a lot of noise. So hot I could not sleep.

Here in these hills I have known a kind of stillness and agreeableness in myself. Is it entirely imaginary that the ground underfoot somehow transmits a character and energy to the person who walks upon it? And now I remember a condition for happiness as defined once by Goethe: We are happy when for everything inside us there is an equivalent something out there. And once, it may be, we lived in such a world, when any stone, tree, or shadow might harbor a speaking spirit; the world alive and sentient, responding to the imagination in shapes of terror and joy. Not this half-dead thing of project and statistic, whose quantified presence confounds us with a spiritual absence. If there is evil in the world, let it take visible form in the shape of a goat, faun, or centaur, or a dragon breathing fire, as terrible as you wish. Not this formless, invisible menace that haunts the crowd of modern people like the atmosphere of a plague, ready to blossom into violent sores.

The wilderness is out there, quiet under the brief, rose-gray twilight before the sun rises again. But the wilderness is in myself also, like a durable shadow. I prowl my region of flesh, my forest of blood, muttering and sniffing, turning many times in search of my own best place.

The tent walls flap, the air blown into the doorway is fresh and cool. I drift into sleep.

By late afternoon of the following day we are back in Fairbanks, threading the holiday traffic. We stop at a pizza parlor on College Road, near the university. We sit quietly in the semigloom, waiting to be served, with music coming too loudly from a speaker in the room. I am aware of traffic on the road outside, of the voices of others in the room, and of a vague but persistent dislocation. I am still partway back in the hills, walking the trail, standing on the dome in the west wind, looking out.

At times it is all but impossible to see our towns and cities, our houses, our cars and roadways, as anything but an imposition, a cruelty done to the earth, and for which we will be punished. And yet this too is our world, and we are all its half-willing conscripts. I recall now something that Robert Marshall wrote at the end of one of his marvelous hikes in the Brooks Range early in the 1930s:

> Now we were back among people in Wiseman. In a day I should be back in Fairbanks, in two more in Juneau, in a week in Seattle, and the great, thumping modern world. I should be living once more among the accumulated accomplishments of man. This world with its present population needs those accomplishments. It cannot live in wilderness, except incidentally and sporadically. (*Alaska Wilderness*, 1970)

Well said and, probably, all too true. But would he have written those words, said those things in quite the same, convinced tone of voice, had he lived through the following decades and witnessed the corrosive effect of another world war and the subsequent and continued degradation of the planet? There is an innocence in those words, understandable and forgivable, for us who are the inheritors of those "accumulated accomplishments" that threaten us now as they have never before.

Meanwhile, we drink our beer, brewed no doubt with mountain water, or with water pumped from some slowly emptying acquifer far under the paved foundations of our thumping modern world.

I think of the sun-lighted hills back there, of Campbell, and of a summer long past: one man alone in the country, taking his rare ease from labor in a camp by a shallow lake:

> June 22. Took a rest. Listened to the birds. A lot of noise around here. I have a mountain bluebird out the door. Old cow moose in the lake. Everybody worked all night, except me and the dogs. *1980-87*

Fables and Distances

Review of Thomas Merton in Alaska: The Alaska Conferences, Journals, and Letters *and* Alaska: Reflections on Land and Spirit, *by Robert Hedin and Gary Holthaus.*

It seems to be the fate of certain places to be written about. Perhaps now more than ever is this the case, as the terrestrial world diminishes and with it the capacity of what remains to nourish us in substance and spirit. As the continental landscape contracts to a "scenic view" prepared for the roadside tourist, and wilderness "experience" is promoted and all but owned by one agency or another, outfitted from one catalogue or another, the baffled human spirit retreats to a kind of no-place within society itself, within the distracted, displaced individual—the last metaphorical cave furnished with plastic trees and tinted feathers, with literal skulls and lacquered bones, artifacts of a life no longer lived, of a world we have outgrown or have simply abandoned. All too evident is a compensatory impulse to ransack the world and expose to public view every remaining secret; an appetite that seems intent on leaving nothing unprocessed and unconsumed.

In extreme moments it has occurred to me that this relentless exposure—this peering and prying, this endless cataloguing on film and paper—is part of that extractive colonial activity so characteristic of imperial societies. As we drill, mine, probe, and cut into the last planetary spaces, so do we seek out, for thrills and profit, the last places of mystery and the last peoples. And it is not that good books do not get written about far places and remote peoples; they do, and we in some way gain from this. Yet the literature that results from this approach to the world is significantly different from that which comes of long familiarity with land and people—a writing that comes, as it were, from within the place itself, rich with its memory of events and persons, and which represents us in a way the other never can. We have only to think of that sometimes dreary academic subject, English literature, and how those thousands of poems, plays, novels, and stories, born of a place named England, have at the same time and in every way returned to it, to become not simply a heap of books and works, but a piece of our lives, as essential as the stones in the fields and the water in the ponds. This writing, a way of thought far older than mere print on a page, part dream, part actuality, embodies equally past, present, and future, persisting in stubborn contrast to our convenient notions of linear time, of progress and improvement.

Very different is the writing produced by that busy class of journalists who venture out from New York or Boston, from London, from Princeton or San Francisco, to do a job on an exotic or newsworthy place—be it Africa, the Yukon, the Amazon, or the Antarctic—and return to certain publication and the promise of another interesting assignment. Increasingly, it seems to me, regions and ways of life are written *about,* and the images that result become more real than the actuality. Is it too much to suggest that this writing *about* things and places is a way of stealing their soul and leaving them empty? It will depend, perhaps, on the motivation, on the quality of the attention, and on the intensity of affection in the author for what he sees and records.

So it is of some interest now to consider in what ways a number of writers and observers have expressed their experience of a place as varied, as vast, as romantically conjured as Alaska, and especially in view of the American preoccupation with a frontier.

Of the two books under review here, the collection of letters, journal notes, and informal talks by Thomas Merton, preserved from a brief visit to the state in the late 1960s, is much the slighter and will be of interest mainly, I suspect, to readers and scholars of Merton. Not being familiar with Merton's writings generally, I can only guess at what additional value may lie in these jottings and impressions. Yet even here, as sketchy as most of the entries are, we sense Merton's very keen reaction to what he sees in the landscapes of southeastern and southcentral Alaska, their mountains and waters and abundant weather:

> Sept. 24: Most impressive mountains I have seen in Alaska: Drum, Wrangel, & the third great massive one whose name I forget, rising out of the vast birchy plain of Copper Valley. These are sacred & majestic mountains, ominous, enormous, noble, stirring . . . I could not keep my eyes off them.

This is, perhaps, a typical response to a new country, though vividly rendered by Merton's descriptive powers. But Merton's sensibilities are alert, humane, and attractive, and we find additionally in this small book abundant intuition of what *place* is, what it can mean for us in that rare freshening of impression by which the world, or a part of it, dulled by routine familiarity, is renewed, and by which in turn we too are to some extent renewed. Whether Merton, who in 1968 was on his way to the Far East, would ever have returned to Alaska, to the solitude he sensed might be there for him, we shall never know. It may well be that what he wanted most was the illusion of solitude, and the immensity of that in Alaska would have been more of it than he would have been able to bear or find constructive use for.

Alaska: Reflections on Land and Spirit collects twenty-two essays by authors well known and unfamiliar, professional and amateur, ranging from early days to the present. Included are contributions from naturalists, eminent jurists, professional bird-watchers, cabin-sitters, and journalists; among them, John Muir, Barry Lopez, Peter Matthiessen, Anne Lindbergh, and the psychiatrist Robert Coles. The quality of the writing varies, but each of the entries is distinctive and illuminating in its own way, and the contrasting moods and sensibilities of the authors have as much to tell us as the actual content of the essays.

The publisher's press release that came with my copy of the book starts off with these words: "Alaska: huge, beautiful, untamed and unknown . . . this 'last frontier,' this last wilderness . . . ," etc. Which is sheer publicist's rubbish by any standards, and sufficient to warn us that anything written about a place like Alaska must contend with these mighty and durable clichés.

As if in confirmation, the editors, in their otherwise useful introduction, feel bound to remind us of the geographical enormities of Alaska, listing the familiar figures as to distance, landmass, population, topographical variety, and so forth. And it is not that all these references to size, elevation, and coastline are unimportant, but that they are a distraction. Of interest primarily to mapmakers and empire-builders, they provide us with little sense of local reality, and fail to answer for us that very immediate question: What must we do to live?

A self-conscious awe in the face of immensity makes up a good part of the substance of the first essay, "Alaska Wilderness," by the late naturalist and nature writer, Sigurd Olson. There are clichés aplenty in Olson, "towering ramparts," biblical quotations, references to a "virgin continent," and a certain amount of worked-up, retrospective emotion. This was, I suppose, a mark of style in nature writing once, but read now the language seems dated and a bit tiresome. Even so, we understand very well what Olson means by the "early morning freshness" of Alaska. Though particularly intense at certain moments in the north country, it is a feeling we have all known at one time or another, in one place or another.

This morning sense of the world is especially acute in John Muir, one of the earliest and most reliable of visitors to Alaska. Where Olson is a bit dreamy-headed, going off into ill-timed ecstasies, Muir, in his "In Camp at Glacier Bay," as in all of his wilderness writings, is factual and observant, knowledgeable as to kinds and species, and with no nonsense. And it is not only his vivid appreciation of geography and weather that I would call attention to, but equally his delight in fellowship, a balance in sensibility increasingly rare. But they were mostly of that spirit, those early wilderness travelers. Witness Olaus Murie's "Dogs Around Denali," a matter-of-fact record of a winter journey by dogsled in 1922, through the country surrounding what is now Denali Park, counting caribou for the federal government. The casual audacity of it—alone on the trail for weeks, camping in snow and deep frost, with no reliable map, no radio, no air support, and above all no television crew waiting to interview him at the end! All in a day's work, and for what would seem now to have been a paltry wage. An able and thoughtful man, Murie, writing down his story years later, wonders "whether it is not misleading to relate such adventures on paper." And he asks, "Why do we look back to those days as something precious? Perhaps there is something there we do not yet understand." Nothing in that thought would seem at all strange to anyone wintering alone in the country today.

It is all the more interesting at this point to turn to "Forest of Eyes" by one of the more recent contributors, Richard Nelson. Where Muir and Murie appear to be at home in the country, at ease with conditions and with themselves, Nelson clearly is not at ease, and must think his way back, step-by-step, as it were, to something like an intimate relation to the southeastern landscape he writes about. The effort involved in doing this, the at times studied, self-conscious style of the writing, is, I think, one accurate measure of the attrition in sensibility we have undergone in recent times. Nelson is watchful, careful in his phrasing, to a degree admirable in his choice of details to convey what he sees and feels—but how acutely alone he seems. Despite references to people elsewhere who are apparently close to him, he is like the last man, never entirely given to what he sees, nor a part of what he walks through, and strange, one imagines, even to himself:

> The long boughs reach out above and encircle me like arms.
> I feel the assurance of being recognized, as if something
> powerful and protective is aware of my presence. . . .

Following Richard Nelson on his hike, standing with him in the midst of an island clear-cut, it is as if we had to learn all over the very thing we have been divesting ourselves of for centuries, and proof that we may have come some grave distance in a deterioration of self and society. If it conveyed little else, writing like Nelson's makes clearer to us the true nature of our modern dilemma: the baffled self-regard with which we relate to the world, and which may be the one thing left to us in the end.

John McPhee is admired by many for his ability to write about almost any subject, place, or event, and make a saleable book of it. This is, apparently, one deliberate way to write: go to a place, a countryside, preferably remote and where something noteworthy is going on; spend a little time there—a few weeks, a month or two—talk to some of the inhabitants, collect a few facts and impressions; then go back to wherever it is you have come from and put together an article, a series of articles, or a book, that will sell both itself and you as a source of current authority. It is a writing suited to a largely urban, mobile audience, one that likes to read about places far from home, knowing that it can probably afford to go there one day, or if not, then the experience can be verified in a TV documentary. We have a number of good people who write this way, some better than others, all of them entertaining and useful to one degree or another. In McPhee's case, however, it seems to me that whatever he writes comes out in the same mechanical, computer prose:

> . . . in a country of mica schists and quartz intrusions, of sharp-peaked ridges, dendritic drainages, steep-walled valleys, and long, flat spurs . . . Circle City was for a time the foremost settlement on the Yukon, and proclaimed itself 'the largest log-cabin city in the world.'

It is efficient and easy to read, it gets you along, and is utterly without character or imaginative depth. His description of Circle City might, with a few changes in names, have been written about any number of places.

In spite of this disadvantage, for those of us who remember what the country was once like, something of the old magic asserts itself in McPhee's narrative, and we are taken back to a frontier that, except in memory or as profitable delusion, no longer exists. The modern world, with its frenzies and achievements, is still far off, and life is concentrated on the river, on the coming and going of the ice, on the local news and its characters. It wasn't a bad life, come to think of it.

Of the writers on Alaska represented in this anthology, Robert Marshall stands out as still among the best. What I miss in many of the more recent contributors, that open and spontaneous joy in discovery and fellowship, Marshall has abundantly. "Toward Doonerak," an exuberant record of a journey in 1938, by foot and by wooden boat, up the North Fork of the Koyokuk River into the Brooks Range, exemplifies the old sense of sharing in one last adventure—in that morning excitement of setting out, of departure and arrival. No pious philosophizing, no musing on the state of one's soul, in or out of tune with nature; but simply pushing on, with a couple of good companions, into the undiscovered country. Margaret Murie's "Geese," a good-natured account of a government bird-banding expedition in 1926, of exploring, with her husband Olaus, their small child, and one other companion, the upper reaches of the Old Crow River, conveys now and then something of the same feeling. For a few hours the official mission is forgotten, and we are caught up in the immemorial sense of travel, of anticipation of something new to be discovered around the next bend in the river. Onward, then! . . . This is the journey, the only true journey, and all others, whether on foot or in spirit, partake of its energy and character. If adventures and places must be written about, let it be in this spirit, in the fervent rush of impressions, and we know where we are, both in the physical terrain and in our hearts:

> ... With snow and faint sunlight, this lofty barren valley with its huge rocks which had tumbled from the surrounding mountains and with its great limestone precipices still rising infinitely into the clouds, seemed an unreal world, unvisited by human beings since the dawn of time.

It hardly matters that Marshall's narrative would not stand up as matchless prose. Here it is mainly the sweep of events and the flavor of the quest that matters, and any attempt to make more of it than this would amount to pretense. Writing of this kind is an accomplishment in itself, and few have managed it as well, as naturally as Marshall. The secret of it lies in the forgetting of self, in paying strict attention to the outside world, hardships and joys acknowledged equally. Yet Marshall is not without occasional subtlety. For one telling moment the party has stopped at an old cabin on the North Fork. In the debris of the cabin Marshall finds a couple of old magazines left behind some years before: "one torn 1930 copy each of the *Literary Digest* and the *Nation*." Thumbing through them, he reads of the "growing depression" that has seized the nation. The nation was at that moment, both physically and conceptually, very far away; but this one brief and surprising reference places the moment with an instinctive exactness.

The sensitivity and acute attentiveness of a good psychiatrist, someone who knows how to keep himself in the background and listen, shows in Robert Coles's "Distances," a brief rendition of an Eskimo girl speaking of herself and her early life on the Arctic coast. These are some of the finest, most illuminating pages in the book. Somehow Coles has done what few others have been able to do: he has seen past the surface, gotten inside the thing itself, and in doing so has left behind for a few moments that ubiquitous, self-aware observer and reporter:

> ... She said one day about the snowmobile: 'It gets you from here to anywhere in a few seconds. There's no space left; you just get inside, and the machine goes, and you sit and watch the land go by, and there's nothing left between you and any place.'

The emotion, the acute, intuitive insight in these sentences, are an appropriate conclusion to this book, personal and poignant, as I'm sure the editors realized. I wish there had been more of it.

There is much to think on here, much of value. Given the variety and abundance of potential material, the editors have done a commendable job of presenting the country through these eyes and voices. I would mention additionally Peter Matthiessen's "Oomingmak," a strenuous romp on Nunivak Island in pursuit of wild musk ox; and David Boeri's sensitive portrait of two old Gambell whalers. I would call attention also to John Hildebrand, whose "Fables" is all the more effective for being part of a personal return to the Yukon River country. Finally, the photographs of Arctic peoples by Alex Harris that occupy a section of the book speak more eloquently than many pages of prose.

What is missing, and which Coles perhaps comes closest to, is that written or spoken expression that results from long and deep familiarity with a place, its history, and its inhabitants; a familiarity that is both physical presence and spiritual resonance. For all the activity, the adventuring and ruminating, I come away with a sense of something oddly diminished. Virtually nowhere in this collection of essays do we find that act of imagination (or it may be more simply an act of being) by which place is transformed into residence, into homeland. And one wonders if this is even possible now, given the steady erosion of local life everywhere and its replacement by an endlessly duplicated social and cultural identity that has as its apparent objective a captive humanity.

One fact about the Hedin/Holthaus anthology will be apparent to the attentive reader. The writing is entirely by non-Natives, most of whom have come from elsewhere and for a brief time only. What remains of authentic local life is encountered and reported in selected episodes. The scene otherwise is dominated by the activities and speculations of the authors, who will in most cases soon leave and return to their lives and professions. Despite the intense interest and concern that this place, Alaska, arouses in them, their real lives are elsewhere. This is, I suppose, a pretty good description of the tourist, and it applies to our intellectual habits as well.

Sorting out various impressions of these two books — the abundant images of wilderness treks and river ascensions, of lofty peaks and glacial vistas, of solitude and animal roundups, I return to a contribution so far unmentioned. Harry Crews's "Going Down in Valdez," an account of Valdez during the oil boom of the 1970s, is good journalism; the writing is spirited and, I suspect, pretty accurate in its details and sense of the moment. It is what a contemporary description of a gold rush camp might sound like, and it offers besides some comic relief to the more solemn nature writing that fills a good many pages in the anthology.

Like any reasonably sane person, Crews has difficulty in making sense of what is happening at that moment in Valdez, in sorting out the talk of fluctuating prices, the shortages of food and material, the short tempers and local resentments that have swarmed over a previously quiet port community. There are some shocking moments, as when shortly after his arrival, while waiting for a taxi at the airport, Crews notices a crippled, legless man sitting on the sidewalk nearby:

> When I started across the sidewalk, the legless man put his padded fists down and gave himself a shove, shooting his little dolly past me. I stopped, blinked. There on the cement where the legless man had been sitting were two symmetrical, perfectly formed human turds.

As one reads on, however, the humor, as crude as it is, begins to wear thin. Following on Crews's forcible initiation by a couple of itinerant tattoo artists, the effect is finally depressing. From these crowded, feverish pages we get a brief look at what it might be like at civilization's end. In the windy, wintry half-dark some vast construction project has been underway, the importance of which no one now remembers. People—unemployed workers and displaced Natives—are wandering about between mobile units under flickering lights. Apparently there is a supply of booze; a couple of prostitutes and their pimps are operating in a reduced market; and we learn of a few sporadic efforts at entertainment. But we no longer sense any purpose in things, and the money still being paid out of some remote corporate account cannot be spent. From one of the metal huts nearby comes the murmur of an interminable drunken conversation lasting into endless night. It is sordid and sad, with no grandeur at the end, no prospect of anything better.

That is one possible, extreme outcome. I would prefer to think that another is also possible: that the painful lessons of the recent Valdez oil spill can be applied to a new sense of state and local responsibility; that regional control of resources can to some extent be reclaimed; and that a local economy more independent of federal and commercial interests thousands of miles distant can be further encouraged. I would like to believe that the inevitable deterioration of a northern environment, one only marginally suited to urban industrial development on a modern scale, can be halted and the energies that fuel it redirected. And that finally a true art, a writing drawn from and expressive of this last, special place, with all of its historical and geographical resonance, will one day emerge. That writing would, I suspect, have to contend at some point with a few questions provoked by this anthology, questions that are for me persistent. What will happen when there are no more hidden, unexplored places in North America, no unfilled spaces on the map? What will happen, for that matter, when none are left on earth? For a society conditioned by the illusion of yet another frontier territory to be opened and settled, for a humanity that has until now existed on this planet with the knowledge that there has always been somewhere else to go—another continent, an island, a desert, a wilderness, some unpeopled, barbarian space—these are not trivial questions.

Meanwhile, perhaps, a few encouraging signs. Contrary to normal expectations, the excitement and critical attention generated by the recent Valdez oil spill still claims a good deal of space in the local papers. A popular indignation (in which one senses at times a certain amount of hypocrisy), added to an apparently serious scrutiny of federal and state resource policies, offers a moderately hopeful alternative to the senatorial news-releases with their tone of belated outrage and behind which one detects the accents of another election. Nor is this all, and one would be entirely negative to discount the many sporadic, individual efforts to define, for Alaska and elsewhere, that shifting and elusive thing "community."

Yet as one drives from the countryside into Fairbanks and is struck once again by the random shoddiness of block after block of malls, shops, and housing—a disorder that goes beyond the normal rough improvisation of a frontier settlement, and is in fact a pretty accurate reflection of the fundamental incoherence of contemporary society; where in walking about the city one discovers in one shop window after another the prominent display of a thick nationally best-selling book titled *Alaska*—one understands all too well that that other and better possibility, if it exists at all, is a long way off.   *1989*

John Muir's Alaska

John Muir's *Travels in Alaska* can be read in several ways, and the sum of them is, I think, something more than the conservationist outlook we are accustomed to.

As an adventure story it reads quickly and well, with any number of splendid views, first ascents, and naming of things, and with a minimum of introspection to slow the narrative. There are hardships and dangers, narrow escapes and momentary disappointments, but the predominant note is one of exhilaration and thanksgiving.

As a study of a nineteenth-century American of energy and genius, the book is also of more than common interest, especially in what it reveals of a continent more open than it has become since to individual exploration and a personal satisfaction. I am impressed by the honesty and directness of the man, that what he sets out to do he does, without preliminaries and without pretense, with nothing more than his nerve, some dry bread, and the clothes on his back. It is Muir's passion for nature, for the wilderness as he finds it, that lifts his narrative out of the ordinary, and without passion there can be no distinction in human life. This dedication, a keen intuition of excellence in the thing itself, and which has nothing to do with self-seeking in the ordinary sense of it, is the stuff of greatness.

Men like Muir, wide-eyed searchers and wonderers (Robert Marshall was another), can be said to continue for us the spiritual reclamation of North America. At their keenest, they evoke for us something of the freshness of an hour and a day when, before the intervention of culture, men saw the world for the first time, as something wonderful and new.

This wonder, without the mediation of style, is a mark of Muir the writer as well. One of the oddly attractive things about Muir is that he is not really interested in writing about the world, and thereby making it into something more, or other, than it is—a tendency of writers—but in calling attention to what he sees and in sharing his discoveries in the most immediate and personal way.

To read Muir's descriptions of the southeast Alaska coast as it was then, to recognize the places he stopped at and explored, and to sense the changes that have come to them, is for me a not entirely charming experience. In these drenched forests and cold, rich waters, we encounter for a last time the original abundance of life, a plenty of bird and fish, of tree life and animal variety. And we learn that we are looking at, and listening to, a world vanished in less than a hundred years.

It is striking and strange to think of Muir at the head of Lynn Canal, having come by sail and oar in a dugout canoe, and to find him camping in a Chilkat village where now the cities of Haines and Skagway stand, where the Alaska Ferry arrives and departs on schedule, and a pair of highways lead over the mountains into the Yukon. Sometime between Muir's earliest voyages Juneau was built, and the old sea-hunting life of the Tlingits was on its way to extinction. Already the tourist had appeared.

And Muir, for all his loving attention to the purely wild, was not immune to that other, all-too-human attraction of a new place. Early in his narrative we find him speculating on the commercial prospects for Seattle and Puget Sound, voicing his loyal citizen's praise of the coal and iron deposits to be found nearby; a sentiment familiar to any frontier society whose attention is unfailingly focused on that something which is always "coming." The same optimistic note can be found in early issues of the *Fairbanks Times*, welcoming the newest gold strikes, or rumors thereof, and predicting great things for the country. It was part of the buoyant mentality of the times. Inevitably, anyone familiar with the country might wonder what Muir would think were he to see it today. Depending on where he was set down, what feeling would he give expression to? Perplexity? Outrage? Sorrow? All of these, maybe, and a good deal more. He would surely find a satisfaction in learning that so much of the land had for the time being been set aside as wilderness, or had otherwise been protected. He would undoubtedly be fierce at this moment in defending the Arctic Wildlife Range from intrusion by oil and gas development. He might be impressed by the road system sprung up in the last thirty or forty years, as periodically dilapidated as it is, and marvel at the ease with which we move about from one range and watershed to another; noting the number of tour buses stopped for a look at the Alyeska Pipeline, he might wonder if this mobility was necessarily a good thing. Otherwise, the mountains and the glaciers are still here, the spaces and the distances are intact, and depending on where you look and how much money you can spend, the wildlife can still be found. Yet in some not easily definable way it has all been subtly altered, perhaps simply as a result of having been looked at, written about, and photographed.

Those of us with a roadside view will have another, more unsettling, impression as we watch the weekenders coming and going: the dipnetters heading out for Chitina, the moose hunters returning, with or without a set of antlers riding in the boats behind them. A seemingly endless summer convoy of RVs and double-tankers reminds us forcibly of the accumulation of machinery (and weaponry) in individual and collective hands; a scene in which the military presence with its occupation of vast tracts of land for one purpose or another appears as an all-too-inevitable complement. Add to this the teetering claims for subsistence rights, for lands and profits, the various competing jurisdictions foisted by statehood—a legal and economic bind for which the more or less forced gathering of Native groups into corporations may have been a singularly ill omen. Add, too, the everlasting clamor for resource development, amounting almost to a hysteria that the least item on the agenda might be overlooked and the smallest parcel go unclaimed. The innocence and enthusiasm of a John Muir cannot be maintained in this atmosphere.

Whatever is most characteristic of contemporary urban America, whether it is fast foods, minimalls, shoddy housing, or just plain noise and ugliness, you can find it here in Alaska, and all the more objectionable for the lack of any originality whatever, and for being imposed on a land that cries out for originality and distinction.

JOHN HAINES   189

We seek out nature for a number of reasons, which amount to but one reason: to return, as we like to think, to our sources; to shed for a time our social self become burdensome and overcomplicated; to renew the alphabet, the grammar of speech and thought, and to refresh our senses in the original of all our arts and skills.

Those who like Muir, like Emerson and Thoreau, saw in nature a link with divinity, were not mistaken. All mythology and religion in one way or another acknowledge that primary relation, the very foundation of the religious instinct. With continual alteration and settlement of the land that connection, lacking an adequate cultural mediation, becomes more difficult to discover and maintain, but to the alert and sensitive spirit the secret of things remains intact. Some may locate it more obviously in the grand, glacial views described here many times by Muir, and which remind us of those exalted, painted frames that so stirred us once in the Sierras and the Rockies: a pastoral view of golden skies and tumbling waters, with Indians at the river ford, and all of it bathed in a classical evening light. I myself return at times to a certain key overlook deep in the Alaska Range, a sweeping expanse of wet, treeless plain, of glacial ponds and brooding foothills, in which it is still possible to feel directly the primordial light and pulse of the land. But even when we are confined to the small and familiar, to conventional woodlands close at hand, to a quiet moment by pond or stream on a summer evening—to nothing more than sunlight on a blade of grass—something of the heart-healing beauty and mystery can still be felt.

None of which, however, will ever quite dispel an uneasiness that exultation in nature, as heady and uplifting as it can be, is sufficient to resolve an old trouble: how we are to live with one another on a diminishing earth. If Jung was right, and every Roman as a result of slavery became in some way a slave, then as a consequence of North American history, every white American carries in his psyche a mutilated and disinherited Indian.

For this reason what I find most memorable in Muir's pages are the isolated human instances, of courage, loneliness, and affection. The people of these journeys and places, not always admirable: the natives sometimes devious and quarrelsome, spoiled by whiskey; the missionary doing his honest best by the situation, unaware of the harm he and his brethren were also doing, but urged by a kindness that might mitigate the worst otherwise inflicted. An old Chilkat shaman, a man of obvious poise and wisdom, welcoming, as he thinks, the white man's superior gift of knowledge. The animal crying of a native child, sudden and strange to our civilized ears. A young Taku girl, sitting on a rocky beach, absorbed in building a playhouse out of quartz pebbles; another with her head held aslant, watching by the fire in curiosity and wonder, and she might be Rachel in the tent of her father. And in all of which Muir reveals, almost as an aside from his main attention, an observant sense of human nature that, had he been so minded, he might have turned to account as a writer of higher rank than he actually is.

And always here in Muir is the strong sense of a world that may have no need of us for its fullest expression, and that goes on its way, spending itself in mud and ice, in wind and rain, fire and smoke, as it has from the beginning. Only in ourselves, perhaps, does this other need arise—a human warmth, the one thing lacking in all that distance and grandeur. After so much trekking and measuring and viewing, what remains with me are the abbreviated glimpses of a world when, for all the abuses otherwise, men were at home with animals as we are not. The Stikine prospector who in his cheerful isolation had taught one of his dogs to fetch pots and dishes to the streamside for washing; the Frenchman LeClair, with his little flower garden, his birds, and his woodchuck. No renegade nor mere adventurer; for the moment solitary, but with a family somewhere, and with entire good nature tending his love as he finds it.

Of roughness and brutality, in and out of nature, we have more than enough. A certain refinement of sensibility can be detected in these solitary individuals, a courtesy of heart, common to Muir, his companions, and to many of the people he meets with in his travels. Together with Muir's characteristic freshness of eye, his openness to and appreciation of the world, it is a quality that seems to me at this moment to be our best hope. *1987*

Days in the Field

Cut wood. Got birch bark.
Picked berries, blue and cran.
Diary of F. CAMPBELL, September 1948

And then the mist burned away above the yellowing birches; the sun shone on the damp, cold earth and warmed it.

We came out early to the field, shrugging away the morning chill, swinging our arms, easing our fingers of their stiffness. The big red tractor started and moved down the furrows, with the yellow digger rattling behind it; and the tawny, earth-flecked tubers spilled up into the sunlight, damp and cold.

By midmorning we were spread out over the field, bending and picking up the potatoes where they lay drying in the sun. Moving slowly east, then west, with baskets and buckets in hand, filling the brown sacks allotted at intervals along the rows. And the dust soon rose above the earth in the brilliant fall sunlight.

There were women among us, housewives come for the outing. A few young men from the military; a derelict or two, seedy, needing the scanty wages. A woman with a small child, who sat in one place and carefully cleaned her potatoes as friends brought them to her in baskets. And from time to time she fed and tended the child wrapped in a blanket and laid on the dusty earth.

Noon came, and a short break for sandwiches and coffee. There was a little time in which to relax, to sit and talk, to smoke, to walk from group to group, remarking on the average size and fullness of the harvest, the autumn distance in the blue sky above us. And then once more to work, moving downslope to where the red machine ran and rattled and turned up the tubers.

Toward dusk, the pickers cleared the field, straggling away by twos and threes. In the gathering light of dusk a big white van backed slowly along the furrows, while the few of us who remained walked before it and swung the heavy sacks aboard to be hauled downhill to the warehouse at the farm.

From the tailgate of a pickup coffee was poured for us by the lean, untalkative foreman, the last strong ration before dark. The last sunlight poured through the dust, ruddy and strong. There was dust in our hair and clothing, dirt in our fingernails. And we stood and drank, and spoke a few final words of the harvest.

The air grew chill, the redness of the light turned into darkness, and we dispersed to the sound of starting engines, voices drifting away over the darkened, sun-warmed field.

On the evening of the third day I picked up my wages and a sack of potatoes gleaned from the rows left behind by the digger. I stopped in town long enough to buy a few needed groceries, and then in the changed fall darkness windy with blowing leaves, I drove back out the long road to Richardson with eighteen hard-earned dollars in my wallet. I went home to my own potato patch on the hill above the river, to the last run of salmon, and to the waiting woodpile.

Each fall, until it seems that the beginning of such things is lost from view—when the birch leaves had begun to turn and loosen, falling in the wind, and with the earth still warm and dry—it was good to stand there in the furrows overlooking the river, to feel one's shod feet on the earth and, bending to that easy work, see the red and yellow tubers turning up and tumbling away from the dry hills. The dry, cloddy clump of plant came up on the face of the shovel: the frost-burned vines grasped, the roots shaken loose of soil, and the whole dead plant thrown aside. Then one more thrust with the shovel into the overturned earth to be sure that not one potato would be lost.

Now and then came a wet, cold September, when the heavy, turned soil clung to the tubers. We had to wash each of them carefully, and wipe them clean one by one. We spread them out on a clean canvas to dry in a brief day of sunlight before packing them away; otherwise they would have rotted in storage.

One year, after the long moose hunt was over, I picked potatoes from Tryph Taylor's frost-bitten field above Harding Lake. In low ground that fall 60 percent of the crop was frozen, a hard loss from an early freeze that drove deep into the hills before the crop could be dug. But those who had planted on higher ground, who hilled their spuds high and late, fared better.

We left the potatoes to dry in the sun for a while, then sacked them and carried them downhill to the storehouse. We left them there to cure for a week or so, then sorted and cleaned them, and put them away into the cellar bins for the winter. They shared space there with cabbages, rutabagas, beets, and carrots. For weeks the dim light of the storehouse, the cool darkness of the cellar, kept the fragrance of drying potatoes, subtle and earthy.

It is morning in mid-July. Peg and I are bending over on a slope above Tenderfoot Creek, picking blueberries. It is the hottest day of the summer, ninety degrees in the sun by midmorning. The heat shimmers on the heavy, damp moss; the mosquitoes, put down by the sun, are quiet. The berries are big and ripe, hanging in clusters with a powdery bloom on their blueness, and the wild smell of them comes rich in the heat as we pick them carefully into our cans. By late morning the sun on our backs becomes oppressive; we quit, and drive back over the hill to Richardson. Not all of our cans are full.

In those lucky, faraway years when blueberries were still abundant at Richardson, the day would come in mid-August when they were ripe on the domes. Campbell and I met at his cabin one bright morning, with baskets and pails, and began the six-mile hike to the top of Buckeye. And once there in the clear sunlight, we bent over by the hour and through the long day, filling the pails. The sun on our backs, the view to engage us from time to time, as we looked south toward Delta or north toward the headwaters of the Salcha; or if it was a cloudy day, with a cool wind in our faces, hoping the rain wouldn't catch us. All through the afternoon we moved from bush to bush, ranging the meadow, until all the pails were filled. And then in the late afternoon we hoisted packs to our shoulders with a grunt, and walked home, bowed under the weight in the long light of the late summer sun.

In the years that followed, the blueberry crop gradually diminished in the Richardson area, and there came a summer when none were to be found. Each summer thereafter, in late July and early August, I caught a ride to Delta with my big basket and half a dozen small pails. From the Junction I walked three miles out on the Alaska Highway to an old burn where the berries were abundant. I had that patch to myself; there was no one else around. By late afternoon, after a long day of picking, I had all of my cans filled. I walked back to the Junction where I eventually caught a ride to Richardson. I got home, late and tired, but with a good load of berries in my pack.

Once the berries were home, the following morning was spent in cleaning them. They were then poured out of the cans and sugared down in gallon jars in the old, sourdough fashion. It was the only way we could keep them without canning or freezing. A layer of sugar in a clean jar, then a layer of berries; another layer of sugar, and so on, alternating berries and sugar until the jar was full. The jar was tapped on the floor to settle the berries deeper in the sugar, and then loosely sealed. We put them away in the coldest place we could find. If it was done right, the berries would keep until frost. Spooned out of the jars later from the heavy, clear syrup, the berries were as fresh, as firm and blue as on the day they were picked.

It was good to walk through the woods in late summer with a basket, gathering mushrooms. Boletus sprang up with the first rains in late July or early August, and in a good year they kept on coming until frost. In the open aspen woods especially, and along the forest roads, clumps of the brown and reddish caps emerged from the thin leaf sod on their pale, net-ted stems. And scattered through the woods, one came on the spread um-brellas of the overripe fungus going soft and rotten.

Walking, awake to the color of things underfoot; a stoop down to look, to pull up the mushroom to see if it was wormy or not. And if the fruit was sound and dry, out came the knife—a quick trimming of dirt from the stem, and over the shoulder they went into the basket with a solid thump. In a good day one felt that gradually settling weight on the shoulders.

Behind Campbell's Richardson cabin there was a particularly favored spot, a patch of aspen woods long since gone to the ravages of a miner's bulldozer, the only place in the country where oyster mushrooms could be found in any abundance. We could never be sure just when they'd be there, early or late. They came up overnight, in late summer or early fall, depending on the dryness of the year, on the late rain, and the temperature. They had to be gathered immediately or they soon became infested with flies. For Campbell, as long as he was alive, it was easy; all he had to do was to walk out each morning into the woods behind his cabin and look. After his death, when the weeds and brush had taken over his garden and the old cabin had sunk even deeper into the soil, it was touch and go whether we would find the mushrooms or not. We came when we could, calculating the day and the hour. Often enough, all we found were a few brown clutches of them, flyblown and useless. But sometimes we were lucky, and there would be great silky gray clumps of them in the small clearings under the aspens. On those lucky days, carefully searching that small patch of woods, we had our baskets filled in a short time.

At home, having cooked and eaten our fill, we turned to that fragrant heap of mushrooms, to clean them of soil, then cut and strip them into pieces and place them on the drying rack above the stove. For days the house was filled with the rich odor of drying mushrooms, until that small room smelled like the house of earth itself.

Each year, in late summer or early fall, I cut hay for the doghouses at a shallow pond not far from Canyon Creek. The native grass stood tawny and dry, cured by the sun, at the edge of the pond. It grew in dense bunches, and was tough and durable stuff. The heavy scythe made my arm ache with the long cutting, but the new hay smelled good where it lay behind me in the cool sunlight, waiting for the fork. When enough had been cut for the day, we piled the old box trailer high with it and drove home slowly, with a weighted canvas over the hay to keep it from blowing out onto the road.

Two such loads at least were needed for the long winter. I kept the hay piled on the ground, covered with canvas if the weather turned wet. When the tomato harvest was over and the vines were cleared from the benches, I forked the dry hay into a loose heap in the greenhouse where it would stay through the winter, free of snow. Now and then I shoved a forkful of it into each of the doghouses, while the dogs frisked and barked and tunneled into the new hay, glad for the clean dry bed.

Sometimes I got to it late, when the hay had been partly bent by frost or an early snow. Then I went carefully with the scythe, pulling the hay upright and knocking it free of ice before I cut it. If the hay was too much broken down, I had to cut it by handfuls with a knife or a sickle, going slowly around the pond edge, while breaking underfoot the thin ice where the last water had frozen in the puddles. I laid the bundles of hay on a clean square of canvas, shaking them carefully free of frost and snow. When I stored that late, damp hay, I turned it from time to time, letting it cure slowly in the cold, dry air.

And there was a fall, late and snowy, when chores kept me from getting enough dry hay. One cloudy day in late October, with the temperature well below zero, I went up to the high, dry ridge behind the homestead. I dug in the shallow snow and pulled up what I could of the bent and smothered grasses. I cut it, beat it free of snow, and carried a load of it home trussed up in a heavy roll of canvas.

Once more it is that time of year, of white smoke, of morning mist burned away by the sun. The leaves are falling, a nearly soundless patter on the root-matted floor of the forest. The last blueberries are sugared down, the pile of birch cordwood grows bigger in the yard; the pink-and-green-mottled chum salmon are running in the river channel. Against the damp green mosses lies the cold red brilliance of cranberries, like the blood of a perishing summer.

We come to them now for the sheer pleasure in gathering them, for the abundant freshness of them, and for the invoked goodness of past years when we picked them out of necessity, ten gallons or more, to be put down beside the sugared blueberries in the darkest and coldest part of the cellar.

We picked them on a dry day when we could, not while the dew or the rain was on them. But some years the fall came on wet, with day after day of rain and fog. And so we waited, doing our chores otherwise, of wood and bark and fish. That calm, dry day would come; we gathered our baskets and pails and headed uphill to the ridge, or down the road to Canyon Creek, wherever the crop was best that year.

And solitary as the work could be, crouched, kneeling, absorbed in the gathering, just the two of us picking in a shared silence along the road; more rarely the berry-picking became a kind of woodsy convocation. I remember how once at Richardson we longtime neighbors went out one afternoon for cranberries in a little gulch east of the Roadhouse. There were four or five of us spread out into the woods, each to his own part of the patch. And after a while we came back to where we had left the car, to find Billy Melvin, eighty-seven years old, lying on his side in the moss, with his head supported by one hand, picking slowly and contentedly into the pail beside him.

The dry, firm berries kept well in a clean flour sack hung up in a cool place, or in a gallon jar with a loose lid. At Campbell's Lake Camp one fall, for want of a better place to store them, we put the jars of berries down in a shallow hole under a pile of hay to keep until November. They were all we had; no store-bought fruit, only the blue and the cran. They were tart, mealy and dry, and would not spoil. Cooked alone, or with rhubarb, or with occasional apples; eaten cold, half-frozen and sweet, with moose ribs and potatoes, there was nothing better.

It's true that those gallons of berries, eaten day after day, would sometimes seem monotonous in a long winter, and we wished for something new and exotic like oranges and melons; but they were entirely free for the labor of picking and cleaning. And there was something else that would always be deeply associated with them, not easily defined, but a rich and persistent sense of having taken part in an ancient ritual, in the last rites of the season.

There are leaves floating in the rainbarrel. I brush them away with the dipper before filling the pail. Dry hay is curing in the sun; boxes of green tomatoes are ripening on the porch; about the house and the outbuildings there is the strong smell of curing onions, the half-sweet, half-sour odor of drying mushrooms. Cold meat hangs in the shade, the skinned quarters red and darkening to redder still, the white, sweet fat turning yellow. Flocks of pine grosbeaks are feeding on the late rosehips and berries on the slopes above the river; we hear, ever so faintly, their wintry cries in which there is always a tiny tinkle of ice. And over the Tanana and the Delta the cranes are gathering, the slow, gyring ascent of flock after flock, the rolling cries echoing over the dry sandbars, as they drift slowly south in the diminished light of the country.

So it must have been in Egypt, following on the annual flood, when the renewed soil gave back life to the sun; in Sumer, where two rivers water the arid plain, and in the high, dry maize fields of the Incas. In these sometimes slavish days of creaking pushcarts, of stacked and bewildering corridors, of green electronic figures winking, mysteriously multiplying an already insupportable debt, it is good to remember that earlier bounty; what it was to stoop down and lift something from the earth, dry tuber or damp mushroom; to close one's hand on the brown, crumbling soil, to sink one's fingers deep into the moss and feel the night and the frost that are waiting there; if only for a moment, to feel oneself once more at home on the earth.

Meanwhile, another day is almost gone. The snowline has dropped a little lower on the foothills, the air is perceptibly keener. The remaining rosehips wrinkle and dry on the thorny canes; dogwood sinks to a cold, dwarfed purple in the shade of the woods. There is a steely gray light on the river at evening, a light on these hills that sinks ever deeper through the yellowing birches. *1980–94*

Shadows and Vistas

There are shadows over the land. They come out of the ground,
from the dust and the tumbled bones of the earth . . .
JOHN HAINES[1]

I begin with "Shadows" as a way of speaking. Laurens van der Post, in *The Lost World of the Kalahari*, acknowledges that he believes in ghosts, in the spirit of the life that the land once held but which cannot be found any longer. Van der Post was looking for the Bushman, who for him signified a lost Africa, one that he had been told about as a boy; but all he could find of it was the changed land itself and a few sites where decades before the Bushman had camped and hunted. According to an old African of his household, from whom he had learned much, the Bushman disappeared because *he would not be tamed.*

I recall an afternoon in October many years ago, when I stood on the edge of that high overlook near Maclaren Summit in the Alaska Range, and gazed down onto the wide sweep of the Maclaren River basin. The cold, late afternoon sun came through broken clouds, and the tundra below me was patched with sunlight. The river, a thin, silvery blue thread, twisted through the subdued autumn coloration of the land, stretching far up into the dark and gloomy hills on which the first light snow had fallen.

I was entirely alone at that moment; no traffic disturbed the gravel road a few yards behind me. The land before me seemed incredibly vast and empty. But it was not empty. Far below me, a few scattered caribou were feeding in the meadows of the river basin, their brown, white-maned forms dispersed among the bogs and ponds, moving slowly upriver toward the mountains. They were the first individuals of a herd that would appear later.

I felt as if I were looking down on a landscape elementary to our being, and that nothing had occured to change it since the last of the continental ice melted from the earth, and the first grasses and shrubs began to grow; and very slowly the animals moved north into the newly restored land, finding their way, feeding on the fresh, undisturbed forage for the first time.

That image has remained with me as one sure glimpse into our past. Even the road that crossed the river on a tiny bridge in the distance did not break the continuity of the feeling I had then. It was all part of an essential vista, a sheer sense of the land in its original presence. On that afternoon, when the guns of the hunters along the road were silent and no cars passed, I easily slipped back a thousand years into a twilight approaching winter; a dusk in which I and a few others, following the game herds upriver, would find meat, fire, and shelter.

That was well over thirty years ago, when the tundra life along the Denali road was still fairly abundant. I have looked over that same view a number of times since, but I have not seen the caribou feeding as they were then. And yet I know that their ghosts are there, that the land contains them and refuses in some mysterious way to give them up, though to the surface view the land appears to be empty.

It is not simply nostalgia, I think, that compels me to believe that this vista, its possibility, needs to be kept. We need it as a kind of model of life, whose images we are bound in some way to resurrect and imitate, even when the original has been destroyed. It is not so much a matter of saving a species, a particular herd and its habitat, but of saving something essential of life and ourselves. And not only our immediate selves, you and I, but those others who were here before us and will come after us, and whose land and nature we have so easily confiscated and misused to our long-standing peril.

It is foolish to believe that we erase life by killing it off, by driving into extinction the remaining game, by paving over the grazing grounds, cutting the forests, and pretending to ourselves that it did not matter after all. Too bad, we say, but let's get on with the business of things. Vanquished in one place, life springs back in another, as at the present time, in spite of all the sophistication in transport and communication, coyotes are barking in the Los Angeles suburbs, and as all the killed and vanished life, animal and people, continues in one way or another to haunt us and question our wasting passage through the world.

As a friend of mine remarked to me some years ago, when in the course of conversation we both remarked on the great physical presence of Kluane Lake in the Yukon: "That place," she exclaimed, "really has spirit!" It does indeed.

And what does that mean? That places, lands, regions, watersheds, etc., all have a life, a felt quality of their own, which we can call *spirit,* and we cannot kill that spirit without destroying something in ourselves. A degraded land inevitably produces a degraded people. It is in fact ourselves we are destroying (and sometimes saving), a possibility of life that once gone will be a long time returning. I say "a long time" and not that it will never come back, because I do not hold with the view that we have the power to destroy life on earth forever. That notion is a part of our problem, part of our arrogance and self-bemusement. We have got it backwards. Life has power to destroy *us,* and do so with our connivance, using our own misaligned means and purposes. A few degrees of climate change, a few more inches of topsoil lost, and our descendants may read the record for themselves.

Is it destined to be a law with us, an iron and withering rule, that anything that cannot be tamed, domesticated, and put to use, shall die? A river, a patch of woodland, a wolf, a small tribe of hunting people? And all the while we preserve a few wretched specimens in a zoo, a controlled park or reservation, or as a collection of images on film, part of an ever-growing catalogue of fossil life.

You can kill off the original inhabitants, most of the world's wildlife, and still live on the land. But I doubt that we can live fully on that land accompanied only by crowds of consumers like ourselves and a few hybrid domesticated animals turned into producing machines. A sure poverty will follow us, an inner desolation to match the devastation without. And having rid the earth of wilderness, of wild things generally, we will look to outer space, to other planets, to find their replacements there.

Today, most of us are familiar with a continuing effort to save some part of a wild heritage, to rethink our lives in relation to the land we drive and park on and from which we draw what certainty we have. And we know the forces assembled in opposition to this effort: There is no need to name or rank them, they all flock under the flag of an ever more questionable progress and enterprise, whose hidden name is poverty.

In *After Strange Gods,* on the occasion of a visit to New England in the 1930s, T. S. Eliot wrote the following:

> My local feelings were stirred very sadly by my first view of New England, on arriving from Montreal, and journeying all day through the beautiful desolate country of Vermont. Those hills had once, I suppose, been covered with primeval forest; the forest was razed to make sheep pasture for the English settlers; now the sheep are gone, and most of the descendants of the settlers; and a new forest appeared blazing with the melancholy glory of October maple and beech and birch scattered among the evergreens; and after this process of scarlet and gold and purple wilderness you descend to the sordor of the half-dead milltowns of southern New Hampshire and Massachussetts. It is not necessarily those lands which are most fertile or most favored in climate that seem to me the happiest, but those in which a long struggle of adaptation between man and his environment has brought out the best qualities of both; in which the landscape has been moulded by numerous generations of one race, and in which the landscape has in turn moulded the race to its own character. And those New England mountains seemed to me to give evidence of a human success so meager and transitory as to be more desperate than the desert.

Certainly, Eliot's description and the feeling it evokes could with a little effort be transferred to many an Alaskan urban landscape, be it Mountain View, North Pole, Soldotna, or one of those lost highway settlements in which it seems as if all the unwanted debris and waste of American life had somehow blown there to settle into an impervious drift composed of tarpaper, crushed plastic, ripped shingles, and foundered hopes. I suppose there are few more unreal and depressing prospects than some of the housing sites, the outlying developed properties in Anchorage and Fairbanks. And what is unreal will sooner or later disappear, the transitory inspiration of a people come to plunder and leave. Van der Post, in another of his books, remarks on the physical fact of Africa as being by far the most exciting thing about that continent. And for him a definite sadness lay in the fact that it had not yet produced the people and the towns worthy of it. By comparison with its physical self, everything else was drab and commonplace.

We who have learned to call this north country home are only at the beginning of a struggle of adaptation between ourselves and the land, and if the evidence so far seems pretty meager, there's a long road yet to travel. The prospect of an Alaska in which a million or so people are on the prowl with guns, snowmachines, airboats, and four-wheelers, is not only terrifying, it is finally unacceptable. An environmental ethic, believed in, practiced and enforced, is not just an alternative, it is the only one, though another name for it may be self-restraint. And it is sometimes possible to sense, behind all the noise and confrontation, a genuine urge toward a real satisfaction, a sane kind of plenitude, a fullness of spirit and being.

And we are all in it together, poet and plumber, even those so far unconscious people out there on the peripheries; and especially those in the halls of academe—our humanists, who surely ought to care but who seem often not to. Mired in their coursework, busily teaching (but what are they teaching?), satisfied to draw their salaries, to save for retirement, to drink the water, breathe the air, and burn the fuel, without a whisper of protest or encouragement.

You may ask what these remarks of mine have to do with immediate politics and practical tasks—the issues, the problems that many of you understand as well or better than I do. And I have no ready answer, no claim that poetic imagery, the personal mythologies of which a writer is sometimes the master, can solve anything. And yet without that dimension of imagination, the instilled power to think and to visualize that poetry, for example, nourishes in us, the solutions, the resolved difficulties seem bound to lack a necessary human element.

So it is a matter of language also, of words common and uncommon, that with something of their original freshness and power have the ability to restore a much-needed sense of reality and reveal to us a few essential things with clarity and concreteness.

Not long ago I saw a marsh hawk, a harrier, hunting the Tanana River islands below Richardson, the first spring arrival of its kind. And that bird was, in a vivid way, rather like a ghost with its gray and white plumage slanting in the spring sunlight as it hovered and sailed over the winter-brown willows and frost-seared grasses. A real spirit, if you like, come back to claim its territory, as it or its ancestors have returned to those flats and adjacent meadows for far longer than our race has existed or can easily imagine. A small but definite image to end on, and returning me halfway to that glimpse into the Maclaren River basin I described earlier, haunted as I am by its persistent contours, and by what seems sometimes destined to become a vanished hope on earth.

And to think, from this diminished perspective in time, from this long vista of empty light and deepening shade, that so small and refined a creature could fill an uncertain niche in the world; and that its absence would leave, not just a momentary gap in nature, but a lack in one's own existence, one less possibility of being.

As if we were to look out on a cherished landscape, hoping to see on the distant, wrinkled plain, among the cloud-shadows passing over its face, groups of animals feeding and resting; and in the air above them a compact flock of waterfowl swiftly winging its way to a farther pond; and higher still, a watchful hawk on the wind. To look, straining one's eyesight, noting each detail of lake, meadow, and bog; and to find nothing, nothing alive and moving. Only the wind and the distance, the silence of a vast, creatureless earth.[2]

1981

Another Country

To be nothing and nowhere. Shreds, particles adrift, a little pallor spun in the dark.

A blankness, a gray film over the eye that saw . . . shadows and a moving brightness. A last deep sigh exhaled from the troubled lungs, and then no breath. Blood stopped and pulse still. In the warm tissue beginning to cool, already a damp decay. And the mosses and the small plants of the soil upreaching, ready to claim the nostrils and the lips.

And so I have stood by and watched a great animal die. And in the stillness that followed the last heave of the flanks, a bloody froth blew from the nostrils, staining the snow. And I who was practiced in death could sense in that silence, that stillness into which a few faded and yellowing leaves were falling, that the hunt was over. I breathed in the damp, rich odor of mortality, and stood for a moment in my own coming death, on the ground of death itself.

It was not clinical death — the sudden stopping of pulse and breath, a gradual rigor in the limbs. It was something else: a sudden space and peace that came to the woods. Before I put rifle and pack aside and prepared for the long job of butchering, I stood for a moment in the oldest stillness on earth. And in that moment, when for this one creature life ceased and its flesh settled into the fixed transience of decay, I could believe in the passage of the soul into another country.

And then there was no time to stand and muse upon the mystery; the animal was down, there was meat to save and work to do.

When the carcass had been gutted and skinned, and the meat cut into quarters, carried off and hung in the air to age and keep, a stained and matted place in the moss kept for a while the imprint of death in life. Blood, body fluids soaked into the snow and the soil beneath; some stray whiskers—hairs that were long and hollow, shading from gray to brown at the roots, and black at the tips—these persisted, along the scraps of trimmed flesh, of fat encrusted with dried blood, freezing in the cold air.

After the kill, and the work of skinning and cutting was over, an odor remained—a warmth, a sweetness of blood and inner membrane, smelt on the hands and clothing, on the knife and axe. That which emerged steaming and hot from the interior of the killed creature cooled to a faint displacement of the dry woods air. And now that I think of it, I cannot dispel completely the persistent odor of death that clings to the woods I have known and hunted.

One morning late in April, after a hard, snowy winter, I climbed to the potato patch on the hill overlooking the river. As I gained the top of the rise, I turned for a moment to look back down the way I had come. On the cleared slope the winter-matted growth of last summer's grass lay warm and yellowed in the sun; here and there some slender, dark twigs of birch and alder sprouted from an old stump. A few yards away, in the shaded woods, patches of snow still lay on the ground, but these were rapidly melting.

Just below me, in a sheltered hollow of the hillside, lay a drift of deeper snow. In the center of the drift I saw a dark brown stain like a shadow, and the snow around it appeared to be discolored, as if the stain were spreading and becoming vaguely pink. Something about that stain in the snow drew my attention, and I climbed back down toward it.

When I stepped off of the path and into the knee-deep snow, I discovered the reason for that stain. Half-buried in the drift, and half-exposed to the spring sunlight, were the remains of a yearling moose calf. It had obviously been dead for some time, and until recently covered by snow. A pair of foxes had been feeding on it, and their well-marked trails led in and out of the drift. The thin hide of the moose had been torn open, parts of the stomach and the intestines were spilled and matted; the snow was threaded with brown moose hair, and scattered about were pink ice-crystals of blood. Much of the half-grown, wasted body had been consumed; what remained had collapsed upon itself like a sodden brown envelope.

A shoulder blade, gnawed and beginning to bleach and dry, was exposed to the sunlight; still attached to it under a flap of hide I could see a part of the rib cage and something of the spinal column. There was very little meat on any of these bones. Even that part of the body so far untouched by the foxes showed me how poor and thin the calf had been. I reached down and pulled from the snow one of the slender leg bones; it was cracked open, and looking closely at it I saw what remained of the marrow: it was thin and bloody, a sign of starvation.

I remembered then that for a brief period during the winter just past we had seen a cow and calf feeding on the hillside below the house and above the river, the two of them in single file treading the deep snow. It was very cold at the time, at least fifty below zero, and the high shoulder ruff of the cow bristled with frost. Severe as the cold was, the cow looked fit and strong, but I thought the calf moved slowly in the troughed snow behind her. Sometime later, when the weather had moderated, I saw the cow alone one day on the hill above the house, not far from where I was standing now, but I did not think then of the missing calf.

A hard winter, deep snow, and maybe a weakness in the calf, that it could not pull down sufficient browse to feed its growing body; weaker and weaker, it failed to keep pace with its long-legged mother in her travel through the woods. One night the calf lay down in the snow and did not get up. Frost drove in through the brown coat of hair, chilling the weakened body. Slowly the blood cooled and the breath came less often. The long ears drooped and stiffened, a cold sleep invaded the bones and stopped the breath.

A vague sadness claimed me as I stood there in the wet, soiled snow, looking down at the pitiful remains. The sun was bright and warm on my shoulder, I could hear a few geese far out on the river, and from somewhere close by came the drowsy, interrupted drone of a bumblebee. I turned away and stepped out of the snow and onto the dark, matted soil of the footpath. Facing the strong sunlight, I climbed back uphill to look over the potato ground for the coming season.

Washed by the spring rains, the snowdrift in the hollow soon melted. Of the young moose, hide and tissue slowly disintegrated, and by midsummer only a stray bone remained in the vigorous new growth of underbrush. Close to the ground, perhaps, in the tangle of grass and flowering plants, there lingered a faint sour odor of late spring and early death.   *1982–91*

Leaving Alaska

Richardson Homestead, August 4, 1991:

Once more I have closed up the house, locked a cable across the drive, and said good-bye to this place, to the familiar yard with its sawhorse and chopping block, and with the hillside above it closing in more and more with the growth of young aspens, poplars, and birches. It is never easy.

In recent years I have taken leave of this place many times, and returned to find it, no matter the season, much the same. A few small changes: an older birch blown down by the wind, the drive blocked by a late snowdrift, the footpath to the creek in need of being cleared once more of brush; growth and decay. Yet, in ways not always easy to admit, everything has changed, changed as the country itself changes, and as the alterations of modern life intrude more and more on all places of a quiet and special nature.

Now I am leaving again, saying farewell to a locked house, to a system of sheds and footpaths, a mailbox, a comfortable writing studio hidden in the woods away from the highway; and have driven out, heading south, on the same road that brought me here, a road that has made possible my residence sixty-five miles from Fairbanks, and that at the same time makes possible, even inevitable, the intrusions that have altered and seem likely to destroy what it was I came for.

And I wonder, as I have many times, while driving back and forth between Richardson, Delta, and Fairbanks, avoiding the frost heaves, shifting gears on the hills, at this perennially restless activity of Americans, always saying good-bye and moving on to that something new that, in our present situation, and despite renewed illusions, seems no longer to exist. Or, we can say, and with increasing certainty, that the new turns out more and more to resemble the old and all-too-familiar.

In my own way, and without intending to, I seem to have entered some time ago on that accelerated American, or it may be more simply, human predicament of arrival and departure. In 1947 I had come north for a set reason, one not clarified at the time. I had come to find, and to know, some part of the American ground, and in that quest to know myself. At twenty-three, too young and idealistic, I had only begun.

In August of 1948 I locked my new house and its one outbuilding, and caught a ride into Fairbanks. I left by plane—my first flight—on August 19. There was ice in the rain puddles on First Avenue that morning. Three days later I was set down in Chicago in the middle of a late summer heat wave. I had run out of money, and had to take a bus the rest of the way to Washington. I thought of my small house on the hillside overlooking the Tanana River, and wondered, sweating and stricken, why I had left it. It was some weeks before the weather cooled and I was settled in Washington, D.C., absorbed once more in my art studies. Life, within as well as without, would never be the same.

I returned in 1954 to a house that, though still intact, lacked by then even a bed or a stove. Young trees had taken root in the yard, and everything of household value had been removed. But in a very short time, once more settled and at home, at work on all that needed urgently to be done, I thought I would never leave again.

Now, over thirty-five years later and after many comings and goings, the hilltop view of this river country I have loved as well as anything in my life, is much the same, though now in order to look down on the river itself I have to cross the highway and climb a guardrail, where once, years ago, I looked directly from the house to see five wolves trotting downriver on the spring ice.

Islands, sandbars, and channels, have shifted and reformed, and even there nothing is quite the same. But the distant and greater view across river to the south, to the foothills of the Alaska Range, to the snow-peaks of Moffet, Hays, Hess, and Deborah, has not changed to the attentive eye. Familiar as they have become, the names seem now to have been carelessly bestowed on those peaks, their syllables, except perhaps for Deborah, which has a darkened and classical tone, not belonging to the masses of snow and rock to which they have been attached.

Traffic on the highway this summer has been heavier and more intrusive than ever. Watching the double-tankers and the holiday homes rolling by, one thinks of this mass of industrial and recreational metal propelled by an increasingly limited fuel supply, of all possible and necessary replacements, and wonders where the parade will end, in what desolated corner of an impoverished planet.

There is something at once inevitable and forboding in the changes that have taken place here in my lifetime, and the more so in recent years: this relentless filling up of open spaces, and the search for yet another space. And the question I have voiced many times repeats itself: What will happen when we at last understand that there is nowhere to go? No more Alaskas, and no more Yukons, no more open and unsettled places on the continent nor on the earth. Will we be able to face that and decide to make a suitable and habitable place where we are? Or, lacking that resolution, will we turn on each other in that ever more limited and constrictive space and destroy everything? No question seems to me more urgent and needing an answer. To face one's history with insight and courage, admit mistakes, and decide to make the best of what remains of time and place: Few things would seem easier to agree on, yet nothing has proved more difficult for humanity, as the history of civilizations demonstrates over and over.

Of one thing we may be certain: Nature will cure everything given sufficient time, and neither the earth nor the cosmos requires our presence in order to fulfill itself. One looks at the ceaseless activity of land, wind, and water, at the immense debris of the past, on the continued evidence of seasonal change and disruption, and observes how it all combines and reforms, how species fail or adapt, return and pursue their fates; and he knows that the worst we can do will not be enough to destroy life, not here nor anywhere else. We can destroy ourselves, render obsolete and useless all of our mechanisms, but that is all. Our inflated claims and expectations amount to very little in the face of that primary perception.

Alaska, what I have known of it, has given me a great deal. I believe, in all honesty, that I have given something back to it and the people who live here. This reciprocal activity, of giving and receiving, seems to me to be what our lives, in respect to the earth and to each other, ought mainly to be about. Yet there are many people—a majority, I fear—for whom, like our current governor in speaking of development in the Arctic, there is "nothing there." And that nothing shall be made into a greater nothing, and its wealth, potential or imaginary, be made to serve a wholly limited and fleeting interest elsewhere.

Unavoidably, then, on leaving Alaska one feels at times that one is leaving behind a project that no longer has in it a great deal of promise, in that undefined, idealistic, and old-fashioned American sense. That unlimited character of land and distance so many of us have felt on first encounter with Alaska, and which must have inspired the first Europeans to see the Far West, has for some time now been fenced and set to corporate and jurisdictional limits; there is little reason to believe that the process can be halted.

It is all too easy to feel, too, on reading of the mounting difficulties of every society and nearly every major city, that the problems of humanity are insurmountable. Every solution, however innovative, brings with it new complications, and the mentality that prevails, despite all efforts to educate it, seems intent on confirming a prophecy voiced by the French artist Jean Arp, that humanity would devote itself "more and furiously to the destruction of the earth."

But I will not attempt to be a prophet here, if only because it is essential to avoid despair, while admitting that however we might wish it otherwise, nothing is likely to remain the same.

With that never-to-be-forgotten sweep of river, hills, and clouds held in mind, one says good-bye one more time, not knowing when or if he will return, nor which, the place or himself, will be the most changed.

1991

VI

The Far Country

Poetry rises from the twilight . . .
all that we make or do stems
from this same obscurity . . .
HERMANN BROCH

Interview with Robert Hedin

*This interview is the result of a lengthy correspondence between myself
and Robert Hedin in 1988 and 1989. Mr. Hedin, a poet, had been an M.F.A.
student at the University of Alaska, Fairbanks in the early 1970s. He has
since retired from twenty years of teaching at Wake Forest University and
lives in Frontenac, Minnesota.*

ROBERT HEDIN In *Other Days*, you call yourself a "wandering spirit" who
"came home to the land" in Alaska. What was it about the interior of the
state, a region so distant and different from anything in the Lower 48, that
helped create a sense of home, of belonging?

JOHN HAINES First of all, I don't exactly call myself a "wandering spirit." I
meant the expression in a more general sense, and felt that I spoke for
others as well, or as representative man.

It's true, of course, that years ago I did come home to the land in a very
personal and immediate sense. Why it had to be that land and not another
is a question that probably has more than one answer.

I see certain aspects of our life as expressions of very old patterns.
What I mean by this is that for thousands, maybe for millions, of years the
life of people was primarily one of movement in search of game and forage: a life of continual change and, I suppose, of continual homecoming. I
suspect that this is a basic pattern for existence written into our brains
and nervous systems, and entirely consistent with what life in nature has
always been. Looked at in this way, wandering, dispersal, exile, and home-

coming are among the few universal themes in human life, and they never grow old. I had something like this in mind when I wrote the sentence you quoted from; it was part of a subliminal content, though I began with my own instance.

RH You have spent a good part of your adult life living what you call "the woods life in all its fullness," attempting to retrieve something "of that native ground, the original and hardly comprehended thing under our feet. . . ." In retrospect, can you point to any single moment or occurrence when you realized your life at the Richardson homestead had suddenly opened beyond its dailiness to take on greater resonance, some sort of historical or esthetic significance?

JH I suppose there may have been such a moment, but what I remember now is more like a sequence of such moments, half-conscious intuitions that the life I was living extended far beyond that moment and that immediate activity, whatever it may have been. I think this feeling can be particularly acute when we are living close to the ancient life of people — in hunting, tilling the soil, tending to animals, and so forth. At any moment, a sudden clarity, and we are, so to speak, *returned*, or, it may be, reconciled, to something forgotten in our natures. I think it is, in part, in the nature of the artist, the poet, and the novelist, to encourage these moments, and to record them, to keep the continuity of things alive. But, in fact, many trades and activities in their own way do this. I recall one cool morning in Madrid years ago when I stepped out onto the street and saw the shopkeepers washing down the sidewalks and opening their shops. Here was something that had been going on for centuries and was part of the life of people. The fact that I was in Spain, in a much older country, heightened my impression. Whether a modern office or factory job retains much of this feeling for things, I doubt. And if not, then I wonder what the consequences will be for humanity cut off from even these rather tentative urban roots.

RH What importance, if any, did some of the early naturalists — John Muir, John Burroughs, Henry David Thoreau, or even Alaskan ones such as Robert Marshall — have in shaping your attitudes toward the kind of wilderness you found in Alaska?

JH There was no direct influence that I know of. I hadn't read any of those people when I was young, did not read them until many years after I had gone to Alaska. I have never read Burroughs, for example. I had, I suppose, been told something about Thoreau, but I think he had no influence on me whatever. As for Marshall, I read his *Arctic Village,* I believe, somewhere back in the early fifties. I remember liking the book very much, and his pictures of the place and the people may have nourished some of my own early impressions.

RH Would you agree with John Burroughs's statement that "the great poet, and the great naturalist, are the same," both in search for what he calls "the vitality of connections?"

JH I like Burroughs's statement very much. It is precise and useful. It is all the more interesting to me because I once wanted to be a naturalist—or I thought I did, not understanding very well what that would have meant. But "the vitality of connections" is a great phrase.

RH As a culture, we've never fully grown out of a transcendentalist view of the natural world. What effect do you think this romantic view has had?

JH To the extent that I understand the problem, and I'm not sure that I do fully, I see it as potentially a confused one. In my introduction to John Muir's Alaska book I suggested that as heady and inspiring as nature can be at its wildest and grandest, that emotion is not enough; we come back to the old human problem: how are we to live with one another.

It's possible that in looking to nature, to the wilderness, without understanding what it is we are looking for, we to some extent evade coming to terms with the real social and political problems that ask of us a deliberate attention. Nature may be an example to us, a lesson, depending on why we go to it and what we are prepared to learn; it can be a temporary escape, but it is not a solution, unless we are prepared to see the eventual triumph of nature as *the* solution to everything.

This may be a roundabout way of suggesting that Americans remain politically naive and innocent of history. Given the power we hold and the way we are disposed to use it, this is a dangerous ignorance.

RH In several poems, I sense you are carrying on a kind of dialogue with our cultural past and, in the course of the exchange, you dismantle many of our country's myths and illusions—Whitman's declarations of the Open Road being one. I am thinking primarily of "Driving Through Oregon," a poem set at the end of the Oregon Trail, in 1973 when America experienced an oil shortage. The poem concludes in Alaska on a very decided note.

JH It's interesting to me that you read into the poem these references to Whitman and the Oregon Trail, things that were not in my mind at all when I wrote the poem.

The poem doesn't end so much in Alaska as at a metaphorical or symbolic point that is at the same time the Far North, the end of the road, and perhaps also the end of an illusion. I pointed the poem in *that* direction, so to speak, because at the time I was driving north. And for a moment (I can't say just when that moment was) it occurred to me that one day we might drive straight north to the Arctic Ocean and be stopped there, inert and silent. This was a powerful image when it came to me, an eerie and disturbing apprehension, strongly supported in its symbolism by seeing so much of a formerly lighted countryside in utter darkness, as if everything had shut down. And, in fact, things had come very close to doing just that.

As for the dialogue, I think that is basic. It has to do with the stupidity, the nonthought we are surrounded by, governed by, influenced by. A poem, a novel, an essay, is a way of challenging this nonthought, of exposing the pseudo-content of the ideas that are so characteristic of society.

But I want to emphasize that a poem, like any creative work, has its own reasons, its own imperative. Once set in motion, it takes a life of its own. If certain elements in my writing seem to "dismantle" some of our so-called myths, so much the better; just don't assume that I set out deliberately to do this.

RH Alongside a sustained longing for home and reconciliation throughout your work, there is a cold, insistent voice that says our culture has fallen short. In "Rolling Back," for example, you depict our culture as an uncoupled train rolling backward out of control. Later you state that "the land will not forgive us." And in "Missoula in a Dusty Light," the birds and brooms whisper, "This land/ has bitter roots, and seeds/ that crack and spill in the wind. . . ." Would you care to expound on these notions?

JH I think you may be crediting me with a philosophical or theoretical consistency I do not have. The main images in those poems were compelling, taken in themselves. The vision of an uncoupled train, for example, may have been with me for some time, and I found what seemed to be the right place for it. In the Missoula poem I took into account the very moment of the poem, the wind and the dust, and the sudden onset of it, like a premonition. But it took me some time to work my way through all of that; one thing led to another, and in the meantime the *idea* that was in the poem seemed to clarify.

There's a rhetorical element to consider. To take one example: It may not be literally true that "the land will not forgive us," though it might be true if we continue to abuse it. But to say a thing in this way is to give it an emotional emphasis; if the emotion is powerful enough and the insight accurate, the statement may be true, may have a *poetic* or a *prophetic,* truth that will outlast any literal or topical truth.

It seems to me that the better part of writing is a matter of acting on suggestions and following up clues. We are engaged in a kind of play, with words and ideas, sounds and meaning. It's a serious kind of play, as poems are meant to be, but it must not lose that sense of play. In the word *bitterroot,* for example, I found a certain resonance, and I made particular use of that. It suggested to me, among other things, that in our displacement of an indigenous population, in our outright theft of the land, our history has these bitter roots. Probably all places and societies have them: crimes, events that are not admitted, not discussed, not even thought about, but they will have consequences. You could say, then, that my writing of the poem was a way of working out one possibility implied in that history.

RH In your talks with composer John Luther Adams, with whom you did the cantata "Forest Without Leaves" in 1984, you state that "any illusions I may have had about the North and the frontier, and about Alaska in particular," had died. What happened to destroy these illusions?

JH Overall, a certain tempering of thought and experience; a belated recognition that no matter how grand and inspiring the physical terrain, nor how apparently rich the human potential of the place, Alaska and the North seem destined to follow the old colonial pattern with only minor changes in the script.

The frontier has been a strong and persistent theme in American life. I doubt if anyone is completely immune to its attraction. When I was young, Alaska seemed to be the one place left on the North American map that allowed the dreamer to imagine a country in the shape of his desire. Is this still true? I doubt it. Or if it is, it is true in a limited way. Reality has changed, and it's hardly possible now to imagine life anywhere without taking into account the social and political forces by which we are all too much governed and influenced. I have lived to see Alaska changed from a nearly limitless open space to one divided among jurisdictions and competing interests: the federal, the state, the industrial, the military, and so forth. This may be lamentable, and to me it is, but it is a fact.

Not even the thinking here has any originality. Nearly all thought and procedure tend to follow the universal pattern more or less imposed by an overwhelmingly bureaucratic state of mind to which money, power, and technology are the answer to everything. Anything really new, in experience and knowledge, in social action, any genuine expression in literature and the arts, has to break through this pattern, or at least change and adapt it. And that, given the power that so many agencies have over us, given the inertia of institutions and the mentality of the mass of people, is not an easy thing to do. It is an added and related fact that modern life with its superabundance of commercial, tourist images has been rapidly turning the world into a cliché. The "frontier" image of Alaska has been exploited and trivialized in this way.

I see all of this from a certain perspective—from, say, forty-odd years of distance and concern. I have also learned to see it in relation to American history generally, for what that may be worth. I think that what is most discouraging about it is that almost no one seems to be aware of the repetitiveness of this frontier history, the utter lack of any creative innovation other than on the most superficial, technical level. And it is difficult at times to escape the feeling that not only is what they are trying to do here somehow mistaken, but that the very effort is evidence that a significant failure has occurred elsewhere.

RH What correlations, if any, do you find in the disappearance of regions, in our culture's destruction of its wilderness, and in the belief that our nation has lost its moral and ethical underpinnings?

JH I'd answer this indirectly, if I may. All nations, all societies and civilizations, to some extent, either accidentally or willfully, displace, alter, or destroy the wilderness—wild nature. Something is lost, and another thing is gained: a cultivation necessary for humanity. How many centuries ago was it that wolves and bears were eliminated from England and from much of Western Europe? In a country so small and crowded as Britain you could not allow these animals to return and roam free; that would only be irresponsible. Yet something is missing, and to someone from, say, the American West, that absence can at times be keenly felt.

Maybe all societies in some way prepare their eventual decline by what they eliminate or destroy: species and peoples. North American history has been particularly swift and brutal in this respect. But there is a strange fact: nothing disappears completely. An uneasy kind of transference takes place: that which you attempt to deny or destroy takes up residence within you. The American Indian, disinherited, sullen, and resentful, is in us.

There's an even simpler way to answer the question: Acts have consequences.

RH In *Other Days* you mention that you have spent a great deal of your life trying to leave "my mankindness behind me." Why? And how does one shed "mankindness" and still preserve one's "humanness?" I realize, of course, that these terms are not synonymous; they are not exclusive of each other either.

JH I don't have the text with me at the moment, but I think I said that I "leave *some* of my mankindness behind me for a *while*. . . ." I don't say I have spent my life doing this, which would be a very different thing. I was speaking for a particular moment in my life.

In one sense—a literary one—this is an expression I use in a heightened, poetic way, to represent my intuition of a certain transformation. This "leaving behind" is pretty much what one does—must do—if he is trying to learn, say, animal ways as a hunter, or even vegetable ways as a gatherer or a gardener. It's essential at times that we leave something of our self-conscious humanity behind us, set it aside for a moment or an hour, or for a few days if necessary, to get out of this terribly burdensome human skin and stop thinking as a purely intellectual being.

I know these things can be talked about endlessly and to the point of boredom and incomprehension; yet the fact remains: It *is* possible to enter another life, to become part tree, bird, insect, or whatever, if only for a brief time. And that is enough; too long a time, and one might lose one's *self* for good. That is a risk of madness that all genuine shamans took. We no longer know, for the most part, what this means, but I am certain that "primitive" man knew it, and was at times terrified by it.

And it may be that we do not know the true extent of our "mankindness" until we have let go of it and entered, to the extent that we can, the life of another being. Isn't this true of what we call *love,* and reason enough for the feeling of terror that often accompanies it? It is the risk of losing one's self.

Admittedly, there can be no exactness in these things, but it does seem that to become fully human, or humane, may require a deep understanding and acceptance of the nonhuman, if not the *in*human. Robinson Jeffers, for example, thought that it was exactly our humanity that was the problem, by which he meant our excessive concern with our selves and with people—a self-infatuation on a universal scale. The cure for this would be found in opening our eyes and our minds to the outside world, to the nonhuman.

RH In an interview with Michael Ryan, poet Stanley Kunitz states that "a poet needs to keep his wilderness alive inside him. He must never avert his face completely from the terror of that dark underworld." Do you agree?

JH Yes, of course. Something like it has been said in one way or another by many poets and thinkers. It implies what Lorca meant by "duende," for example.

Ways of talking about this kind of thing became all too common and clichéd back in the late sixties and early seventies, with the interest in surrealism and the so-called "deep image." But it is nothing new; the real poets have always known that terror, akin to love, to chaos and death. Among other things, it implies that one's true attention be always left open to the irrational, to what may appear to be the accidental, but which is an acknowledgment of something for which we have no adequate name, the fundamental material of art and poetry, of magic and religion; an admission that there is something *out there,* outside our normal understanding, asking for expression.

The notion implies, too, that there is nothing so deadly to poetry and to thought as having an opinion: One's mind is made up, closed.

But we shouldn't be careless in talking about these things. The same element that in art and poetry may constitute the soul of things, turned loose in the world, has consequences we dare not invite. People once understood this instinctively, which is why what we have learned to call *art* was originally a very serious matter, and nothing to fool around with.

RH How would you distinguish between "nature" and "wilderness?" In reading through your work, I feel they are not always synonymous terms.

JH Like many people, I suppose I've sometimes used the terms indiscriminately. But let me define them in this way: *Nature* is the more general and inclusive term; it stands for the world as we know it and receive it through our senses. It includes everything that is not cultivated: land, water, climate, the elements, etc. But it also includes us, our history, our notions of good and evil, and so forth. It includes a whole world of things about which we know very little directly, other than for their effect on us: pests and diseases, for example.

Wilderness, on the other hand, is that part of nature we have not interrupted to any degree, have not tamed and made useful to us — I mean useful in an immediate, practical sense. Wilderness as such *is* useful to us, necessary in all sorts of ways; in a more specific sense than nature, it is our original home.

But wilderness has also meant a place of abandonment — spiritually and psychologically a desert, an internal space in which we are lost, as surely as we can be lost in a physical wilderness to which we have no map, no path, no sign of direction.

I doubt if we can define any of this exactly, nor should we expect to. It's interesting to think that the need to distinguish among these things is one result of civilization. For Native Americans, for example, as for all "primitive" people, wilderness as we think of it did not exist; what we call by that name was simply their home.

RH Your landscapes are forever populated with old human remains — gravestones, fallen cabins, vanishing paths and trails — a rich presence of human history. Often I sense the narrators of your poems have arrived at the very last moment of things and are able to catch a glimpse before the past takes it over. How does this fit into your interest in origins, your desire to track down and record what you call "the original murmuring and whispering of primordial powers?"

JH It's true that in certain situations I have felt like that — like the last, or next to last, arrival on the scene, and that something rich and populated, never again to be witnessed, is passing. But this is an old feeling and an old theme for poets, so there must be something universally valid in it. Perhaps now, especially, as at certain times in the past, a feeling that an epoch, or a phase of existence, is closing, is particularly acute . . . the end of an age. The landmarks are disappearing and we face the unknown. Once again we feel the need to return to first principles and to sources.

Meanwhile, so-called "normal" life becomes a kind of facade. I often have this feeling about much of modern life—a sense of the "no longer and not yet" that Broch made so much of in his novels. Behind the facade something is at work, preparing the world for what we have yet no conception of. The gods, the primordial powers, are awake, at the same time creative and destructive, forces for both good and evil.

RH Among other things, your writing embodies a kind of tribal history. By that I mean it chronicles not only your life on the Richardson homestead but also the lives of other homesteaders in the immediate area, many of whom were old Klondikers who turned to the land after the gold fields ran fallow. You state in "With an Axe and an Auger," for example, that "they were my people, if the phrase now means anything, and the best of them I have loved with a deep appreciation that has never left me. They were friends and teachers, and I do not expect to see their kind again." Do you feel a responsibility to keep their lives and stories from dying out?

JH Well, you are referring to a part of my writing, that which deals with a certain frontier experience in Alaska. But I would agree with the observation generally. Certainly it is true with respect to what I've written about Richardson, in verse and prose. And, without having made a program of it, I do feel a responsibility there. No one else will have known those people and that place, not as I knew them; it's too late now. And I suppose that within certain limits I do feel that they were my people; at least I am at some liberty to claim them. Their lives and persons have that special meaning we attach to people we have known under very special circumstances—a familiarity that, if it is not love precisely, is close to it.

But more recently I've had to consider another responsibility, and it has to do with the significance of these people having come north in the first place. Thinking about that has taken me some distance from Richardson and contemporary Alaska. What are we to make of these more recent intrusions into the North? How do they fit into North American history and its consequences? Is this just another dispiriting phase of the same greed and expropriation of what is left of a wild continent? And just where will that leave us in another two or three decades? These are some of the questions I ask myself now. They are questions I would not have asked myself perhaps even ten years ago.

RH This chronicling of lives, then, is what you meant when you wrote in "Snow": "I have imagined a man who might live as the coldest scholar on earth, who followed each clue in the snow, writing a book as he went. It would be a history of snow, the book of winter. A thousand-year text to be read by a people hunting these hills in a distant time. Who was here, and who has gone? What were their names? What did they kill and eat? Whom did they leave behind?"

JH Yes, you could say so, though what I had in mind was more like a rhetorical, or metaphorical, figure. I liked the *idea* of it, you see, and this followed more or less naturally from thinking about snow and the life I once lived in the snow. If you follow the thought, there is a close relation between reading the snow—reading signs in the snow—and reading words on a page. In fact, the relation between these is at the heart of much that I have written and talked about in one place or another.

Anyway, think of it: "a man who might live as the coldest scholar on earth. . . ." There's a lot of resonance in that figure. But don't confuse that, literally, with me. Though I may have begun with myself, once I invented that figure it was no longer me; it became a thing with its own life.

RH In several poems you cast the individual as witness to great natural events, placing him in the context of migrations, epochal arrivals and departures.

JH I like to see human activity against the background of that older and greater world—the great stage of things: spaces and distances, migrations, conflicts, and so forth. I like the perspective we gain from having the landscape, nature itself, as one of the protagonists. This is something I have always admired in Jeffers, for example, the way his narratives are set in relation to elemental things: sea and mountain, fire and storm, etc. Just recently I read a long story by Chekhov, "The Steppe," in which a few people make a long journey by foot and wagon over endless open distances; the story and the persons gain another dimension for having been placed there. The story is told from day-to-day and from hour-to-hour, between nightfall and sunrise; reading it, we have the feeling that something timeless and obscurely purposeful is being enacted, and we are in some way a part of it.

I suppose that what you see of this in my own writing owes much to my having lived for so long in circumstances that more or less compelled me to see human activity on a background of such elemental scale that even today, with all the changes that have occurred, earth and the weather tend to overshadow nearly everything else. Yet it takes very little human interference to change things: One word spoken in an absolute stillness, one shout, one rifle shot, means more, changes more, than a thousand people marching in a city, where noise is the first element.

RH Shadows play a significant role throughout your poetry and prose. Perhaps the finest example of this is the Prologue to *Stories We Listened To,* a highly expressionistic account of the ghosts of our near and distant past reclaiming the land. How does this relate to the kind of language that you have chosen to use throughout your writing, that in one essay you call "shadow-language?"

JH The word itself, "shadows," has for me tremendous resonance. It suggests, among other things, the half-lit world in which much early experience takes place. It speaks to me of what we don't know, cannot admit, wish to avoid, to keep hidden: a shadow-self, for example, which most of us have whether we know it or not.

My use of the word refers also to the evidence we have of past life that has left something of itself behind, like a fossil. Life itself casts a shadow, literally and symbolically. As for "shadow-language": can you think of a better, a more suggestive phrase for those signs we read in the snow, left behind by creatures we have not seen, may never see?

It's important to keep in mind that very old human adventures — presentiments, imaginings, spiritual journeys, are in one way or another continually being reenacted, even when, as is the case most of the time, appearances are deceiving and the meaning is kept from us. Only perhaps when the immediate and the temporal disappears, is put aside for a moment, do those older shapes become visible, and the true significance of the solstice, for instance — the departure and return of the sun — with its intimate relation to harvest, to birth and death, is revealed to us.

I think one reason why poetry continues to be important to us is that it can on occasion recall to us the original meaning of things, and restore, if only for a moment, something of the lost vitality in our connection to the world.

Somewhere in this I think we discover the reason why a poetry concerned mainly with the personality of the poet, which is often the case now, is an inadequate art. It has little to tell us of any consequence, and is really a form of gossip. The true poets have always been open to what I call the *time-ghost* in things: the universal spirit of time and place, which is in essence all times and all places and all peoples.

RH Often throughout your work the natural world takes on a decided religious quality, nature providing a sense of the sacred and restoring a capacity for belief and wonder. Yet you never lose sight of the indifference of the natural world.

JH I assume that the physical universe *is* indifferent to us, as a species and as individuals. The suspicion that this is the case has driven us to invent, or propose, a god, or a set of gods—a concerned and loving presence in the world. I can't see that the probability of indifference in the world contradicts the religious feelings we also have; in fact, the knowledge of that indifference might in some way enhance or intensify this feeling.

RH You have made the statement that all human forms, our whole sense of structure, is rooted in the natural world. Could you explain this further?

JH This ought to be self-evident. From where else can our sense of things have come if not from nature? I am speaking of that sense of order, of proportion, or of right relation, that we all make use of in one way or another whether we are aware of it or not. Whatever it is that provides us with a practical or esthetic satisfaction, in building, in making or thinking, would appear to have its source, its model, somewhere in nature. We could show this fundamental relationship in all kinds of ways—in the way that an insect, for example, is put together, in the way in which it functions. To anyone who has really looked at a piece of machinery the resemblance is obvious, and in fact children will often see this.

People were once so attentive to nature that they understood these things instinctively. For the most part now we learn it all at second- or thirdhand—from books and teachers, from tools and objects, from the example of other people, from social rules, and the like. But these cannot always be counted on to be true; periodically a few individuals—artists, inventors, and thinkers—feel the need to return to primary sources.

Perhaps this is one reason why wilderness has become so important to us. Without that part of the world we have not changed—what we call the *wild*—we lose sight of that original; we are abandoned to our own imaginings, to the example of our own makeshifts. Or to put it another way, we are abandoned to our demons.

RH How, then, does this translate to writing? Rather than being an act of creation, it essentially becomes a process of recovery and recreation, rediscovery and reenactment.

JH Well, to an extent you've answered the question yourself. Every artistic creation, whether a poem or a painting or a temple or a musical composition, is an attempt to recover something of that original sense of order, of right proportion. You can call this an *ideal* if you like, but then where does the ideal come from? Probably there is never more than a partial recovery exemplified in certain works, in certain epochs throughout the ages, and to which we turn repeatedly for confirmation. I think that this is, in part, what is meant by tradition, why we feel the need to honor it, and why we also feel on occasion the need to challenge it. Perhaps in that fundamental argument a creative energy is released.

In talking about these things as I have, I've been aware of simplifying something that is immensely complicated; but it's worth having at least a rudimentary appreciation of, because it seems to me to be *the* principle at work in everything we make or attempt to do.

The Eye in the Rock:
Toward the Understanding of a Poem[1]

.

•

.

The Eye in the Rock

A high rock face above Flathead Lake,
turned east where the light
breaks at morning over the mountain.

An eye was painted here by men
before we came, part of an Indian face,
part of an earth
scratched and stained by our hands.

It is only rock, blue or green,
cloudy with lichen,
changing in the waterlight.

Yet blood moves in this rock,
seeping from the fissures;
the eye turned inward, gazing back
into the shadowy grain
as if the rock gave life.

And out of the fired mineral
come these burned survivors,
sticks of the wasting dream;

thin red elk and rusty deer,
a few humped bison,
ciphers and circles without name.

Not ice that fractures rock,
nor sunlight, nor the wind
gritty with sand, has erased them.
They feed in their tall meadow,
cropping the lichen a thousand years.

Over the lake water comes this light
that has not changed,
the air we have always known . . .

They who believed that stone,
water, and wind might be quickened
with a spirit like their own,
painted this eye that the rock might see.

JOHN HAINES, 1975

It is an actual place on the west shore of Flathead Lake in western Montana, and is known locally as Painted Rock Point. In company with five other people, I went there one day in early summer a few years back. We had come, as I recall, on a personal mission related to an environmental project for the Northern Rockies, and were exploring some of the Indian past of the countryside.

We came by small boat from a landing two or three miles farther north on the lake shore. The late morning was calm, the sun bright and warm. As we approached from offshore, the rockface came into view, and what appeared from a distance to be rusty splashes of lichen, or patches of a reddish mineral color in the rock, resolved into a scattered arrangement of small painted figures.

Roughly vertical, rising thirty to forty feet above the lake, and with numerous faults and planes, the rockface with its red-painted figures dispersed among the gradations of rock color, was like a weathered mural, faded from its original brilliance but, in full sun, still glowing and subtly dappled with light from the water below.

There is an irregular shelf of boulders below the face on which one can stand and view the paintings at close range. That morning we tied our boat to a length of driftwood lodged among the boulders at water level, and climbed up to the shelf. There we could move around and explore the face at our leisure.

From close up, the painted figures tend to blur into shadings in the rock surface and have not the definition and seeming coherence that they have when seen from the water. The figures are simply, even crudely, rendered in a bright rust or red brick pigment that could be ferrous oxide; they are recognizable representations of bison, elk, and deer, with many additional designs and markings, perhaps abstracted from something in nature, dispersed among them.

The figures are arranged in no immediately discernable pattern, mounting from somewhat below eye-level to a height out of reach of even the tallest man. The animal shapes are in profile, facing toward the left as one stands before them, and appear at times to be drifting across the face of the rock. Here and there a figure will be partly obscured by a break in the rockface; then, stepping a short distance to one side and shifting one's angle of view, another partly erased figure will reveal itself.

The rock faces east, across more than a mile of water, into the rising sun. I am not certain now what kind of rock it is; pink quartzite is common in that part of Montana, but it is not that. The color of the rock ranges from tawny to a dusty blue or green, depending on the light and the time of day. According to one informed opinion, the figures are perhaps eight hundred to nine hundred years old, and may not in all cases be contemporary.

The most striking figure on the rock is an eye, an obviously human eye, many times life-size, painted at the far, or north, end of the face, and somewhat above average head height. The eye is painted as if looking back, into the eye-corner. Arranged around it are a number of vertical and diagonal slash marks. Neither the eye nor the markings around it appear to have any relation to anything else on the rock.

I had brought a camera with me, and in the course of the morning and early afternoon I took several photographs in color of the rock and its various sections, from the water and from the shelf. Whatever conversation passed among us that day concerning the eye and the other figures, it is clear to me now that none of us had any real understanding of the significance of what we were seeing. It was not until later, when the film had been processed and the slides returned to me, and I had spent some time in studying them, that I realized that the eye which had so puzzled us was part of a face in the rock, that it had been placed in exact relation to a profile in one jutting edge of the rock, a profile that included a mouth, a nose, and a chin. It was clear also that the other markings around it—behind, above, and below it—all contributed to form the face, a portrait perhaps of someone marked with ceremonial decoration. Once seen, the effect was so striking it was remarkable we had not noticed it at once. They knew what they did who painted that eye, and there was surely nothing haphazard in the arrangement of the other figures on that rock.

I can't recover now all the stages that my poem went through. I recall it as being rather easy to write. With nothing more than memory to go on, I'm willing to say that the poem probably began with a few notes made on the spot, and was written out later that summer.

I have just written, "the poem probably began with. . . ." And having said that and thought about it for a moment, I realize how tentative must be anything said about the origins of a poem. At one time, during the early 1970s, I made an intensive study of rock art in central California. I combined a good deal of reading on the subject with several backpacking trips into the mountains of Santa Barbara and San Luis Obispo counties. With the help of a local authority on rock art, I was able to explore a number of remote and little-known sites. I camped alone in the hills at night, and by day I explored the rocks and caves, photographed and made extensive notes on what I saw.

When I went to Painted Rock Point that day some years later, I had already an informed background from which to view it. And it might be as fair to say that as a consequence my poem had its beginning, not there on Flathead Lake, but some years before, on a sweltering forenoon in early summer when I first saw the sandstone redoubt of Pool Rock; and that somewhere in the underground of the poem there may also be some strange and still-unsorted emotion recalled from a night when I camped in a certain cave high in the Santa Ynez Mountains west of Bakersfield.

With that much said, I suspect that my sense of the poem's structure took shape early, and that the first lines, falling as they did into a three-line group, gave me a clue as to the overall form the poem would take.

This three-line stanza is repeated at intervals, and its occurrence illustrates a convenient working principle: that by following what the poem suggests to us at any moment, we can shape it toward a possibly unforeseen conclusion.

It may be, in this case, that the ending of the poem was formed early and I wrote the rest of it in order to get myself there. But what I *can* be sure of is that certain lines, images, and combinations thereof, revealed themselves and served as keys. I am referring mainly to the third, fourth, and fifth stanzas, and to lines like "not ice that fractures rock," and to the image of painted animals "feeding in their tall meadow." Around these elements the poem grew. And, "that the rock might see" was surely a perception worth writing toward.

The alternating long and short lines create a visual as well as an aural pattern. I notice, too, that the lines in most instances are long enough to contain the phrases and parts of sentences without breaking them. This is, let's say, a matter of choice at any given moment, but it cannot be arbitrary; every device employed, every part of "craft," must justify itself.

The very obvious rhyme that occurs toward the end of the poem was partly deliberate, though as nearly as I can now tell what was deliberate in this took its clue from the accidental. A certain amount of repetition of sounds seems to occur naturally to an ear attuned to language. I don't know how apparent this will be to a reader used to *seeing* a poem as print on the page, but if one reads the poem aloud and listens to it, the echo of syllables and consonants will soon be clear enough in the repeated sounds of "green," "grain," "men," "rock," "back," "lichen," "light," and so forth.

At one time I might have written a shorter, more compact poem out of the same circumstances. I will assume that all poems offer a kind of meditational process; but there is more than one way to meditation in a poem. There is that something brooded upon for a long time, possibly for years, and the result given expression in a brief and concentrated poem. For me, this sort would be represented by a number of poems in my first book, *Winter News,* and by many subsequent poems. And there is the poem in which meditation itself is in process and clearly given its full due, as rumination and extended commentary. Much traditional poetry is like this, or, to name a poet of our own time, many of the poems of Czeslaw Milosz. I would say, just for the occasion, and assuming that such categories are useful at all, that "The Eye in the Rock" is a poem that falls somewhere between these two: that it is both immediate and discursive.

The foregoing discussion of some of the technical elements in the poem happens to be the least of my own interest in this poem and its circumstances, and for reasons that I hope will be clear.

My interest in rock art is that of an amateur, but it is of a piece with my passion for landforms, for earth history, and for all that belongs with and adorns these. I have sensed, and all too keenly at times, that in our time something may be dying: an ancient life-relation, and each of its manifestations become the more valuable as they become rare, are cheapened or defaced, or disappear entirely from one cause or another.

A phrase in the fourth stanza of the poem, "blood moves," refers to the color of the pigment used in the rock paintings. Was the color red chosen because of its availability, or because of its closeness to the color of blood? Were there originally other colors on the rock that have since faded? I don't know. But my phrase also implies the feeling I had at the time that the rockface took on life from those painted figures, and that both the rock and the figures gathered a life-energy by virtue of the light and the moving water below.

What the eye may have meant to the people who placed it there is, so far as I know, impossible to say exactly. That is, I cannot know with any certainty what the "Indian's belief" was. And since I can know very little of the original thought and purpose behind the eye in the rock, nearly everything in the poem is a projection of mine. But to the extent that I can recover in myself something of the mind that looked on nature in a way very different from our habitual attitude of "use"—a nature that was alive in every detail and filled with meaning, with *spirit*—it may be that my projection verifies a felt truth.

It could be said that the eye and all that surrounds it, the rock of which it is part, constitutes a fossil language, decipherable now only to a limited degree. The figures and the markings, the rockface itself, are evidence of a communication with the visible and invisible world. We have lost the key to that language, but if we had it we could read the rockface as a book. Or, to put it another way: If we were able really to see with the *eye of the rock* we might read the entire history of the earth—past and future, mineral, seed, and flesh.

I would say, then, that the tone of the poem is that of reverence mixed with a keen sense of loss. A remark by Ortega y Gasset in his *Meditations on Hunting* seems to make an appropriate connection here:

There are people who believe in good faith that we have no obligations toward the rocks.

This observation makes an intellectual event out of what was once an immediate kinship with the elements. In our time we must think our way back through many centuries in order to regain a kind of understanding in place of what was once intuitive.

It is "only" rock, to be sure; but then this is "only" earth, and we are "only" flesh, and finally, perhaps, nothing but dust. And yet it's true, even from a plain geological viewpoint, that the rock *does* give life—gives it back continually in the work of centuries of consolidation and soil-building. There is also, alas, a point of view from which we can all now-adays be seen as "sticks of the wasting dream."

It is I who speak the poem, as representative man muttering to himself some interior thing, but assuming at the same time that he will be over-heard. Perhaps because I saw the rock in company with other people I was led to speak in terms of "we" rather than of "I." But I notice that among the poems of which "The Eye in the Rock" forms a group, from my book *In a Dusty Light,* how consistently I have used the pronoun "we." This is something I had not thought much about until now. Here, at any rate, I seem to have written as if "we" were the natural self.

There is a sense in which I could speak of this poem as having been "found." Maybe all worthwhile poems (and things and persons for that matter) are found. They are found by us in the act of living, of walking and looking, and often in the act of thinking. Now, I know that it is possible, with a little skill and practice, to write poems about almost anything, and by taking any clue in the world around us as a starting point. But let me be clear about this: I do not believe in using the world as a source of egotistical aggrandizement—in going through the world looking for things and events to set a poem in motion. This is a trick that can be learned, but to me it is the literary equivalent of that material exploitation that in one way or another is wasting so much of the life of this planet.

I believe in the poem as a gift. I believe in that fortunate meeting of attention and object which results in an essential and necessary recognition of the thing felt, understood in a way that precludes any choice or equivocation. I believe also in silence, in keeping still when one has nothing to say.

JOHN HAINES   237

Rereading my poem now, rather like a distant friend of the occasion, I find in it things that please me. After the preparatory ground of the opening lines, I note a certain gathering of energy, a breaking forth in the third stanza, and again with intensity in the fifth. And from there on it seems to me that the poem sustains itself pretty well to the end. Assuming I'm right about this, none of it, naturally, was plotted out beforehand. Only an inborn sense of balance, of *rightness,* allows these things to happen in the right order and with the right weight of emphasis. (But who is to say that we aren't all originally gifted to some degree with this sense?) The effect is similar, I suspect, to the way a good piece of music reveals itself with alternations of tone and pitch. And somewhere here, *craft* turns into *vision,* though as I say those words I know how trivial they can be made to sound.

As esthetic object the poem satisfies me. If it were worthwhile to try and reduce the poem to its message, it seems to me it could be expressed in this way: "Here is something you have not thought about, fellow citizens. You think that rock is dead matter, and that these red daubings are the play of children now gone. But you are wrong. This rock and these figures are alive, and they are telling you something: that the past is not past, and that despite your certainties and amusements, life has not changed much in these thousand years. What *has* changed is your perception of values. But keep looking, for if this rock and this poem say nothing to you now, some day they might."

Reviewing what I have written about this poem, I feel that the explanations I have offered are substantially true, that things occurred as I have said and with their approximate meaning. At the same time, the reader should be aware of taking at face value anything said in this way about something as mysterious as a poem. I know that the poem itself says more fully and deeply what it means and is. Any attempt to say more about the eye, the rock, and their combined significance would require another approach than this brief essay—an approach more nearly poetic, though not necessarily another poem in verse.   *1985*

On Hunting

Review of Deer Camp: Last Light in the Northeast Kingdom *by John M. Miller and* A Hunter's Road: A Journey with Gun and Dog Across the American Uplands *by Jim Fergus*

Hunting. The other morning I was hunting for my green sweater. The next time you're in town hunt me up. I have been hunting all over for you . . .

I make a point of these expressions because they are essential to an understanding of the persistence of activities like hunting and fishing; in these pursuits we reenact something fundamental in our being. Though most of us, I suppose, do not actually hunt in the field with gun and dog, we nonetheless hunt among the books on our shelves, and we fish among thoughts, whether we think of it this way or not. The vocabulary and the habit of thought remain with us long after the old pursuit of prey has ceased to compel us.

Here are two books concerned in one way or another with hunting. One of them, *Deer Camp,* is largely a photographic format; the other, *A Hunter's Road,* is a prose narrative of a journey by pickup and camper across the country, from west to east, and from north to south, in pursuit of game birds and, not incidentally, the people who hunt them.

The two books differ from each other in several ways. Mr. Fergus is a hunter; Mr. Miller is not. One book concerns itself with the hunting of a large animal, deer; the other with game birds like grouse and quail. The deer hunt comes off as something of a social activity; bird-hunting, on the other hand, as mainly a solitary pursuit. Both books have their merits and can be said to complement each other.

Miller's country is backwoods Vermont. His people, who retire to their hidden and often makeshift camps in season, hunt for meat but also to maintain a stubborn pride and manliness in subsistence. They are friends and neighbors, fathers and sons, posed before the camera with their guns, their beer cans and cigarettes, in a kind of rough defiance, as if to say: "You can cut my wages and foreclose my house, but you cannot steal my manhood."

It is clear that this hunting activity, confined to a brief annual fall period, is precious to those who take part in it, and that they would literally fight to keep it. Miller invades this largely male enclave, the hunting club, housed perhaps in nothing more elaborate than an old trailer parked away in the woods at the end of a road and accessible mainly to its members. He comes to them armed with a camera, to be greeted characteristically at the door by someone armed with a gun. But they let him in, give him a beer, and he is accepted for what he is, someone interested in what they are doing and in how they feel about it.

As with most books of this kind, it is the photographs that tell the story best. The text, though interesting and supportive, is hardly necessary, and is moreover written in a ubiquitous present tense that I personally find rather tiresome. Miller's photographs, however, are superb, and the quotations spaced throughout the book, from farmers and sawmill hands, from maintenance workers, retired game wardens and others, are succinct and poetic, full of a personal character: ". . . We don't have no phones here. We lug our water. . . . We don't even have a radio in camp. . . . We don't want to know what the outside world is doing. . . ."

One amateur hunter, none-too-energetic, stays in camp one morning while his friends go out early to look for deer. He sees a good buck from the camp window, grabs a gun and shoots it right there in the yard, to the muted exasperation of his fellow hunters when they return later in the day without a deer.

As crude in some respects as the activity of these vacation hunters with their gas lanterns and poker games may appear to many of us, there is at the same time something appealing and energizing in their determined independence — a kind of last-ditch defiance in the face of an impending global unity of mind. Snow comes, the season is over for the year; the hunters close their camp and go home, a few of them with a deer, all of them with something nourished in that brief outing.

Jim Fergus takes on another project altogether. He leaves his Colorado home one day in September and sets out across western America, heading east through Montana, the Dakotas, through Wisconsin, Michigan, and Pennsylvania, to New England; then south to the Carolinas and Florida, and west again to Texas and Arizona. From the open sagebrush country of the West to the briar thickets of the eastern woodland, he hunts both birds and land. He camps along the roads, in vacant parking lots, and in the yards of friends, his only companion a female Labrador retriever named Sweetzer. His wife remains at home, or she is elsewhere except for a brief meeting with her hunter husband in New York City.

Often he will phone ahead to arrange a hunt with an individual or group prominent in local bird-hunting; or he will pay a respectful visit to a celebrity like George Bird Evans. He meets and hunts with fellow writers like Richard Ford and Jim Harrison; joins briefly with a gun club made up of lawyers and stuffy professional types; has briefly to do with people most of us would prefer to avoid. He hunts with a French count in Florida, with a coarse Cajun bully in Louisiana, with a young Chippewa woman in Michigan, and with a one-armed policeman in New Hampshire.

It's an odd sort of trek, boyish and enthusiastic, contemplative, reminiscent, and revealing of character. The writing at its best has an honesty and immediacy that is attractive. Each of the chapters is prefaced with a quotation from a text related in some way to hunting or to land conservation. Among the writers quoted are Tolstoy, Turgenev, Ortega y Gasset, and Aldo Leopold. Many of the chapters close with a recipe for preparing and cooking the various birds, often roasted over the coals of an open fire.

Fergus has done his homework. He is knowledgeable and persuasive in his account of persons, places, and situations; whether it is the fate of sage grouse in Montana or the disappearance of habitat in the West generally. His description of an aspen wood in Minnesota, of its ground cover and the natural succession of fire and new growth is, to this northlander, convincing. Additionally, we learn something about the encroachment of private hunting preserves, that increasingly the available hunting is becoming a privilege for people of means and property.

For me, not being a bird-hunter, the best parts of the book are not the hunting episodes, which are all pretty much a matter of birds and dogs, of doubles and missed shots, but the encounters with people. I do not, for example, know the art of Russell Chatham of Montana, but I am grateful to learn about someone who, from the description of him given here, appears to be a man of grace and restraint in his relation to the land he lives on. A chapter called "Dawn on the Rez" with its telling portrait of Joe Kipps, a Blackfeet Indian, has some of the best pages in the book. Hunting with Kipps one day, Fergus is taught something of the Indian's intimate relation with the land they are hunting over; that in thousands of years of use and occupancy the soil underfoot is composed of the bones of his ancestors: ". . . as long as my sons can go outside and pat the dirt lovingly, I know that they are Indians." From such things one learns far more than hunting.

Perhaps the most poignant moment in the book comes when Fergus, as he is about to dispatch another prairie chicken, quotes from Paul Johnsgard a brief description of the last male heath hen in North America, who returned each spring to its mating ground on Martha's Vineyard in Massachussets, "where it displayed alone to an unhearing and unseeing world."

About halfway through this book it struck me that Fergus's wife must be an extraordinarily patient and indulgent woman to have put up with this adolescent wandering and maiming of things. I myself at times became impatient and irritated with the comparison of one shotgun to another, with the body count of birds, the holding and cooking of the dead. But on balance perhaps it was all worth it, when Fergus and his dog finally come home to his cabin in Colorado in the deep of winter, himself in some way satisfied and completed; worth it for the trip itself and, one hopes, for the lessons learned.

Altogether, hunting is a decidedly mixed business, filled with contradictions as are most human activities. Despite its evident attraction for many people, the thought persists that this mania for guns and slaughter belongs to humanity's childhood, and we will have to find another and better way of facing the world or we will destroy everything. It is true also, and worth remarking on here, that deprived of the opportunity to hunt birds and beasts we are inclined to hunt each other and, as Shakespeare put it, "make perforce a universal prey. . . ."

I haven't hunted in twenty-five years, and have no wish to. Yet, on reading through these two books I have thought back at times to a magical and frosty September, to my old mentor, Fred Campbell, the two of us sitting on the bare hill overlooking his Lake Camp: waiting, watching, and above all, listening, for that one possible moose who for us that fall never came.

I think of my friend Lee Merrill in northern Wisconsin, who lives for his forays into the field, to hunt and fish in season. And of Bob DeMott in Ohio, with his annual "game dinner" and its choice of venison and fish, grouse and woodcock. In the chaos and confusion that society seems increasingly prone to, with the falseness and pseudo-life imposed on us hourly and daily, why not now and then go hunting? Enjoy the morning and the day, and refresh oneself in an ancient act of re-creation—if not for the sake of society, then for oneself. It may be better than bombing the Kurds, better than selling junk bonds. *1992*

To the Wall

To the Wall

To the wall that holds up night
come these chained, myopic figures:
the faded nominees, envoys
without portfolios, past presidents
and shunted candidates . . .

Heroes with guttering torches,
ill-starred drummers
in the thickets of policy.

They stand, hollow and waking,
trying to see through
the course fabric of illusion;
and fall, as another volley
echoes in the reddening
canyons of our dawn planet.

And the wall advances,
trailing its broken ivy,

hour by hour,
with the sound of wind
through a slot.

May all the laboring captains,
junkmen, raiders and dumpers
—life-wreckers
whose seared lips blow
on the forges of sunset,

stand before that wall.

JOHN HAINES, 1973–1990

"To the Wall" was first written sometime early in the 1970s, though I cannot be certain now of the exact date of composition. Behind the title, and echoing throughout the poem, is the cry that was heard so often during the Cuban Revolution at the end of the 1950s: "A la pared!" — *To the wall* — when the supporters of the overthrown dictator Trujillo were being rounded up and executed. That cry, its force and apparent meaning, remained with me for a long time, to finally find a place in this poem.

As nearly as I can now reconstruct the poem's development, I would say that, in response to events that were then taking place toward the end of the Vietnam period, I wanted to find a way to include in a poem some of the representative figures of our own history—the infamous, the corrupt, and the merely incompetent. To that end, and taking the poem more or less stanza by stanza, I imagined a wall, not of stone, but a wall in time and space, before which these figures would be brought and forced to stand, symbolically chained and blindfolded, not understanding their fate, but obliged to accept the judgment that was theirs.

Once, in an early version of the poem, I compared these individuals to figures in a zodiac, a constellation of failures and discards. These were the people, elected and appointed, who had deceived the public and betrayed their trust: congressmen and candidates, officeholders and plain liars.

Here were the heroes and pseudo-heroes, with their torches guttering in the wind of time, whose mistakes and misjudgments had betrayed them and us in those rank thickets of policy whose continual regeneration makes of public life a never-ending crisis. I imagined them standing before that wall in a cold dawn light, in the customary situation of executions, "hollow and waking," trying vainly to see through the rough masks placed over their faces—that "coarse fabric of illusion," the failure of promises and programs. They stand and fall, as the echo of a volley of rifle shots, or of sounds that might be shots, rattles through some dimly lighted canyon of our planet.

And the wall itself, rather than standing still, fixed in a particular place, is advancing through history, trailing behind it what I call here a "broken ivy," which can be understood as the debris of historical hopes, broken treaties, and the like. The wall, with its figures standing or fallen, comes on hour by hour and decade by decade, as if toward some final reckoning, with a sound like a strong wind blowing in a confined space—a slot in a canyon wall.

This, then, is the immense and open stage on which the poem is set. Though the poem itself is relatively brief, the scope of things, the events and persons, are as vast in conception as the space through which the earth is spinning, and as weighted as their accumulated crimes.

In the final stanza I project the poem into the future, and call upon more recent and contemporary figures: the bureau chieftains, the market manipulators, corporate thieves, and so forth. These are the life-wreckers whose activities, unchecked and unrepaired, bring a society to ruin. My intention, plainly, is to bring them before that wall.

There are no names in the poem, only those archetypal figures who stand for political wrongdoing in all of history. These, and their motives, hardly change. What changes is their means for mischief and oppression, and the scope of the harm they do, as represented by the many "gates" we have passed through in recent times, whether or not we have called them by that name.

I have sought, from time to time and in one poem or another, a vocabulary, and through that a means of bringing a poem to bear with a more deadly accuracy on the persons and events that play so prominent a part in our lives, and with so often drastic consequences for us all. It is not easy now for poetry to take on that responsibility—to assume, instinctively and justifiably, that a word, a verse line, or a stanza, might in some way change the world. Once, and it was not so long ago, both the will toward this effect and the potential for it could be assumed to be part of nearly every poet's ambition.

My poem, if only on a limited scale, seeks to engage public and historical events in a way that may bring to them a new meaning for our time, and which may awaken in the reader a renewed sense of seriousness and purpose in poetry. To an extent, perhaps, the poem can be read as a kind of prophecy.

I published an early version of this poem in a journal whose name I no longer remember. Looking at it years later, I was dissatisfied with it and eventually rewrote both the first and last stanzas. It seemed to me that in my original version my characters were too vague and generalized, that the words I had chosen to describe them lacked sufficient force, and that I did not have a firm enough sense of the setting of the poem. Meanwhile, other events, and the ascension of even more sinister persons seemed to have worked even more thoroughly to the deterioration of society.

What I worked for in this poem was a certain force and resonance, in its sounds and its images, and in the meaning of the poem itself. If I succeeded in this, then perhaps it can be said that the poem *moves,* not only in terms of its emotional impulse, but in the progress of its lines and stanzas down the page, and moves also through the space into which I have, in a sense, cast the poem.

If the poem succeeds, and it seems to me that it does, it will be due in great part to the particular force of the conviction in which I wrote the poem and later revised it. To say again: I believe that poetry must find a way to regain a more direct address to public events, to confront them and the individuals who stand behind them, and to regain thereby an authority it once had so abundantly. My poem is an attempt in that direction, an early one on my part, but one I am pleased with.

To turn for a moment to details of the poem's structure, and for what interest these may have, I note the alternating short and longer lines, and the grouping of these lines into their stanzaic pattern. I might point to certain key words: "to," "come," "stand," "fall," "advance," "trailing," etc., to their strategic placement in the poem, contributing to that sense of movement I have described. Much of this, and especially in regard to a poem composed in free verse, can, I suppose, be said to have been intuitive; if so, it is an intuition founded on much practice.

Recent arguments over the opposing merits of free verse and traditional measures notwithstanding, I am not convinced that there is significant difference between deciding initially upon a more "formal" pattern, and the alternate method of allowing a poem to develop in the form that seems latent in it. Both approaches imply a certain intuitive sense of the shape of the completed poem, even when, as is often the case, that shape cannot be initially defined. In the present case, I doubt that the poem would have succeeded in quite the same way had I written it in a more traditionally formal pattern—one, for example, in which all of the lines are of equal measure, or in which only so many lines may be used.

But to analyze the poem as a classroom exercise is not my chief concern in this brief essay. As interesting as that may be to specialists, it seems to me that no discussion of verse measure, of lines and stanzas, of formal structure, is of much consequence unless joined vitally with the substance of the poem. And here I would like to quote once more from Wallace Stevens on the subject:

> Poetic form in its proper senses is a question of what appears within the poem itself. It seems worth while to isolate this because it is always form in its inimical senses that destroys poetry. By inimical senses one means the trivialities. By appearance within the poem one means the things created and existing there. . . .

I believe this to be true, and believe further that whoever fails to understand what Stevens is saying here has little hope of comprehending the form, the content and direction of this poem, or of any true poem.

Finally, "To the Wall" interests me because it is perhaps the first instance in which I conceived a poem on a scale that, to some extent at least, places it outside the bounds of earthly time. I have come to feel that poetry must begin to attempt this. Whether we wish it or not, emotionally, intellectually, historically, and in other respects too, we have outgrown the planet Earth. Or so, at moments, it seems to me. *1992*

The Far Country of Sleep

Of the death of my father over twenty years ago I recall most vividly those time-suspended moments in a funeral home in Washington, D.C.: standing before an open casket, while looking down on that distant, long-silent man enclosed in a cushioned box, and on his gray, sunken features the final peace of departure.

I had flown from the West Coast with my brother in mid-December after hearing the news of his death. Though we knew that he had been gravely ill and would not live much longer, the news nonetheless came as a shock; following on the death of our mother three years before, it seemed to close a long chapter in our lives.

Shortly after arriving in Washington, we gathered with my stepmother and some of my father's fellow officers, friends and their wives, at a funeral home in the northwest part of the city. The atmosphere was typically heavy and somber, vaguely obsequious and hypocritical in its apparent attitude toward the elemental fact of death, as if we who were still living might somehow escape if only we kept up a certain appearance and continued to speak, or to murmur, the words for which there was now no answering belief.

The casket was open; we mourners filed by, stopping briefly to look down on the dead, then wrote our names on the page of a large register that stood near.

Deeply moved as I was, and oppressed by the conventional piety of the occasion, I withdrew from the immediate scene, found a chair in the corner of the room, and sat down. I wanted at that moment to be as far removed as possible from that plush parlor, in thought if not in fact.

Out of intense confusion of grief, of shock and loss, my thoughts converged on the potential earth-imagery that surrounded me, taking form and substance from the burnished wood of the casket, from the tall, thick candles burning at head and foot of the dead, and from the fount of water in a stand nearby. Among these things, in the heavy red somberness of the parlor, a few people came and went, talking in low tones.

Seated there, alone for the moment, I took out a pen and a notebook, and began to write down a few thoughts as they came to me half-formed in lines of verse. In what I wrote, I turned back to that imagery of thicket and woodland, to a scene already transformed in my mind. The water in the fount became a forest pool in which the candle flames mysteriously flickered. All became shadowy and subdued. And one by one, as the living passed before the dead, they dipped their fingers in the water and wrote down their names on a tablet of wet clay.

Soon afterwards came a chapel service, followed by interment in Arlington Cemetery. But for me these events were already past importance, dominated as I was by the thoughts and words set in motion during those moments in the funeral parlor, thoughts that the more I dwelled on them suggested to me another domain altogether. In some way not clear to me at the time, that symbolic return to a natural setting, to something close to a primal stillness and darkness, was a last tribute to my father, who took me at an early age into the woods and introduced me to the life that was there and to an affection I had never outgrown.

Many years later I came on a passage in Robert Musil's *The Man Without Qualities* that recalled vividly and directly my own distant occasion. In the passage given here, the main character, Ulrich, and his sister Agatha, on the death of their father, have returned home for the funeral and to take care of family business. As Ulrich observes the activity around him, the funeral arrangements and the many small demands of the hour, the following thoughts come to him:

He had never before realized how many people are always politely waiting for someone else's death, and how many hearts one sets throbbing the moment one's own heart ceases to beat. He was considerably astonished, contemplating it: a dead beetle lying somewhere in the woods, and other beetles, ants, birds, and flickering butterflies gathering around. For in all this commotion, this profit-seeking activity, there was everywhere a fluttering and stirring of darkness as in the deep woods.

Musil's quiet irony arises from a sensibility different from my own, yet I found in his sentences a confirmation of my own intuition. In the poem I later completed I went even further than that symbolic comparison. I felt directed not only to remove the proceedings from that plush parlor, but to do something additional, and I placed the poem in the voice of the one who was dead—a man who, unable to speak aloud but still half-conscious in the world, saw and heard all that was taking place around him in the half-light of a waking dream. I found it important also that something of the ancient rite of burial, of preparation for the voyage of death, as perceived by people for whom an afterlife truly existed, be present in the poem.

The Incurable Home

Then I came to the house of wood
and knocked with a cold hand.
My bones shone in my flesh
as the ribs in a paper lantern,
the gold ring slipped from my finger.

The door swung open, strong hands
seized me out of the darkness
and laid me in a bed of wood;
it was heavy, weighted with shadows,
lined with cloth woven from wheat straw.

Four posts stood by the corners;
thick candles were lighted upon them,
and the flames floated

in pools of forest water.
The air smelled of damp leaves and ashes.

People whose faces I knew and had forgotten
wound a chain about my hands.
They dipped their fingers in the water,
wrote their names on a clay tablet
and stood aside,
talking in the far country of sleep.

1970–91

VII

Early Sorrow

Somewhat closer to the heart . . .
but far from close enough.
PAUL KLEE

Early Sorrow

There was a girl, eleven or twelve years old, who sat at a desk in front of me in a schoolroom in Vallejo, California. I can no longer be certain of her name, but I think it was Shirley; that name, at least, has a sound that is close to what I remember of her. She was chunky and round-faced, with short, curly brown hair. Her complexion was not very good, but there was something attractive about her, a manner at once bold and shy, sensitive and appraising.

We never saw each other except in school. She was the daughter of a navy petty officer stationed at Mare Island, and they did not live in our neighborhood. I remember that she was brought to school by car every morning, and called for again when school was over. Our being together had that tentative, searching character I seem to associate with so many early relationships, based on little more than a closeness of desks, a loaned eraser, a shared lesson, with all potential intimacy and permanence diverted into casual play.

But even had we lived closer to each other it is unlikely that our friendship would have survived the limitations imposed on it by the class structure of navy society. Shirley was the daughter of an enlisted man, and that meant that she was somehow of a lower order in the scheme of things than I was as the son of an officer. In the service then, and it may be so still, you never forgot that *class* did exist; any but the most casual or superficial mixing was frowned on and discouraged. Whatever might have been the outcome of our brief friendship, sooner or later we would have been faced with the consequences of an obscure and fundamental law that determined one's life before it was lived.

I was twelve, at most thirteen, already somewhat withdrawn and thoughtful. I was puzzled by a disparity between myself and others, dimly aware that I stood at the border of a world apparently unacknowledged by those I knew; and that the world whose representatives I faced at home and at school was not and could not be wholly mine.

Can one be truly in love at that age? I don't know, but surely I had more than a vague crush on this girl, and though she half-teased me with preferring another boy, I knew that something in my feeling was returned. From time to time during that winter I felt that the potential woman in her was playing a subtle game with me, trying to draw me out of my too obvious shyness. And it was she who on the school playground one recess period recited to me the obscene verse I have never forgotten:

> There's a cowgirl way out west
> Who has melons on her chest;
> There's a nest between her legs
> Where the cowboy lays his eggs.

This verse was all but incomprehensible to me. Shirley, though she probably understood little more of its meaning than I did, found the words uproariously funny. Out of some crudity or down-to-earthness in her background, she was wise for her years in ways that I was not. Looking me in the eye in a way that I found disturbing, she repeated the verse. And with a mocking little smile, she skipped off to join another group of children, leaving me to stand there on the gritty pavement puzzled and, in some part of my youthful being, deeply shocked.

The events I am writing of are what remain imperfectly after forty-five years: an image of a schoolroom, of a playground and a face. And overlaid now with a still-keener sense of a neighborhood and its landscape: of tall frame houses set along the steep streets of the town above an arm of

San Pablo Bay; of sunlight and fog, of dry, grassy hillsides dotted with groves of live oak and eucalyptus. Beyond the street on which we lived the countryside seemed to stretch away, the fields empty and half-wild, with abandoned cisterns, warped sheds and broken fences of farms and ranches that in the widespread poverty of the 1930s were gone back to quail and thistles. But there was a sweep to the countryside, an openness that, limited as it must have been and would seem to me now, spoke strongly of mysterious frontiers. To the west, across the water, lay the Mare Island Shipyard where my father's ship was stationed, and of which I recall little more than a uniform grayness of metal and paint.

I remember the slaughterhouse, a low-built structure of brick and wood standing beside a county road not far from home. It could not have been far, for it was within easy walking distance of our neighborhood. I recall with exactness the reek of that place, the sickening, sweetish stench that in a downwind permeated the countryside. The smell came from the cast-off animal parts, the chicken guts and manure rotting in piles outside the building, along with bales of hides and great broken bags of feathers. Water standing in a ditch at the roadside was clogged with blood and body fluids that shone with a muddy irridescence in the cloudy sunlight.

Over the hill from the house we rented was an abandoned quarry and brickyard. It lay at the bottom of a steep, rocky bluff on the slaughter-house road. Open and isolated as it was, the brickyard was used locally as a target range. On weekends some of the neighborhood men and women came to fire their pistols and rifles at targets set against the bluff. I and my friends often went to watch them. When the shooters had gone home, we picked up some of the cartridge cases that were left behind, and if we felt really serious about it we would spend an hour or two digging into the loose sand of the bluff, hoping to find a spent slug.

At one edge of the brickyard there was a small depression with tumbled bricks at the bottom; in the rainy season it filled up with rainwater. Grass and weeds had taken root at its rim, and the pool made a sort of rough oasis in the waste of rock and gravel. One cool day after school I came there alone with an empty fruit jar taken from my mother's kitchen. The jar had a tight lid, and inside I had placed one of my old painted lead soldiers cushioned on a wad of cotton, and with something else of value to keep him company. There was enough weight in the jar to sink it. I tied a string around the jar and let it down into the water to the bottom of the pool. The significance of this pastime is no longer clear to me, but is vaguely associated with some inner distraction. I sat there at the edge of the pool, holding one end of my string; looking down at the jar under the water, I imagined some deep adventure at the bottom of a distant sea.

From the back of our house a path led uphill into open fields where it soon joined a seldom-used dirt road. Walking that road one Sunday morning in spring, I met death in the form of a rabbit freshly killed by a hawk. The blue bulge of the rabbit's gut lying by the roadside in the sunlight woke me to a loneliness I had not known before.

That loneliness was enlarged by my growing sense of the world outside our family, and had been further intensified by the continual uprooting of the family as we moved about the continent from one city or navy base to another. Each move meant that new friendships had to be formed and old ones abandoned. As I became more conscious of the social world, of the seeming impermanence of neighborhoods, of schools and friendships, this continual dislocation brought me more pain than I was able at that age to understand or admit to myself. I concealed that pain for many years, and it became a vast, empty space within that I attempted to fill from time to time with imaginary creatures and absent friends.

There in Vallejo I was often with neighborhood chums, taken up after school and on weekends with the games and adventures of a normal childhood. But sometimes, following an obscure impulse, I chose to be alone, away from the house, alone with the grass and the sun. One day in spring, walking the windy fields, seized by a sudden and inexplicable desire, I took off my clothes and sat in the grass, utterly alone. The sun was hot, the grass rose high and yellow above my head mixed with the vibrant green of the new season's growth. Not far from where I sat, on a rise of ground, a tall grove of eucalyptus guarded an old wooden water tank. The iron belts of the tank had rusted and broken, the unbound seams gaped and made a dry and spooky sound in the wind.

As I sat there, heated by the sun, the world seemed to grow at once smaller and more immense. It vanished at the skyline of grass where not a single housetop showed itself; or it was concentrated for one intense moment in a two-inch square of soil at the root of a grass stem where a small red ant struggled with a particle of sand. The leaves of the eucalyptus scraped and whispered, a mourning dove called, hidden in the foliage. The memory of that moment is so strong that I can still recall, as if it was a taste left in my mouth, the sharp and bitter smell of the eucalyptus leaves, the dry, sunburnt odor of the grass.

For a while then, too, I was intensely interested in birds, chiefly in hawks and owls. I spent hours looking through the one bird book I had then, a large, thick *Birds of America* I had been given the previous Christmas. The book was well illustrated with black and white pho- tographs, with drawings and watercolors by a famous bird artist of the time. I copied with a pencil many of the more striking illustrations, trying to render exactly the hooked shape of the hawk bill, the strong curve of the talons, and the bold edge of the bird shoulder. I made no at- tempt to imitate the colors, nor so far as I know did I learn the use of watercolor.

I was not capable then of systematic study, and apart from the pencil drawings my bird-watching had little focus. I knew the meadowlarks and the red-winged blackbirds, but not much else. I was mainly excited by a glimpse of some hawk of passage, and once by the limp feathers of an owl shot by a local boy.

The town library was within walking distance of home and school. From that small, square brick building on the bluff just above the bay I took home some of the first books I had begun to read independent of school. I can only guess now what the books might have been, but I am certain they included stories of the far north woods, a few of the Western novels of Zane Grey, and stories of Middle Earth by Edgar Rice Burroughs. I have misty memories of places like the Tonto Rim, and of a region called Pelucidar where dinosaurs and pterodactyls survived to threaten a band of brave explorers. I am certain too that one of my authors was Ernest Seton, for I seem to remember that a favorite story was that of Lobo, the great outlaw wolf of the southwest plains.

Periodically the family went to San Francisco for a day or a weekend. In those years before the big bay bridges were built, we took the ferry from Carquinez, a twenty-minute drive out of Vallejo. Then followed a long, re- laxed ride across the open bay during which we left the car and were free to roam the big upper decks of the ferry. Standing at the damp, salt rail, we watched the gray forbidding hulk of Alcatraz loom and pass, the city skyline and the downtown docks drawing closer.

When the shopping and sightseeing were over for the day, my parents often stopped off for an hour or two at a speakeasy called THE BLUE FOX, whose heavy, slotted door opened into an alley not far from the water- front. The bar had survived from the prohibition period not long past, and though there was now no need for secrecy and surveillance, the bar and its approaches kept all the appearance of a special and not-quite-lawful resort.

My brother Bob and I were left to wait in the car parked in the alley or on a nearby street. We watched the clients come and go, and speculated on the gangster aspect of things, all that was still very much alive in films and radio plays. A man or a couple would walk up to the entrance, knock on the door or ring a bell; a small slot in the door would slide open, and the customer was identified. The main door opened, and we heard for a moment the sound of voices and glasses, the background tumbling of a piano; then the door closed, and all that mysterious, forbidden world within disappeared and left us to the discord of city traffic, the anonymity of voices that passed and faded on the street.

Midway in the late afternoon one or both of our parents came out to the car to see how we were getting along with each other, to bring us a glass of Coke and assure us that they would not be inside much longer. But it was otherwise a strained and boring time for two restless kids. When we had counted the cars going by, named the years, the makes and the models, there was little to do but squirm and wait. I particularly remember one warm afternoon when a boy passing on the sidewalk waved to us with a broad smile and dropped a leaflet through the opened car window. The leaflet announced in bold type that a film entitled "Anna Christie" was to be shown soon at a theater in the city. That leaflet brought a brief surge of excitement into our boredom, and "Anna Christie" gave us something to talk about. The name, of course, meant little to us, but we liked the sound of it, suggestive and mysterious, belonging to a world of importance far beyond that locked and stuffy car by the curbing. When my father and mother finally came out to the car and we started home, we showed them the leaflet and begged to be taken to see the film. We were badly disappointed to be told that it would not be suitable for kids, and so far as I know we never did get to see it.

Spring and early summer came to the hills and the bayshore. Meadowlarks and blackbirds returned to the fields and the tidewater marshes. For me, and sometimes for Bob too, there were early Saturday morning trips with my father to Rector's Canyon, a small rock stream that tumbled out of a gorge in nearby Napa County. Early in the season, fishing a small hook baited with a single salmon egg, we caught the young trout planted there by the county or the state. I have a photograph taken about that time, showing myself posed beside the water with my rod held high, a creel at my waist, and a small, silvery fish dangling before my face at the end of my line. I had short, uncombed, sun-bleached hair, wore sneakers and a sweatshirt, and faded dungaree trousers. In the picture I appear subdued and self-conscious, holding up that terribly small trout for the camera.

With the beginning of warmer weather, there were family Sundays on the Russian River, a large stream in a valley north of Vallejo. These Sundays were my father's concession to my mother who was never really at ease in nature and never quite understood my father's addiction to whole days and weekends out on some creek or pond. Fishing was for him a serious and mainly solitary occupation, but he could not justify spending entire weekends away from the family. So, on these Sundays we settled for a kind of family picnic, with a blanket spread on a sandbar, fried chicken from a hamper, and bottled drinks cooled in a shallow of the river. We seldom caught any fish on these outings; the day amounted to some wading or swimming, playing with the dog, and taking pictures. What I remember of those Sundays now is something like a general dissatisfaction, as if no one was doing what he really wanted to do.

But early one cold and rainy spring morning, while it was still dark, my father went with a friend to fish the Napa River for steelhead. He came home late that evening, wet and muddy, but quietly satisfied. When he had dumped his soaked gear in the kitchen, he took from the game pocket of his stained and smelly fishing coat the one fish he had caught that day, a steelhead some twenty inches long. He laid the fish in the sink, and we all stood there to look at it. It was bright silver with a rainbow flush along its sides, and a dark, steel blue cast on the top of its head and upper back. As steelhead went, it was nothing to brag of, but it seemed to me bigger than any trout I had ever seen or could hope to catch. As he cleaned and washed the fish, he told us of the long wet day, and of the big trout he had seen rise and turn from his bait in the muddy, rain-swollen river.

In those months of passage, while the rains came and went over the hills and life alternated between the routine of the classroom and the freedom of the open air, between companionship and solitude, girls began to trouble me seriously for the first time. This new thing came to me in the form of an emotion I did not understand but instinctively feared. It came as a stealthy awakening, a secret and unbidden guest to my heart, the meaning of which I was somehow given to understand by parents, by priests and nuns, I was not to ask about, for there would be no explanation. Only in the casual talk of the men and older boys whom for some reason or other I sometimes found myself with, did I catch the vocabulary of a further and obscene mystery connected however vaguely with a confused imagery of white bodies, of limbs, lips, and secret recesses.

So, of a girl named Judy whom I watched one day as she danced with a group of other children on the school stage during a noon-hour performance, it was chiefly her slim legs and bare knees that attracted me. She was the close friend of a redheaded, freckled boy named Roy, who was also a neighborhood friend of mine; but for me Judy was all too cool and distant. I was envious of their easy and companionable closeness in which, for all I could tell, lay nothing of the torment I was beginning to sense would be my own experience of early love.

Toward the end of the school year a play was put on in which I was given a part. The play was *Punch and Judy*. By an odd coincidence, the girl Judy played Judy; Roy was Punch. I had the role of the Devil, and for reasons not hard to imagine I took a kind of fiendish satisfaction in the part. I appeared near the end of the play in full red costume, with a wooden pitchfork and a long, barbed tail. At the critical moment I burst onstage, and in as deep a voice as I could manage I spoke the only line I was given: "Punch! Your time has come!" And with ferocious authority, lashing my tail and jabbing my fork, I forced Punch off the stage and into Hell.

Then, by an obscure train of circumstances I was drawn to the girl named Shirley who sat before me in class, and who from time to time gave me such bold and mystifying glances. It may have been partly our closeness to each other in the classroom, or a feeling of solidarity in our service background. For me it may well have come as a kind of compensation for what I did not have: a companionship I had observed of others, and for which I yearned in secret. Whatever its cause, the attachment grew in me, grew to be a periodic distraction that I carried away from school and brooded upon. On one level it was no more than a tentative reaching toward someone who might relieve the oppressive separateness that had already become part of my nature; on another and deeper level it did not occur to me to doubt that what I felt was love.

I was unable to speak of my feeling, and that tormented me all the more. Then came the news, announced one day in class, that Shirley was leaving. Her father was being transferred to another station, and she would have to leave before school was over. I was deeply distressed by the news;

aside from my deeper feelings, it meant that another attachment was about to be broken, and who could know if we would ever meet again? Somehow, then, before she left, I must find a way to speak to her of my love.

As a result of one of my expeditions to the brickyard I possessed a large caliber pistol cartridge from which the lead slug could be removed and reinserted. It was a treasured thing, and I often carried it in my pocket. This, I decided, would be both my parting gift and a means of confession.

On the morning of what was to be Shirley's last day in school, I wrote the words "I love you" on a scrap of paper. I signed it, folded the paper to fit into the cartridge case, and sealed it with the slug. I carried the cartridge with me to school, and all that day I waited for the moment when I could give it to her. I am not certain how I intended to do this; I could not give it to her outright, for then I would have to explain my reasons, and in my pent up, tongue-tied state I was sure to be misunderstood. I hoped that however I managed to do it, she would open the cartridge when she was far away, read my note, and understand.

The exact sequence of events that day has long since slipped my mind, but their probable course is not hard to reconstruct. There was a class break. Shirley went out of the room for a short time, and left her purse behind at her desk. In the confusion of the break, and with most of the students out of the room, I somehow got hold of her purse. It was held closed by a little clasp. In the partial concealment of my desk I opened the purse and placed my cartridge inside. I intended to hide it there as deeply as I could, so that she would not find it immediately but only later when she had left school. But I was too hurried and nervous to do more than drop the cartridge inside. I replaced the purse on her desk just as the students began returning to the classroom.

Already, as the desks filled and attention focused on the front of the room, it began to dawn on me that I had done a reckless and witless thing. My youthful and overexcited imagination had woven something impossibly romantic out of our very limited being together; but now, once set in motion, events would take their course.

Shirley returned to her seat. To her casual greeting I managed only an embarrassed murmur and could not meet her eyes. The classwork resumed, an English exercise in a notebook. And then what I feared most happened. Shirley opened her purse to look for something, and digging into its contents immediately found my cartridge.

I heard her give a gasp of surprise, and from that moment I knew I was done for. She turned to look at me, the brass cartridge casing with its dull lead slug lying in the palm of her small hand. Did I know how it got into her purse? No, indeed I didn't. She turned to the others around her to ask the same question; but no, not the girl who sat in the row next to us, nor the boy on the opposite side.

Our teacher had already noticed the confusion in our part of the room, when Shirley raised her hand and asked to speak with her. The teacher, a Miss Ferguson, a thin and homely woman in her forties, called her up to the front desk. And with her purse in one hand and my pistol cartridge in the other, Shirley went up.

Over the rows of desks with their suddenly attentive heads I saw Shirley bending at Miss Ferguson's desk, heard the murmured exchange of voices. Miss Ferguson turned to the class with an expression of concern, held up my cartridge, and asked: "Class, do any of you know how this got into Shirley's purse?" Thirty-odd pairs of eyes looked around the room; there were whispers and blank expressions. I alone sat silent and stricken, my eyes glued to the notebook page on my desk.

Roy, who was the class custodian, was called to Miss Ferguson's desk, and he and Shirley and Miss Ferguson huddled over my cartridge. Roy left the room for a moment and returned with the school janitor. Another examination of my cartridge followed. By this time it would have been noticed that the cartridge was not new, and that it had been fired at some time in the past. With a word of assurance, Roy and the janitor went off to the school shop with my cartridge. Shirley returned to her seat, and the class settled down to its assignment.

I sat very still in my seat, unable to concentrate on the lesson, dreading the return of Roy and the janitor, knowing that my secret must soon be known. And it was Roy who returned alone with a small, knowing smile on his face. I saw my note and the empty cartridge pass from his hand to that of Miss Ferguson. I watched as she read the note, and heard her speak a low-pitched "Oh . . ." I heard her thank Roy, and I saw him return to his desk. He passed down the aisle next to mine with that sly, freckled smile on his face while I pretended not to see.

I shrank into my seat and thought frantically of some way to escape. Reality receded into a loud buzzing, as though an invisible cloud of insects swarmed about my head. I heard Miss Ferguson call Shirley to her desk. Peering aslant from my own desktop, I saw her speak something quietly to the girl, and saw her pass my note. And once again I stared fixedly downward as Shirley walked slowly back to her desk with lowered eyes. Miss Ferguson called the class to order, and the period went on to its close.

All through the rest of the class period I sat huddled in an agony of self-accusation. I would have given anything to have disappeared from the face of the earth. Why had I done so stupid and awkward a thing? It would soon be known to everyone; I was shamed and revealed. Even now, it seemed to me, I caught more than one whisper and amused looks in my direction.

I remember little now of what went on in the classroom. My attention wandered between my desktop and the back of Shirley's head. Once, during the twenty or so minutes that remained, she half-turned in her seat and looked at me. I caught a puzzled, half-frightened look—that one glance only, and she did not say anything to me.

The time was mercifully brief, and soon everyone was picking up their papers, gathering their coats, and leaving the room. In the blur of confusion and pain that surrounded me, no memory remains that Shirley spoke to me before she left; probably I did my utmost to avoid speaking to her or to anyone. But before I could escape, Miss Ferguson called me to her desk. While I stood there, numbed and waiting, she gave me back my cartridge. She was a kind woman, and sorry for my embarrassment. She understood that I meant well, but I had not only frightened Shirley, I had caused some alarm and trouble in the class. Perhaps in the future I ought to find another way to communicate my feelings? I don't think I said a word in reply. What could I have said?

I did not see the girl again. She never came back to school, and we heard that she and her family had left Vallejo and gone east. Somewhere in my confused memory of the time there exists an uncertain clue that she wrote me a note; more likely, nothing of the sort happened, and the uncertainty represents no more than a tiny, implanted hope.

At school, contrary to what I had feared, a strange and considerate delicacy followed on the incident. No one spoke of it to me, though it is unlikely that it was kept a secret. Now and then it seemed to me that a boy or a girl looked my way with an expression of concern or amusement, but this may have been only my overwrought imagination. Only Roy, the boy who had gone to the shop with the janitor, once or twice looked at me with that freckled smile of his to let me know that he at least was in on my secret.

And who knows what concealed emotions I had stirred by my act? Was anyone else in love, or thought that he or she might be, and had no way to express it? And Miss Ferguson—had she once known that fleeting intensity of affection? Had anyone, ever, written her a shy note of confession?

My own pain soon lapsed into a dull and familiar ache. I had received a tiny wound to my sensibilities, self-inflicted in a moment of awkwardness; in a moment of folly, a fondness badly expressed.

Thereafter a mist seems to have closed over events, over an entire period of time. Out of the days and weeks that followed, a few images and episodes only stand out in no clear sequence. They are confused with another and separate year in Vallejo, another house on the same street, other faces and voices.

There was Hazel, the young farm girl who came to keep house for us for a while. We loved her for her uncomplicated friendliness and good humor. For Bob and myself there was a rare excitement in this seventeen-year-old girl living in the house with us like an older sister. When our parents had gone for an evening, Hazel would read aloud to us before bedtime. I remember a kind of deliciousness in our huddling together on the sofa in our pajamas, while Hazel with a strong bare arm around one or the other of us, pronounced the words of a favorite story. And I think it was not the book or the story that mattered most, but that plain, warm feminine closeness with a voice that spoke with affection and assurance. She was more like ourselves, not yet of the adult world, in some odd way both friend and parent.

Hazel had a boyfriend of whom we were mildly jealous. He was a sergeant in the Marine Corps, a man several years older than she. Dressed always in a clean, pressed khaki uniform, he came sometimes to spend the evening with Hazel while she was keeping us. The two of them sat together in our living room, holding hands and smiling at us, now and then exchanging a quiet kiss. Bob and I did not get read to on those evenings; we were taken upstairs and put to bed with a friendly threat that if we were not quiet we would not get read to next time. We lay in bed in the dark with the door open, listening to Hazel and her friend murmuring to each other downstairs. One evening, consumed with curiosity, we crept halfway down the staircase to listen. A step in the stairway may have creaked, or we made some other noise. Hazel discovered us and flew into a momentary temper to find that we were eavesdropping on her. Much later, after we had left Vallejo, we had a letter from Hazel, telling us that she and her man had gotten married and were housekeeping on their own.

And then, one day late in spring, at the end of the school year, we left Vallejo. With most of our household belongings in storage, we took ship from San Francisco, bound for Hawaii. In writing these words, I know how much time and how many drastic alterations my own brief life has contained. It still comes as a surprise to me that almost no one flew anywhere in those days. We went by ship or by rail, and it was still an adventure to drive the continent by car. What is missing now is that increasingly rare mysteriousness of departure, and the sense of a whole new adventure beginning, and which I suspect lies near the heart of the human experience of life on earth. The evening darkened over the coastline, the city skyline faded, and the open sea took us in with its gentle rocking and promise of tomorrow. I do not think travel by air preserves any significant part of this. And all that I speak of here seems to belong to another age, closed off from the present by some transparent material that both divides and reveals.

We had five calm days at sea on one of the big white Matson liners. They were easy days of sunlight, of shipboard games and freedom from school, with the anticipation of a new place. Then came a summer and part of a school year in Honolulu. Seven months later we were back in California, once more by ship on a rougher, more wintry sea. A year later, in 1938, we returned east to the Navy Yard in Washington, D.C.

It may have been three years following our winter in Vallejo that I was in Annapolis with my parents, watching the last half of a football game. It was a frosty fall afternoon, and we were cramped and chilled from sitting in the cold. During an intermission toward the end of the game, I stood up to stretch myself, and as I did so I looked up into the open benches behind me. Three rows above, by the side of an older man in uniform, sat a girl in a dark blue suit and a blue cap. She looked down at me, our eyes met, and some vague recognition seemed to pass between us. It was no more than a glance, and our attention was almost immediately distracted when the game resumed and a man seated in a row between us stood up to shout something to someone lower in the stands. When the game was over, and people began climbing down from the cold bleachers, I looked again for the girl on the seat above me. She was gone.

Was it Shirley? I believe it was. She was taller and slimmer, her face had lost some of its chubby roundness, but I knew that gaze, direct and searching. It seems likely now that, following our winter in Vallejo, her father had been transferred to Annapolis, or to some station nearby. Chance circumstance, fate, brought us both to the game that afternoon, and to the one glance exchanged above the crowd.

Would we have found anything to say to each other? When I thought of that—of facing each other and finding the necessary words—the suppressed memory of my own folly and embarrassment returned with a rush, and with it a stumbling inability to speak. There remained that slim blue question mark in the cold stands, and scattered like dust or pollen over the wrinkled vastness of a continent the improbable elements of a story that no one would ever write. Though, as I say this, it occurs to me that it has already been written many times.   *1984–91*

Notes

ON ROBINSON JEFFERS

1. John Haines, "Roots," *Living Off the Country* (Ann Arbor: University of Michigan Press, 1981).

2. Since this essay was written, a number of writers have sought to revive Jeffers's reputation. Dana Gioia especially has done so with grace and insight.

FORMAL OBJECTIONS

1. *The Letters of Wallace Stevens,* ed. by Holly Stevens (New York: Alfred A. Knopf, 1966), p. 590.

SOMETHING FOR OUR POETRY

1. Carolyn Forché, *The Country Between Us* (New York: Harper & Row, 1981).

2. Czeslaw Milosz, *Selected Poems* (Hopewell, N.J.: Ecco Press, 1973).

3. Octavio Paz, "The Poetry of Solitude and the Poetry of Communion," 1942).

ON A CERTAIN ATTENTION TO THE WORLD

1. The lines I have quoted from Kundera are taken from an interview with that writer and transposed by me from their original sentence form into verse lines, in keeping with their poetic character.

2. James Hastings Nichols, Introduction to *Force and Freedom* by Jacob Burckhardt (New York: Pantheon Books, 1943).

SHADOWS AND VISTAS

1. John Haines, "Shadows," *The Stars, the Snow, the Fire* (Saint Paul: Graywolf Press, 1981).

2. *Ibid.*

THE EYE IN THE ROCK

1. This essay was first published in *45 Contemporary Poems, The Creative Process;* ed. by Alberta Turner, Longman 1985, and was written in response to questions put to me by the editor regarding the genesis of the poem, its structure, and its meaning.

About the Author

Born in Norfolk, Virginia in 1924, JOHN HAINES studied at the National Art School, American University, and the Hans Hofmann School of Fine Art. He homesteaded in Alaska for over twenty years. He is the author of several major collections of poetry; a collection of reviews, essays, interviews, and autobiography, *Living Off the Country* (University of Michigan Press, 1981); and a memoir, *The Stars, the Snow, the Fire* (Graywolf Press, 1989). Haines has taught with distinction at several universities, including the University of Washington, Ohio University, George Washington University, and the University of Cincinnati. He has received numerous awards, including two Guggenheim Fellowships, a National Endowment for the Arts Fellowship, the Alaska Governor's Award for Excellence in the Arts, a Western States Arts Federation Lifetime Achievement Award, a Lenore Marshall/ *The Nation* poetry prize for *New Poems 1980–88* (Story Line Press, 1990), and a 1995 Academy Award in Literature from the American Academy of Arts and Letters. He currently lives with his wife Joy in Alaska.

This book was designed by Will Powers. It is set in Minion and Castellar type by Stanton Publication Services, Inc. and manufactured by Quebecor Book Group on acid-free paper.